THREE-WAR MARINE

THE PACIFIC · KOREA · VIETNAM

THREE-WAR MARINE

THE PACIFIC · KOREA · VIETNAM

by

COLONEL FRANCIS FOX PARRY, USMC (Ret)

Introduction by General Leonard F. Chapman, USMC (Ret)

Pacifica Press

92
P2498t

Requests for permission to make copies of any part of the work should be mailed to: Permissions, Pacifica Press, 1149 Grand Teton Drive, Pacifica, California 94044.

Designed by Toni Murray

Printed in the United States of America

First edition

Library of Congress Cataloging-in-Publication Data

Parry, Francis Fox.
  Three-war Marine.

  1. Parry, Francis Fox. 2. United States. Marine
Corps—Biography. 3. Marines—United States—
Biography. I. Title.
VE25.P36A3   1987   359.9'6'0924   [B]   87-14854
ISBN   0-935553-02-9

GUIDE TO
ABBREVIATIONS

ARVN	Army of the Republic of Vietnam
CCF	Communist Chinese Forces
CO	Commanding Officer
COC	Combat Operations Center
CP	Command Post
DI	Drill Instructor
DMZ	Demilitarized Zone
DUKW	Amphibious Truck
FDC	Fire Direction Center
FFI	Field Force I
FFII	Field Force II
FO	Forward Observer
G-1	Personnel (division or higher)
G-2	Intelligence (division or higher)
G-3	Operations and Training (division or higher)
G-4	Logistics (division or higher)
GCT	General Classification Test
H&S	Headquarters-and-Service
HQMC	Headquarters, Marine Corps
I-I	Inspector-Instructor
J-1	Personnel (joint staff)
J-2	Intelligence (joint staff)
J-3	Plans and Operations (joint staff)
J-4	Logistics (joint staff)

J-5	Long-term Plans and Operations (joint staff)
J-6	Communications (joint staff)
LST	Landing Ship, Tank
MACV	Military Assistance Command, Vietnam
MAF	Marine Amphibious Force
MSR	Main Supply Route
NCO	Noncommissioned Officer
NKPA	North Korean People's Army
NVA	North Vietnamese Army
OSD	Office of the Secretary of Defense
RCT	Regimental Combat Team
ROK	Republic of Korea (Army)
S-1	Adjutant (regiment or lower)
S-2	Intelligence (regiment or lower)
S-3	Operations and Training (regiment or lower)
S-4	Logistics (regiment or lower)
UDT	Underwater Demolitions Team
VC	Viet Cong
VT	Variable Time (fuse)
WAC	Women's Army Corps

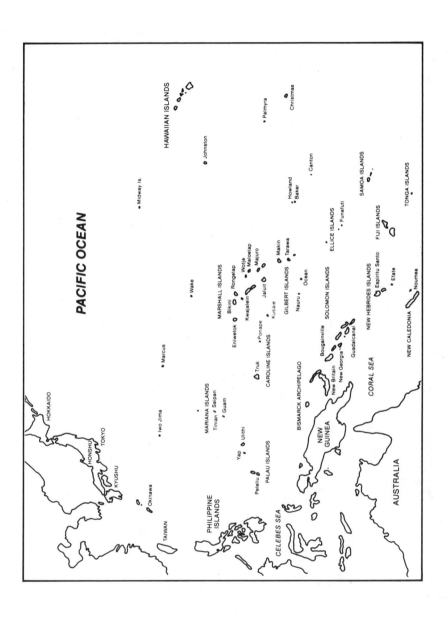

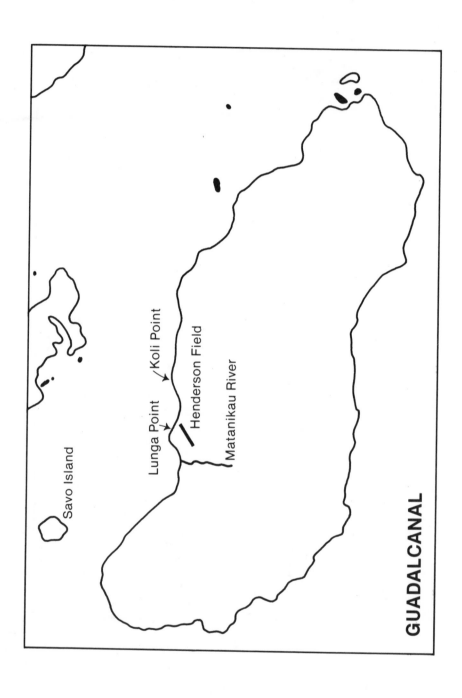

Savo Island

Lunga Point

Koli Point

Henderson Field

Matanikau River

GUADALCANAL

OKINAWA

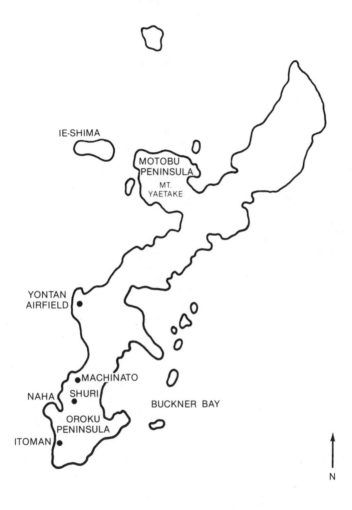

IE-SHIMA

MOTOBU
PENINSULA
MT.
YAETAKE

YONTAN
AIRFIELD

MACHINATO
SHURI
NAHA

BUCKNER BAY

OROKU
PENINSULA
ITOMAN

N

0 1 2 3 4 5 6 7 MILES

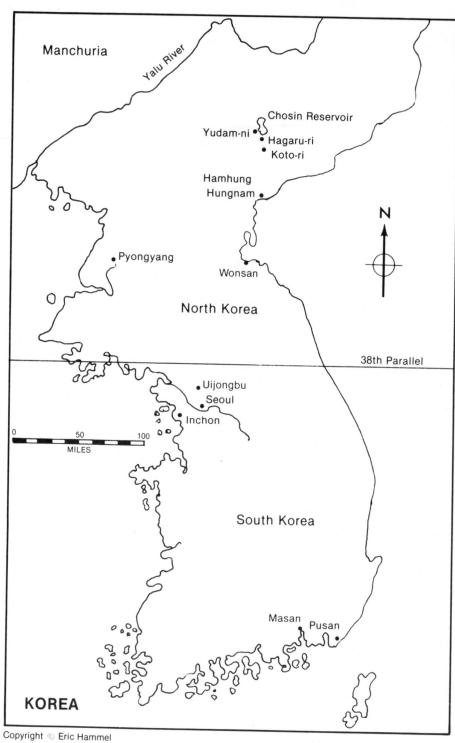

Manchuria

Yalu River

Chosin Reservoir

Yudam-ni •
• Hagaru-ri
• Koto-ri

Hamhung
Hungnam •

N

• Pyongyang

Wonsan •

North Korea

38th Parallel

• Uijongbu
• Seoul

0   50   100

• Inchon

MILES

South Korea

Masan
• • Pusan

KOREA

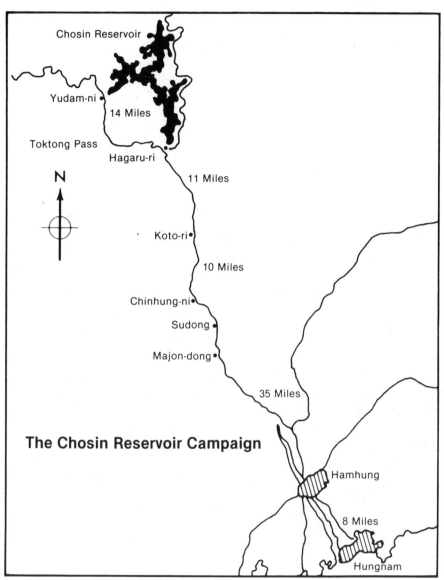

Chosin Reservoir

Yudam-ni

14 Miles

Toktong Pass

Hagaru-ri

N

11 Miles

Koto-ri

10 Miles

Chinhung-ni

Sudong

Majon-dong

35 Miles

The Chosin Reservoir Campaign

Hamhung

8 Miles

Hungnam

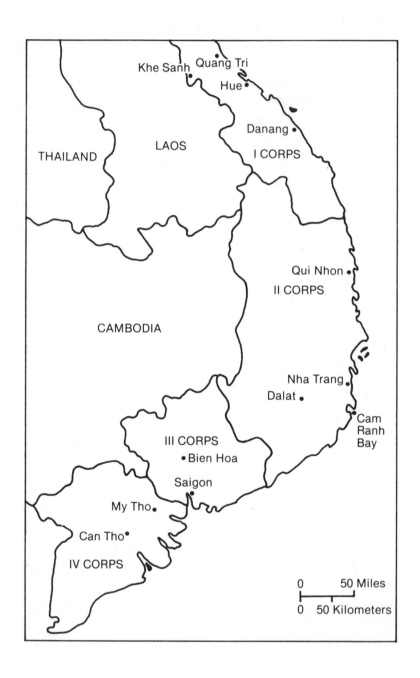

Khe Sanh

Quang Tri

Hue

THAILAND

LAOS

Danang

I CORPS

Qui Nhon

II CORPS

CAMBODIA

Nha Trang

Dalat

Cam
Ranh
Bay

III CORPS

Bien Hoa

Saigon

My Tho

Can Tho

IV CORPS

0   50 Miles

0   50 Kilometers

Introduction

Although this is primarily Francis Fox Parry's story of his professional growth throughout three war-glutted decades—of his experiences during and views of the stirring actions in which he
participated—it is also about his generation of Marine officers and
some of the senior officers who inspired them. Most particularly, it
is a tribute to Marine field artillery and its largely unsung role in
battle.

Who can read Fox Parry's dramatic account of his battalion's
actions at the Chosin Reservoir in November and December 1950
without wondering why we have heard so little over the past 37
years about the artillery's contribution to that Marine epic of heroism and survival? This has been the case too often. Infantry commanders often credit their field artillery brethren in private with
the crucial nature of their battlefield contributions, but their role
often goes unnoticed in public. Field artillery is not often in the
front lines, it gains or holds no ground, and it sustains a far smaller
percentage of casualties than the infantry. Nevertheless, its contribution to success in battle is frequently vital. At the Chosin Reservoir tanks played no significant part, and air support was often
inhibited by horrendous flying conditions. So the field artillery had
to shoulder most of the supporting-arms burden alone. Few field
artillery battalions in history have been thrown into battle with as
little training as Fox Parry's 3rd Battalion, 11th Marines at the
Chosin Reservoir. This book affords us all an opportunity to accord
Marine field artillery battalions of recent wars a grateful "well
done!"

Fox Parry and his contemporaries are a unique breed. Volunteers all, they are men of noble spirit and patriotic disposition.
Brought up during the Depression years, when civilian career opportunities were not abundant, they saw the profession of arms as
an honorable one and a military commission as an opportunity for
service to their country as well as a means for personal advance-
ment. Many of these officers stayed in the Marine Corps after the
Pacific War and became the commanders and key staff officers of

the Korean and Vietnam wars. Two of the most distinguished Marine artillerymen of the '40s and '50s were Bob Luckey (later lieutenant general) and Bigfoot Brown (later major general). I served with both of these officers and can readily understand the importance of their tutelage in the maturing of Fox Parry. Fox's firm hand yet easy rapport with his officers can be easily traced to Bob Luckey's influence; the importance that Fox attributed to an intimate relationship with the supported infantry surely had its genesis in Bigfoot Brown's early guidance. The excellence of the Army Artillery School's gunnery course at Fort Sill also had its impact. These as well as other influences all come together in the battalion commander we see in the middle chapters of this book.

But this is more than a story of a highly successful field artillery battalion commander. It is a gold mine of information about Marine field artillery in action on Guadalcanal, Okinawa, and Korea; of the handicaps under which it labored; and of its effectiveness. The vicissitudes of training at Quantico during World War II and at Camp Pendleton in the early '60s shed additional light on the artilleryman's way of life. The lessons learned in Korea should be gospel to the direct-support field artillery of today.

There are many rewarding insights to be gained from this book. The inside look at the U.S. Naval Academy before World War II and the problems faced by young lieutenants growing up in the Marine Corps are interesting. Fox's peacetime experiences as an instructor at the Marine Corps Schools, as a colonel in the Office of the Secretary of Defense in the Pentagon, and on troop duty in the early '60s all contain useful lessons.

Many will find Fox Parry's insights into the Vietnam War as a well-placed senior colonel in General William Westmoreland's headquarters in Saigon instructive—a different angle on that unhappy experience. His role in the Cuban Missile Crisis provides insights that will be welcomed by many military men.

Anyone who is interested in the events and lessons of our recent history will do well to ponder the lessons—explicit and implicit—of this exciting, thought-provoking memoir of a Marine artilleryman in his three wars.

—Leonard F. Chapman, Jr.
General, USMC (Ret.)

THREE·WAR MARINE

THE PACIFIC · KOREA · VIETNAM

Prologue

The War Generation

This is a book about several members of a generation of Americans that was brought up during the Depression years, that went to war to defeat the Fascist oppressors, and that stayed on in the military to defend the world they had helped to free. They are members of the "war generation." Although they seldom analyzed their motives, they were idealists—even crusaders—who believed in the virtue of their country's mission to promote freedom and in their obligation to serve their country in pursuit of it. Confident of success and that the achievement of it was worth real sacrifice, they strove to improve whatever situation confronted them anywhere.

Often, the sacrifices demanded of these men and their families were great. Absence of material gain, poor schools, frequent uprootings on short notice, marginal living quarters, long separations, and often dreary duty stations added up to a tough life. Some who were brought up in the military tradition were equipped to deal with these problems; most lacked such a background and had a difficult time coping. For the most part, however, they all embraced the service ethic, accepted the sacrifice, and met the challenge.

As the years passed—as the war generation matured—some disillusionment set in. The system rewarded some with early promotion, coveted duty assignments, or combat awards. Others, though equally deserving, went empty-handed. Despite these perceived imperfections, the war generation did not falter; it resolutely kept the faith and tried to win through.

If *Three-War Marine* illuminates the profession of arms as a nonmaterialistic brotherhood more united in purpose than most, one that can laugh at itself, and one that is not ashamed to reveal human emotion and weakness, then I have achieved my purpose. If you sense that there was more than a strain of nobility in the war generation, my purpose is twice fulfilled.

—Ambler, Pa.
1987

PART I

Annapolis & Before

1

A Military Family

My military career, which spanned thirty years and three wars, began unexpectedly in a confrontation with Father in the small den of our home in Chestnut Hill, a northwest section of Philadelphia. It was during the spring break of 1936, my senior year at The Hill School, a private academy in Pottstown, a Philadelphia suburb. Judge Parry, my father, fastened me with a penetrating stare and announced, "I've managed to get an alternate appointment to Annapolis, and I want you to go. John wants to go, but he can't pass the eye exam, so you're it."

Although a year younger than I, my brother John was also a senior—he had completed two grades in one year. Always intrigued by ships and the sea, John had clearly been a candidate for a naval career.

A naval career was fine for John, but I had other plans. I declared, "I don't want to go to Annapolis; I want to go to Harvard."

Judge Parry knew well that I had already been accepted to Harvard, his alma mater. Used to having his verdicts accepted without argument, he smiled without warmth and declared acidly, "You're not listening. Unless you want to be out in the street, you're going to the Naval Academy."

Further protest was useless; Father was not easily defied. I knew that his father had sent him off to the coal mines at the tender age of seventeen, so I recognized the likelihood that obstinacy on my part might earn me a similar fate.

That I should now be pointed in the direction of a naval career was not altogether coincidental. My oldest brother, George, had become enamored of the Naval Academy during his days at Saint John's, a liberal arts college in Annapolis, just outside the Academy walls. He had landed there after being expelled from Harvard along with a handful of others for conduct unbecoming gentlemen students. They had been apprehended in or in front of a house of ill repute—the precise location depended on the account of the escapade you heard, the university's or George's. While attending Saint John's, George had befriended several Naval Academy professors and had managed to have himself assigned as an Associated Press correspondent on the annual midshipmen's summer cruise to Europe in 1930. George bunked in officers' quarters aboard a battleship, ate in the officers' mess, and roamed about Europe with relish. He returned home singing the Navy's praises.

Perhaps George's high opinion of the Navy influenced Father. He was not unreceptive to the suggestion that a son attend Annapolis, but appointments were not easy to come by. When one came within reach, he did not hesitate. Educating seven sons during the Depression years was not easy, and the lure of a good free education for one of them was irresistible.

There may have been more to Father's decision than solving the problem of my schooling, however. Although unknown to me at the time or, indeed, until after my retirement from the Marine Corps, I had several illustrious military forebears. Perhaps Father felt that he should follow family tradition by nudging at least one son toward a military career.

Two of my forefathers distinguished themselves in military service in the early days of the eastern seaboard. Major William Bradford (son of the Governor of Plymouth Colony) was the leader of the Plymouth Forces in King Philip's War against the Indians, in which he was wounded. Colonel Miles Cary, leader of the Armed Forces of Virginia, was killed in 1667 by the Dutch. It is the Harris and Frazer families, however, from which our military traditions primarily spring.

William Harris enlisted in the Revolutionary Army in 1776 at the age of eighteen. A sergeant, then a lieutenant, and finally a captain, he fought at Brandywine and Germantown. He was later made a brigadier general of the Pennsylvania troops, but he died in 1812 without seeing service against the British in that war. Two of his sons served in the armed forces with distinction.

Thomas Harris entered the Navy for the War of 1812 as a surgeon and sailed with Commodore Decatur against the Barbary pirates in 1815. Later, President Andrew Jackson called on him to extract a bullet acquired in a duel twenty-five years before. Thomas Harris was the Navy's Chief of the Bureau of Medicine and Surgery from 1844 until his retirement in 1857.

John Harris joined the Marine Corps for the War of 1812 and lived to become its Civil War colonel-commandant. He also sailed with Decatur against the Barbary pirates, and he fought against the Creek Indians in Alabama and the Seminole Indians in Florida. During the Mexican War he commanded a battalion of Marines at Alvarado, near Vera Cruz. He is also notable in that he introduced the lima bean to the United States.

My great-grandfather, Stephen Harris (1798–1851) was a doctor, and he married Marianne Smith, the granddaughter of two notable Revolutionary War figures: Lieutenant Colonel Persifor Frazer and his beautiful wife, Mary Taylor Frazer. Colonel Frazer fought at Brandywine and was captured later while on a scouting mission. He escaped, reported to Valley Forge, and commanded the 5th Regiment of the Pennsylvania Line at the Battle of Monmouth. He was made a brigadier general of militia in 1782.

Mary Taylor Frazer is an unsung national heroine who displayed her courage and fortitude on many occasions. When the British invaded her home near the Brandywine battlefield, she stood her ground, demanding respect and exacting a measure of courtesy even as they looted her farm. Later, on several occasions, she rode unescorted through enemy lines to bring food and encouragement to soldiers of the Continental Army who were prisoners of the British in Philadelphia. One day, after being searched by the British, she rode 50 miles through heavy rain and past drunk and brawling soldiers to ford a raging river and deliver a secret message from the prisoners to George Washington at Whitemarsh. The following winter she led foraging parties from her farm to supply the cold and hungry army at Valley Forge.

My grandfather, Brevet Major Henry C. Parry, served with bravery as a military surgeon in the Union Army during the Civil War. Due to the poor field sanitation, he contracted recurring amoebic dysentery and malaria. These diseases were treated according to the medical practices of the day—with opium, morphine, and ether. Henry Parry soon became narcotics dependent, and the condition grew worse. After the loss of his job as an insurance examiner in

1874, he was unable to support his family. Support was thereafter provided by his father and then by his wife's brothers. As a result of Henry Parry's drug dependency, my father never knew his own father as a self-supporting, self-respecting man. It was probably because of this unfortunate relationship that my father passed on so little of the family history to his sons.

My father, George Gowen Parry, missed the Spanish-American War while he was in Gold Rush Alaska, but he joined the Pennsylvania National Guard in 1900. An incident from his first week in the National Guard gives some indication of the self-confidence and opportunism which, along with integrity and courage, would distinguish his later career as a member of the bar for almost sixty years. During a regimental revue, the colonel came along the line and asked the privates their General Orders. The results were indifferent. Finally he came to Private Parry and ordered him to repeat General Order Number One.

Private Parry answered by reciting all ten of the General Orders, without missing a syllable.

Colonel (impressed): How long has this man been in your outfit, Captain?

Captain: One week, Sir.

Colonel: Make him a corporal.

Private Parry: I don't want to be a corporal, Sir. I want to be your adjutant!

Colonel: Captain, make this man a second lieutenant.

After serving seven years, my father resigned as captain and adjutant of the 2nd Pennsylvania Infantry in 1906, having seen active service during the Anthracite Coal Strike of 1902 and Regular Army maneuvers at Manassas, Virginia, in 1904. When World War I arrived Major Parry—at that point of the Army Reserve Corps and over forty-five years old—was not called to active duty.

In 1936, as I faced my future, I knew little about my military past. Perhaps Father did pass on the legacy, however, by instilling in me the values and temperament that would sustain me in the military life. I catch glimpses of these features in my character as I review my earliest recollections.

2

Schools and Camp

My mother, Sara Valentine Fox, whose forebears numbered many Quakers, was a sweet, self-sacrificing lady who seldom challenged my autocratic, mid-Victorian father. But when it came time to name Father's fifth son, she got her back up. My four older brothers had been named after Father's family and English kings—George, Edward, Henry, and Richard. Mother held out for some relief from the English-king syndrome. For the months that this struggle lasted, Father dubbed me Quintus. Eventually, Mother's quiet determination won, and I was named after her childless older sister, Frances Fox Brockie. In the meantime, however, with one of my first intelligible sentences I had protested the obnoxious Quintus and opted for Wawa, my word for water. It took me many years to live that nickname down.

Growing up as the fifth of seven sons, competition for attention was inevitable. This spilled over from the dinner table, which was raucous, to academics and athletics. We were imbued at an early age with the will to succeed and taught to prize integrity. We were also subjected to sometimes heavy-handed discipline by our tough, self-made father. This frequently engendered rebellious behavior. In one incident typical of the period, Father locked me in my third-story bedroom for some misdemeanor. I escaped through the window by jumping to the second-story roof and then to the ground. After I had had a chance to reflect upon the possible penalty for my disobedience, getting back in my room was not so easy.

The seven Parry boys all went to Germantown Academy, one of the well-respected older schools in the country. Father had been in the Class of 1889, in which he had excelled as a mile walker (then an important track event) and halfback of the championship football team. He had been an indifferent student, however. Most of his sons, on the other hand, were good students, ranking near the top of their classes. Ted, Frazer, and Dick had all been on the tennis team—Ted and Dick were captains their senior years. Dick had also been basketball captain.

I had done well enough at Germantown Academy. I stood near the top of my class and performed with distinction on the junior athletic teams. In ninth grade my name had been inscribed on a plaque as the student most exemplifying excellence in "Scholarship, Athletics and Integrity." I am grateful to the school for a solid grounding in the three "Rs." The most enduring legacy that I took from Germantown Academy, however, was an understanding of the meaning of perseverance. The school seal depicts a garden upon which the sun is shining. Water sprinkles from a watering can held by a disembodied hand. Around this garden scene is the inscription: "By persevering we shall see the fruit." For some time this admonition puzzled me; I could not comprehend why "preserving" would let you see any fruit. So I asked Papa. He explained to me the meaning of perseverance, and I have never forgotten.

By 1934 Mother's health had begun to deteriorate. She had brought six children into the world over an eleven-year span, with her first coming when she was almost thirty. There was no effective way in those days to treat her resultant high blood pressure. Papa decided to reduce mother's responsibilities at home by sending John and me away to boarding school.

The fall of 1934 found me at The Hill School, 30 miles west of Philadelphia. Despite the beautiful campus and friendly students, my arrival at Hill marked my first time away from home, and homesickness undoubtedly influenced my performance for a while. Even after I adjusted to the routine, however, my two years at Hill were not happy ones. I did well enough academically, but I could not make any of the athletic teams. I had always been prominent in athletics at Germantown Academy—it was frustrating for me to warm the bench. I would have enjoyed Hill more if I had repeated a year, as did most of those transferring to boarding schools in those days. Whereas I do not fault Papa for seeing no reason why I should repeat a grade (and stay on the family payroll another year), the fact that I did not influenced my performance in athletics. In my final football season at Hill I weighed only 145 pounds; nine months later I weighed over 160 pounds.

Despite what I viewed as my failure in athletics, boarding-school discipline doubtless did me some good and certainly prepared me for the demanding regimen of Annapolis. The stiff collars we wore at dinner at Hill, for example, were a full-time fixture of the Naval Academy uniform.

Perhaps my most significant pre-Annapolis experience took place in 1935 when I was packed off to Camp Kipawa in Quebec. After a few weeks of hiking, canoeing, and swimming to acclimate us and determine our relative capabilities, the twenty-odd campers were divided into two groups—a small group of older boys and the remainder. My seventeenth birthday was only two months away; I was the youngest in the small group. We prepared for a long canoe trip through interior Quebec.

Our trek, which lasted thirty-seven days, began with a rugged 7-mile portage northward out of the Ottawa Valley. We then headed north and east through a wilderness of lakes, rivers, and streams. About three weeks out Boyd Chapman, the other boy in my canoe, and I were traversing a large lake (Grand Lake Victoria) in a rain squall. We had fallen far behind the other two canoes, which were almost out of sight. When a crisp breeze came up, we rigged a sail by fastening our pup tent to a paddle, which I held upright in the bow. Soon we were moving along smartly. Chapman ignored my caution, however, and wrapped the tumpline, which he was using as a sheet, around a thwart. About halfway down the lake, the inevitable gust materialized, and we turned over. I righted the canoe and pushed it toward a small island about 50 yards away, attempting to keep all the contents within the water-filled canoe. Chapman thrashed around in his poncho, yelling for help. Inasmuch as the entire food supply was in our canoe, I thought it more important to attend to it than to Chapman, who I knew would be an adequate swimmer once he could disentangle himself from his poncho. After beaching on the island and inventorying our remaining stores, we saw that we had lost almost everything. Much of what we had saved soon fermented. The other two canoes had long since passed from sight when, after reloading, we headed after them. It was twilight by the time we reached the bottom of the lake and were confronted with a vee, with no clue as to which arm of the river to follow. Fortunately, we chose the north fork, and after a twenty-minute paddle in the gathering gloom, we saw the campsite.

It was not a joyful reunion. Davis, the leader, could hardly fault us for losing all the provisions—he had planned what each canoe would carry. The fact that he had abandoned us to fend for ourselves did not speak highly of his leadership either. Our diet for the next week consisted primarily of fish and blueberries, although twice we varied the menu. We rooted around in the weed-glutted garden of an abandoned trapper's cabin, found some turnips, and boiled them. A few days later we heard porcupines in a large pine, chopped it down, beat one of the stunned animals over the head with sticks, then skinned and cooked him. The meat wasn't bad.

Most evenings we paddled until midnight so that we could reach the Hudson Bay Company's post at Lake Barriere in seven days. There, we assumed, Davis would procure supplies. When we finally arrived, Davis got into a controversy with the company about adding to his already bulging charge account. So it was three more days of forced march on empty stomachs before we joined up with the other group at Lake Kipawa.

The final few days back at camp were anticlimactic after the ill-starred thirty-seven-day canoe trip. Toward the end of August, all the younger boys departed. Davis had decided that we should linger a day or two longer to enjoy the beautiful weather. Our final morning we awoke to a blinding snowstorm. We had to paddle up the Ottawa River 4 miles in the driving snow to where the cars were parked.

All in all, I loved the Canadian wilds and certainly matured during the summer. One lasting blessing has been my lifelong abstention from tobacco. Along with the food, the tobacco had also gone to the bottom of Grand Lake Victoria. For days I watched my fellow campers become increasingly irritable as they burned their lips and fingers nursing the final puffs out of cigarette stubs. Later, they rolled the husbanded ends into yet another gruesome fag. I saw smoking as a sorry habit that I determined to do without.

In September 1936 I headed for Severn School to acquire the mathematics and science I needed for entry into the Naval Academy. Having scrupulously avoided math and science at Hill, I now paid the penalty with a diet of college algebra, trigonometry, solid geometry, physics, and chemistry. The only relief from this rugged regimen was the required course in English.

Attractively situated on Round Bay, about 8 miles up the Severn River from Annapolis, Severn was a small school of less than one

hundred students. Discipline was more relaxed than at Hill, probably because most in attendance were strongly motivated toward a
service career and did not require a tight rein. Students came from
all parts of the country, many were Navy juniors (sons of naval officers), and practically all came from high schools.

The fact that we were both from private schools was probably
the reason that Arthur Hutchinson "Tom" Terry from Kent School
in Connecticut and I were assigned as roommates. Tom, by any
reckoning, was an out-of-the-ordinary character.

Tom came to Severn with many of the trappings of a sailor,
which, indeed, he was. He had a sextant, facility with Morse Code,
familiarity with all things nautical, and the curiosity to learn more.
Stocky, nonathletic except for water sports (he had been on the Kent
crew), Tom was a formidable character with forearms like Popeye's,
determination, and a glittering eye. Often seen trying to locate Severn by sextant star sight using an artificial horizon (a can of oil)—
he was never able to do closer than about 50 miles—and conversing
in language richly spiced with nautical terms, Tom was promptly
dubbed The Mariner. One of his winter enterprises was to rig
up a Morse Code key by which he communicated by blinker light
from his desk in our annex with a like-minded agent in the main
building.

To learn something about what we were in for, The Mariner and
I visited Annapolis frequently on weekends, an easily negotiated
distance by the rickety trolley line from Baltimore to Annapolis.

In the autumn of 1936, Annapolis was a picturesque fishing
village. The Naval Academy nestled alongside ponderously, if pre-
cariously, hemmed in by the Chesapeake Bay to the east and the
Severn River to the north. Although the Governor's Mansion stood
in close but forbidding seclusion in the center of town, the state
government had not yet established a significant, year-round presence. During the week the little town kept the noiseless tenor of its
way. Only on weekends, when 2,200 midshipmen poured forth from
behind the 8-foot-high masonry wall of the Academy, was the town
roused from its somnolence.

The quaint, winding streets and circles of Annapolis were not
designed for vehicular traffic, a fact that made the town more inviting to the midshipmen, who were not allowed to own automobiles.
Flooding the streets and alleys like an incoming tide, the invaders
in blue, gold, and white swarmed to the inns, fish market, movie
theaters, and shops. They wandered through the cobblestone streets

and byways in search of diversion and that scarce local commodity, feminine companionship. Some of the local inhabitants extended their hospitality to the young men far from home—especially if they had eligible daughters—but for the majority of the lonely midshipmen there were few, if any, doors open.

A highlight of Annapolis weekends was the arrival around noon on Saturday of the "toonerville trolley" from Baltimore. After rocking along through the woodsy Maryland countryside at speeds of perhaps 40 miles per hour, the trolley delivered scores of breathless, nubile beauties to the tiny station on the western fringe of town. Equally excited, if not so shaken up, young ladies arriving by bus and car joined these gaily clad girls. Impatient upperclassmen ("plebes"—freshmen—were not permitted to "drag"—date) eagerly awaited the start of an all-too-brief romantic adventure. Strolling with their uniformed escorts through the Academy grounds by seawall and boat basin, along campus paths and—for the venturesome—up the Severn to the secluded cemetery, the feminine incursion transformed the gray and granite of the Academy "yard" into a throbbing, lively place. Then, almost before you knew it, Sunday Evening Formation in front of Bancroft Hall was over, the midshipmen marched off into their massive, cavernous dormitory, the feminine tide receded, and the yard relapsed into sterile masculinity.

It was this intriguing scene that Tom and I observed when we visited Annapolis for the first time in September 1936. We returned many times that fall and winter. Besides the obligatory pilgrimages to the Academy and the government buildings, we once paid a call on Lieutenant Commander Weems, U.S. Naval Reserve, who graciously explained his new system of navigation to us and showed us his trove of nautical gear. Another time, armed with a letter of introduction from a Terry family friend, we had a brief audience with the governor, although this led to nothing.

My heavy academic load, together with athletics, kept me busy. Although no standout in football, I did make the team as blocking back. In winter I was a sometime boxer, but we had no team. In the spring I was recruited for lacrosse, as were all footballers not already playing baseball. I immediately liked the game and made the team as midfielder. I also played on the tennis team when it did not conflict with lacrosse.

One early spring afternoon before sports had started, Tom and I took a long walk through the hinterlands, which included borrowing a rowboat and crossing one of the many inlets of the nearby Chesapeake. On the way home, as we approached the school annex where we lived, a delegation of boys came running up the road to meet us. Our room, they said, had been gutted by fire during our absence. This proved all too true. What furniture and clothing the fire had not destroyed, the foam from fire extinguishers deployed by over-enthusiastic, fire-fighting students had ruined. For three weeks Tom and I had to camp out with others in the main building while our room was rehabilitated.

The insurance company poked around for a few days and eventually accepted the explanation that the fire resulted from a short circuit in the elaborate wiring for Tom's signal apparatus. Tom and I, with straight faces, allowed as how this could well have been the cause. Had I not had an indelible picture in my mind's eye of Tom emptying his pipe in the wastebasket just before we departed on the walk, I might have agreed more convincingly.

A few weeks later, in April, the results of the Naval Academy exams arrived. Tom failed, as did about 50 percent of those examined. This was an abysmal record—one which, if repeated, quickly could have put the school out of business.

The football coach and math instructor interviewed me along with others to determine the cause of the fiasco. I told him of the extensive cheating I had observed during our regular Saturday-morning practice exams. The cheating explained why some of those for whom the faculty had had high hopes and who had achieved constantly good grades had failed the Academy exam. (They expected me to fail because I had flunked test after test. Finally, however, I got the hang of the tricky algebra problems. By exam time I had mastered them and had little difficulty getting a 3.6 (90), even though my cumulative grade for the year was undistinguished.) The faculty was stunned, and I am sure they overhauled the testing system the following year.

That evening a preoccupied Tom and I walked down to Round Bay, swam out a hundred yards to a moored sailboat (owner unknown), and went for a long moonlight sail. Upon return about 11:00 P.M., Tom packed his bags, bid me farewell, and walked down to catch the last trolley for Baltimore. He said good-bye to no one but me. He did not even check out of school.

3

Annapolis

In late June 1937, after a brief vacation with the family, I arrived in Annapolis for the final pre-entry physical exam. Annapolis was like a ghost town. Most of the midshipmen had departed on old battleships for the summer cruise to Europe. Half of the second class (the juniors), the only class remaining, were off on an East Coast destroyer cruise. Those present were helping indoctrinate the plebe class, which was being augmented daily by new recruits. The town was quiet indeed. Those few of us awaiting the results of our physicals, preoccupied with our imminent adventure, wandered aimlessly around the deserted streets. With stiff upper lip we contemplated our future with a mixed sense of excitement and foreboding.

Then, abruptly, there I was on a warm summer day standing at attention in the rotunda of Bancroft Hall. With about twenty nondescript youths from all regions of the country, I took the Midshipman's Oath as a member of the United States Navy. It was July 1, 1937, and already the inevitable hustlers among my classmates who had been arriving over the past three weeks and taken the oath earlier were belaboring us with the quaint idea that since the government fiscal year ended on June 30 we would always be their juniors by one year. Most of us were seventeen to nineteen years old. There were also a few in their twenties and a handful who were only sixteen. Some were so naive as to give credence to this absurdity.

Immature though I was, the sheltered product of private boys' schools, for better or worse I was now in the Navy. But there was little time to consider the significance of this fact. For the next few weeks the Academy staff and second classmen struggled to mold the raw material from high schools, colleges (some plebes had had one to three years of college), and the Fleet into a semblance of military conformity.

My roommate plebe summer was Victor Delano. His father, a Navy captain, skippered a battleship. Although not close friends, we had been classmates at Severn. It was evident, however, that my conscientious roommate and I, still in doubt as to my commitment to a military career, would not be compatible over the long haul.

Just down the corridor was a ruggedly handsome, easygoing, athletic type from Little Falls, a scenic village in upstate New York. Allan Lloyd Feldmeier had graduated from Taft School and then gone on to Dartmouth, where, as a member of the freshman football team, he had attracted Navy recruiters. About 5 feet 10 inches and 180-odd pounds, he had also attracted the attention of the captain of the football team, who delivered an overenthusiastic elbow to Al's mouth during a varsity-plebe scrimmage in September. The upperclassman knocked out three of Al's top front teeth. The mishap marked Al as a class character from that day forth. The medical department considered it foolish to give him permanent false teeth until his football-playing days were over, so Al went through the next three years with a temporary bridge, which he occasionally neglected to wear. This earned him the nickname of Bucky, but more often he was known as The Count or Basie after his favorite musician. The Count and I had met in August, when we vied for the position of stroke during a lifeboat drill on the Severn River. Gradually, this prickly introduction ripened into friendship. We decided to room together.

From the beginning the Class of 1941 was different. The smallest class for several years, it was also the last class to have plebe year in the old mess hall. A massive basement room extending almost the length of Bancroft Hall, the ceiling of the hall was supported by innumerable pillars. These pillars effectively reduced the visibility of the officer of the day, who sat at a centrally placed table. More than two thousand midshipmen ate in the mess hall, and at least two thirds of them were thus obscured from the officer's view. This relative immunity from detection seemed to provide whatever encouragement was necessary for hazing of the more physical sort, such as making a plebe sit at attention through the meal without a chair, pouring catsup over a plebe's head, and what we called beating ass with tin trays. During the summer of 1938, the ceiling of the mess hall was raised, arched, and reinforced; the pillars were removed. Although this renovation did not eliminate hazing during meals, hazing did require more ingenuity than it had in the old mess hall, and it was far more risky to resort to blatantly physical variations. As the years slowly passed and the war in Europe sucked us inexorably into its vortex, other, more dramatic, events would distinguish the Class of 1941.

Academics were not of great interest to either The Count or me. An engineering school had not been the first choice of either of us. My preference had always been the language arts. Although more scientifically minded than I, the Count was no more motivated to excel academically. In fact, our easygoing, noncutthroat attitude toward scholarship probably led to our initial rapport. Fortunately, mathematics came easily to both of us, and we were not overwhelmed by the fast pace during plebe year, when each course consumed only six weeks. The pace of the curriculum accounted for almost all first-year attrition, or about one third of our classmates. We did our homework, except when we ran out of time before lights out, but it was not a labor in which we had much interest. We usually had novels or other reading matter in which we buried ourselves at every opportunity. We cleaned our room, made our beds, shined our shoes, attended to our laundry and other domestic chores without relish, and managed to get by without too much notice. At drill there were more uncoordinated plebes who absorbed the drill masters' attention. Of course, there were some upperclassmen who viewed our casual attitude toward our lowly plebian status as threatening, and they periodically chastised us for it. One happening was memorable.

A hallowed tradition at Annapolis is the "spoon," the occasion when an upperclassman shakes hands with a plebe. The handshake indicates to one and all that the plebe can relax in the upperclassman's presence, call him by his first name, and come to him for protection. One January day after the evening meal, a crowd of second classmen and youngsters (sophomores) intent upon mayhem had gathered in our room. The ass beating and hazing had already begun when a loud, ring-induced rap sounded on the thick, half-glass door. (This was a first classman's or officer's way of announcing his imminent entrance—only they had class rings.) Festivities halted abruptly while our chastisers waited to see who was about to enter. The door swung smartly open, and there stood John Leydon, the regimental commander, with five gold stripes gleaming on each sleeve. He was the senior of all midshipmen and impressively tall. John dated Helen Allen, who lived next door to us in Chestnut Hill. He had spooned on me in the autumn, and he was a welcome sight indeed. Calling "Johnny," we shoved aside our tormentors and went off with him to his room until the bell for study hall permitted our safe return. Of course, in later ass beatings, we paid dearly for this moment of triumph, but it was a source of gratification nonetheless as word spread throughout the regiment of this glorious, if transitory, victory of the hares over the hounds.

About a month later the Academy weekly paper, *The Log,* mentioned in a sports write-up that Midshipman 4th Class Parry was undefeated in wrestling at 165 pounds. A few upperclassmen at my mess table Friday evening queried me facetiously about my wrestling prowess (I had won five straight bouts) and made me suffer for my victories by forcing me to eat five apple dumplings complete with hard sauce. Saturday afternoon I won again but felt poorly and related the mess-hall incident to the coach. He was so exercised about the affair that he promptly established a plebe training table for wrestlers. So The Count (who wrestled at 175 pounds) and I escaped our tormentors, during meals at least, for another month.

Plebe year was finally staggering to an end but not without a surge of hazing during the last days before graduation. The final night of plebe year we had been forced into the shower several times, and after each drenching had to crawl up on top of our clothing cabinets (where our mattresses had been hoisted) to "sleep." All our bedding was soaked after the third cycle of this childishness, and our patience was wearing thin. An upperclassman from our corridor who had been harassing us throughout the year appeared around midnight and ordered us into the shower for yet another dunking. As The Count crowded into the shower with me, our tormentor reached his hand in, felt the warm water, and ordered me to turn it to cold. The Count and I exchanged glances. Then we both stepped aside as I turned on the cold water and The Count wrapped a meaty arm around our incautious adversary and held him—full-dress uniform and all—under the icy water. The Count released him. Kicking, screaming, and dripping wet, our tormentor sloshed down the corridor and endeavored to arouse his classmates to retribution. The only responses he managed to evoke were threats of violence to his person if he did not shut up. How he could possibly have dried his heavily padded full-dress uniform in time for graduation, I have no idea. In any case, our final night as plebes ended on this satisfactory note. Distasteful as plebe year was to us, The Count and I never indulged in any hazing whatsoever of underclassmen throughout our three remaining years at the Academy. We gave no credence to the allegation that such treatment was beneficial.

My class standing plebe year was in the middle third. Although I was unable to do better in football than third string, I did at least make the squad of forty-eight, which some high-school captains failed to do. With no prior wrestling experience, I made the team the first week. I was undefeated at 165 pounds and twice claimed as one of my victims Bea Weems, a senior at Severn. (He was later Navy's eastern intercollegiate 165-pound champion.) In lacrosse I was center midfielder. The promise of these accomplishments gave no indication of the disaster lurking ahead.

On the summer cruise to Europe, Ace Leigh, the varsity wrestling captain, and I worked out on a mat on the main deck of the USS *Texas*. Ace was 145 pounds, fast, and strong. I was learning a good deal from him until my right shoulder came out of the socket. This proved to be only the first of many dislocations that ruined my athletic career, although I had no premonition of such ill fortune at the time.

Our flotilla made ports of call at Le Havre, Copenhagen, and Portsmouth, from which we sallied forth to Paris, London, and other nearby points of interest such as Elsinore, Stonehenge, and Winchester. It was during a bus tour through the countryside near Copenhagen that I got into trouble. We had just visited the old royal castle at Fredericksberg and were reboarding the buses. I was seated by a window in a near-empty bus when a first classman entered and told me to move because he wanted my window seat. As newly anointed youngsters, we were supposedly no longer subject to petty harassment; I declined to move. With many first classmen and youngsters as observers, he remonstrated. I ignored him. Feeling uncomfortable on the ride to Elsinore, I purposely dallied on the ramparts there and returned alone to Copenhagen later that evening on the train. Although I realized that I had incurred one first classman's wrath and perhaps that of a few of his narrow-minded classmates, I had no inkling of how devastating his resulting "blackball" would be. Continued success in wrestling and lacrosse would have mitigated my indiscretion, but this was not to be.

Despite the use of several different types of restraining harnesses, I threw my shoulder out of joint five more times while wrestling and once more during lacrosse practice just before the first game. The doctor who looked after Academy athletes ordered me to refrain from contact sports before I became permanently disabled. The prohibition thoroughly deflated me—I had always loved athletics and participation in contact sports in particular was an important facet of my self-image. Not mature enough to handle this disappointment, I allowed it to poison my attitude. In addition, athletics at the Naval Academy, unnaturally devoid of feminine companionship, provided the principle avenue for venting nervous energy and frustration. Without this vent for releasing steam, I began to look elsewhere for diversion. June Week provided an opportunity.

June Week, a highlight of the Academy year, is a period of festivities just before graduation. The week features afternoon hops and evening formal dances and parades. During June Week midshipmen have considerably more freedom of action than in the rest of the year. My youngster June Week was highlighted by a memorable cruise.

During the winter Robert H. "Moon" Mathew and The Count had purchased an old boat with an inboard motor. About 25 feet long and reasonably seaworthy, they christened it *The Good Ship Broadbeam*. Possession of such a craft, much less plying the waters in it, was not sanctioned by Academy authorities, so the *Broadbeam* was secreted in a boatyard in Eastport, a poor suburb of Annapolis. There The Count, Moon, and I would repair and discard our uniforms in a boatyard shack. Suitably disguised in old clothes to look like fishermen, we would take to sea for weekend outings. Fortified with beer obtained from a waterfront store in a cove nearby, we spent many pleasant Sunday afternoons cruising the unfrequented waters within sight of Annapolis.

One evening during June Week, Moon and I decided to take our ladies for a cruise. Emboldened by the darkness and an afternoon of drinking, we went aboard in uniform and chugged out into the bay about 2 miles. We decided that the occasion called for a refreshing swim. The girls, who under normal conditions were discretion itself, were soon carried away by the ardor of the moment. Clad only in their underwear, as were we, they jumped into the water to join us. Splashing noisily about, we became aware too late of the ferry boat bearing down upon us. Fortunately, the Annapolis–Matapeake ferry channel ran about 50 yards to the north, but we were scared to death by this escape and quickly scrambled back aboard. In our excitement we forgot that the tide had come in during our two-hour voyage. So as we passed under the bridge from Annapolis to Eastport, our 10-foot mast, on which was mounted the running light, was snapped off and Moon, who was at the wheel, was almost decapitated. Befuddled by darkness as well as booze, we headed for the nearest cove and anchored near the beach. Holding our clothes over our heads, we waded ashore. Making ourselves presentable was another thing, and we had no solution to the girls' drenched hair. Bedraggled, we started for town on foot. After a few blocks we were able to flag down a taxi which, to our embarrassment, was occupied by a first classman. Hardly able to keep a straight face as the four of us piled into the back seat, he graciously dropped us off at the girls' accommodations without a word of admonition. The Count had to find and return the *Broadbeam* to safe anchorage the next day. He was so furious at Moon and me that he addressed us only by our last names for a week.

Two escapades during our second-class destroyer cruise in June and July are illustrative of the many times during our last two years that we inadvertently tempted fate. First we had a layover at West Point, during which we fraternized with our counterparts at the U.S. Military Academy and danced with their dates. Then we steamed up the Hudson to Poughkeepsie to watch the annual rowing regatta. That evening I routed out a Hill School classmate and he rounded up two Vassar girls. After an evening of good fellowship, we arrived at the dock several minutes before my motor launch was scheduled to depart for the ship. While I was overly wrapped up in leave-taking, the launch pulled away without me. I had to settle for a seat in the last launch of the night, which made the rounds of all seven destroyers delivering, for the most part, drunken sailors who had missed their own boats. I was the only midshipman so marooned and did my best to look inconspicuous amidst the rowdy seamen as we came alongside the USS *Decatur.* I sighted the officer of the deck at the head of the gangway and felt certain that I was a goner. As a drunken sailor was being assisted up the ladder, the officer of the deck left his station. Seeing my opportunity, I darted up the ladder and disappeared into the bowels of the ship just before he returned. I will never know whether he gave me this chance or whether a passing vessel momentarily distracted his attention.

A few weeks later our destroyers sojourned briefly in Newport, Rhode Island. Two of my running mates (Bleecker P. Seaman and

Walter B. "Pinky" Shrout) and I decided to visit some girls summering in Watch Hill, Connecticut. We took the Newport–Jamestown Ferry and then taxied the rest of the way. After a pleasant afternoon and evening, the girls drove us back to the ferry. Misjudging the time, we arrived as the last ferry was pulling away from the dock. We sprinted down the pier, intending to leap the slowly opening gap. Fortunately, a heavy chain strung across the slip entrance about 10 yards from the water intervened, or we surely would have landed in the water. As it was, Bleecker, lacrosse captain and the fastest of us, reached the chain first, tripped, and sprawled headlong onto the dock. Why he was not badly injured, I have no idea—probably his ample load of spirits. Pinky and I were able to pull up short of the water after leaping over the cable. We then talked the girls into driving us as far as Providence, whence we taxied to Newport. Arriving there almost an hour before liberty was up at 7:00 A.M., we decided to have breakfast at a waterfront cafe. Our watches were slow or the coxswain shoved off early because once again we missed the boat. Embarrassed, we had to wait for the officers' boat at 8:00 and ride that to our respective ships amidst the raised eyebrows of returning officers, who magnanimously refrained from putting us on report.

Inserted between these adventures, I had distinguished myself as midshipman officer of the deck. After exiting New York harbor in late June, our squadron of seven destroyers ran into a violent storm off Sandy Hook. The officer of the deck was so ill that he was unable to remain on his feet—he had to retreat to the captain's sea cabin just aft of the bridge. As midshipman officer of the deck, I now had the conn. Besides the helmsman, I was the only one on the bridge who was not seasick. Throughout the tempestuous night, we managed to stay on course and keep position within the squadron.

The next day I was complimented by the captain. Two or three days later, the USS *Decatur* was acting squadron leader during maneuvers. The ensign officer of the deck was less than impressive in executing turns and keeping in line, and the skipper lost patience. He directed me, as midshipman officer of the deck, to take over. As fate would have it, I performed flawlessly again and received the captain's accolade. Of twenty-six midshipmen on the *Decatur*, I stood number two at the end of the six-week cruise. Despite the fact that this amounted to half the summer's grade, I stood close to last in the class for second-class summer. With this unequivocal evidence that I was blackballed beyond redemption, I turned maverick.

From then on I made the minimum effort to get by.

Second-class year, traditionally a pleasant one, was blighted by fratricidal warfare between first and second classmen. The Academy administration instituted in the fall of 1939 what at the time seemed to be a radical policy; it certainly had far-reaching effects as far as my class was concerned. All first classmen were reassigned to different battalions. The reputed objective of this unprecedented shift was to break up cozy friendships that had developed over the two previous years between first and second classmen who had lived down the hall from each other. As the reasoning went, this would lead to more objective assessment of second classmen and more equitable selection of midshipmen regimental officers for first-class year. In fact, this reassignment created confrontations and bad feeling. Harassment by immature first classmen reached such proportion that open rebellion almost erupted. In an effort to gain some relief, the leadership of the second class obtained an audience with the commandant of midshipmen, who subsequently censured the more flagrant offenders from the first class. Bad blood persisted between the two classes right up until graduation. As a result of this shocking situation, an unprecedented number—over half of my 400 classmates—requested assignment to the twenty-five available billets in the Marine Corps. The Class of 1941 was indeed unique.

In November 1939 Moon Mathew, John C. "Black Rufe" Bangert, and I latched onto a bottle of whiskey in town. We polished it off and returned to the Academy grounds well before taps. With thick fog adding to our sense of security, we indulged in some boisterous horseplay as we ran down the boardwalk then encircling the front half of the chapel, which was undergoing enlargement. As we came clattering over the boards onto the pavement in front of the superintendent's quarters, we almost ran into Rear Admiral Wilson Brown, who was walking his dog. Outraged at our unseemly behavior, he commanded us to report immediately to the officer of the day. We returned to Bancroft Hall, where with the aid of sympathetic classmates we endeavored to sober up. But getting three half-bombed midshipmen shipshape took some doing, and before we knew it the better part of an hour had elapsed. In the meantime the admiral had told the officer of the day to be on the lookout for us. The thought crossed our minds that we might be able to brazen it out, that the admiral might not be able to identify us since he had only glimpsed us briefly in the fog and had not taken our names. But the consequences if we were ultimately apprehended were too ominous to contemplate. Failure to obey a direct order from the superintendent himself on top of conduct unbecoming midshipmen would guarantee our dismissal. We decided to pay the piper. Just when the officer of the day was about to panic and send out an all-points bulletin, Moon, Black Rufe, and I sheepishly presented ourselves. Pay the piper we did, with 100 demerits apiece and thirty days of confinement to our rooms, a period that bridged most of the Christmas holidays.

Christmas in deserted Bancroft Hall with only Moon, Black Rufe, and myself to ponder the echoing silence was a bleak experience. It would have been more so were it not for the unquenchable ebullience of Moon. On our way to Christmas dinner in the mess hall, a messenger intercepted us and ordered us to report to the officer of the day. There, to our astonishment, were Mr. and Mrs. Robert H. Mathew, who had journeyed from Nebraska to be with their son on Christmas. They graciously included me in their Christmas dinner in town, after an appeal to the Academy hierarchy had resulted in our release from confinement for a few hours.

With the advent of the new year and 182 demerits (out of an allowable 200) already racked up as a second classman, I expressed the fear to my father that I could not make it to June without incurring more than eighteen demerits. This called forth a reply from the judge:

February 1, 1940

Dear Wawa:

I don't know what to say to you. You come home at Christmas with 170 demerits. That leaves 30 for you to go during the year. You get 12 more in four weeks and express the fear that you can't get through the rest of the year on 18. Somebody ought to take you down to the dock, tie a brick around your neck and throw you in. Young Jack Walsh was at Annapolis four years and got 32 demerits in the whole time. He, I should say, is far from bright and by no means a model of discretion but if he could get through, you can't scare up a decent excuse for not doing so.

I told you when you were home that I'd been tipped off that your officers thought you were going with a bum crowd and ought to break away from them but of course you would a damned sight rather get fired than do anything like that. There is no reason in God's green earth why you should have got any demerits during the last month and there is no reason why you

should get any more from now until the end of the year if you
take a little trouble, but I suppose you'll do as you damn please
and grouse around for the rest of your life telling everybody how
badly you were treated.
Buck up.
GGP

Despite this "psychological lift," I might not have made it if my
12th Company commander, Otto Trainer, had not gone out of his
way to protect me. He believed that I was being unfairly bedeviled
by two of the most disliked first classmen, my squad leader and his
roommate, the commander of the 11th Company. On more than one
occasion Otto tore up reports authored by them. The two even sent
their plebes around to our room "to buy your full-dress uniform
cheap because you aren't going to be around long." With Otto's help
I went demeritless the last four months. The harassment took a toll
on my grades, however, and I entered the final exams as unsatisfactory in six or seven subjects. With concentrated effort I pulled them
all above passing.

Due to my flirtation with academic as well as behavioral disaster, June Week found me without a date. There were two reasons,
the more prosaic being that I had no funds to speak of. My father
had the quaint idea that midshipmen were paid an adequate wage.
Actually, most of our compensation was arbitrarily saved for us so
that we would have wherewithal for our leave periods and to purchase uniforms upon graduation without going into hock—or at
least not much in hock. Besides, I had never liked asking Father for
spending money, and with my horrendous scholastic and conduct
records it seemed inapppropriate to solicit him for a contribution to
my social life. The other reason was that, due to my preoccupation
with career survival, I had not kept up regular correspondence with
the Philadelphia girls. A further complication was that The Count
and I had not purchased class rings for the highlight of our June
Week, the Ring Dance. We had fully intended to but had procrasti-
nated. To our chagrin this delinquency brought The Count and myself to the attention of the commandant, who admonished us.
Believing this to be a private matter and resenting the pressure, we
declined to buy rings at all. We may well be the only Naval Academy graduates to have never had class rings, a distinction of which,
I think we are neither proud nor ashamed.

Fate was smiling upon me, however, for a member of the Class of
1942 had invited his sister down from Rochester, New York, and she

was without a date. A classmate arranged an introduction and I spent the latter part of June Week with a pretty, compatible charmer with whom I carried on a brief romance that summer.

I began my year as a first classman auspiciously enough: The three old battlewagons of the midshipmen squadron—*Arkansas*, *Texas*, and *New York*—ferried us to Panama. There, according to our tastes, we saw the sights or wallowed in the fleshpots of Colon, Cristobal, and Panama City.

While we plowed eastward along the coast of South America enroute to Rio de Janeiro, we brushed up on our skills as future deck officers, navigators, and engineers. (On the youngster cruise, in contrast, most of our jobs had been enlisted men's duties.) We also tried out our Portuguese. But Rio was to remain a dream, for the French capitulated to the Germans early that summer, and the high command of the U.S. Navy decided that we should return to the cozier confines of the Caribbean. So the three battleships split up, and my new destination was St. Thomas, Virgin Islands. Liberty in St. Thomas was a far cry from liberty in Rio but better than no liberty at all.

After forming up again, the squadron proceeded to Guantanamo Bay, Cuba. There I had a chance to glimpse the harbor and roam some of the surrounding terrain, an area that, many years later, came ever so close to playing a dramatic role in my career. During our stay in Guantanamo Bay, an old destroyer manned by naval reservists on two weeks of active duty made an overnight run to Santiago de Cuba and offered to take some midshipmen for a ride. It was enlightening to observe the comparatively casual way in which the reservists went about their chores. The 10-mile haul up the narrow, curving channel to the small, picturesque inland harbor was scenic. So was the hillside town, although beyond the welcome extended at brothels, it did not open its arms to us. It was easy to see how the Spanish warships that had taken refuge in the harbor in 1898 were destroyed when they tried to run the gauntlet from the channel to the sea past the U.S. Fleet standing offshore.

The twenty-odd days of leave during the first weeks of September are a time for midshipmen to recharge batteries, and they make the most of it. It was at a shipwreck ball at the Stone Harbor Yacht Club in early September 1940 that I first saw Vera Corey Henderson, a strikingly beautiful, long-haired blonde three months short of her eighteenth birthday. Wearing a sarong that did little to hide her superb figure, she was dancing with my youngest brother, Steve, who (I learned later) was her escort. I cut in and promptly asked her for a date. A little while later I danced with her again and asked her for another date. The next day my mother remonstrated with me for moving in on Steve's territory, but by then it was too late. For the remainder of September leave, I was with her almost every day—I even managed to double-date with her on those occasions for which she had previous engagements.

With the war in Europe at a crucial if not calamitous stage, the Academy shortened our senior year by half and graduated us in February. The expanding U.S. Fleet badly needed junior officers, so the academics we needed most were compressed into the allotted time. Winter sports were truncated and for us, the spring schedule was canceled. It had finally dawned on the military hierarchy that the times were not normal. Oddly, there was not as much thought of war among us as one might think. Perhaps the day-to-day demands of the curriculum permitted little time for concern. Even with France defeated and Britain hanging on by her toenails, we seemed oblivious to the war. There was practically no discussion of it in class and little among classmates. The Count and I never talked seriously at length about the war and the implications of it, although I believe we knew that eventually we would be involved. The uncompromising grind, the unyielding schedule where every waking minute was committed to study or class or inspection or drill or athletics tended to insulate us from the real world. In a broader sense, however, the midshipmen reflected the national indifference to the plight of our traditional allies; we mirrored American myopia.

My final brush with academic disaster came in the last exams in January 1941. I had done so poorly in electrical engineering that I needed a 3.2 (80) on the final to pass the course. I crammed for the exam and answered each of the eight questions correctly. My grade was 3.8 (95), more than enough to pass. Nonetheless, I was annoyed because I knew I had "maxed" the exam and should have received a 4.0 (100). But I was uncertain how an inquiry would sit with the instructor who, like teachers everywhere, abhorred underachievers. So I left well enough alone and never discovered how he had contrived to deny me a perfect grade.

In the final standings, I had been last in "aptitude for the service"—an absurd assessment—and last in conduct. Together they comprised 30 percent of the final grade and proved too heavy an anchor for my good subjects—English, history, and French—to overcome.

I had invited Vera for that part of our graduation week for which she could get away from her boarding school, Low–Heywood, in Stamford, Connecticut. In January she was put on probation by school authorities because she had been overheard "swearing" by a teacher. This precipitated a school controversy when it became known that she might be denied permission to go to Annapolis. Most of the students and teachers urged compassion. But the headmistress was adamant, and only days before my graduation festivities Vera was told that she could not leave school. Once again I was without a date with graduation week only days away.

Due to our compressed senior year, June Week in 1941 was February Week, and it was a poor substitute for the traditional, glamorous summer send-off. It was bitterly cold, and most of the Severn River and all its estuaries were frozen solid. My mood was as icy as the weather. In an attempt to rally my spirits, I took Emily Bonsall, a cute Chestnut Hill girl, ice skating one afternoon. There was a limit to which I could muscle in on other's dates, however, and John Davenport, her escort, was a friend of mine. Denied Vera's company and too late to ask another girl, I was feeling rebellious. When my brother John, a senior at Penn, showed up the afternoon before graduation at the house we had rented for the week in the Annapolis suburbs, I was ready for some action.

There had been many highjinks during our four-year grind, but my final gesture of defiance was unquestionably the most foolish. We had been drinking beer all afternoon, and as the time for our final evening formation drew near we had the brilliant idea of dressing John up in my uniform to stand formation in my place. After all, John had been the one who had wanted to go to the Academy in the first place; I used his appointment when he could not pass the eye exam. In our euphoric state this seemed like a dramatic statement against what we considered a flawed system. Although John was about 20 pounds lighter, we were almost the same height and he did not look too bad in my uniform. Moon Mathew, who stood beside me in the last squad of 1st Platoon, took him in tow and off they went. Back at the house with the four girls, none of whom was my date, I sobered up too late. My fantasy of having fun with one or more of the girls during their dates' absences quickly evaporated. Visions of failing at the eleventh hour with Mother and Father already enroute to see me graduate flashed through my aching head. Without wheels or uniform, all that I could do was hope for the best. The more than two hours until John's return seemed like two years. Although there were some questioning looks at John as he stood in my place, marched down to the mess hall, and ate dinner with the regiment of midshipmen, the escapade was outwardly successful. But the worry that ate away at me (and I believe at John also) rendered our coup a hollow one.

I am not proud of my Naval Academy record. Although it can be argued that being last is in many ways an achievement comparable to being first (there is no margin for error in either case), it is not an "honor" that is easy to live down. It cost me many dollars because of belated promotions throughout the years and may have cost me prestige in ways of which I am unaware. Although my standing as anchorman at graduation certainly penalized me less in the Marine Corps (where I was last of twenty-six) than it would have in the Navy (where I was last of about 400), it was a handicap nonetheless.

In fact, however, I was not that poor a student. Lazy, unmotivated certainly—especially after youngster year—I never shaved it so close that I was required to take a re-exam, the fate of more than a hundred classmates whose standing was higher than mine.

4

Shavetails

Quantico

That twenty-six second lieutenants ("shavetails") reported to the Marine Corps Schools, Quantico, Virginia, in late February 1941 instead of the allotted twenty-five was the result of an appeal by William McReynolds to the Secretary of the Navy. Bill's father had been a Marine officer, and Bill believed this sufficient reason for him to be appointed to the Marine Corps. The secretary concurred.

Even before Bill appealed to the Secretary of the Navy, the Marine Corps commissions for 1941 had been subject to intense behind-the-scenes activity. Naval Academy authorities had been embarrassed by the magnitude of midshipmen who had originally applied for the Marine Corps—208, or over half the class. As a result, an aggressive campaign of persuasion was conducted in which most of the applicants were interviewed privately by staff naval officers. (The Count and I had the dubious distinction of not being summoned for interviews.) The interviews succeeded in whittling the number of applicants down to the true believers. Therefore, seventy-eight of us gathered in the office of the commandant of midshipmen to draw envelopes for the twenty-five Marine commissions. Within each envelope was either a blank slip or a slip with the typed message "Assigned to U.S. Marine Corps." Bill McReynolds's was blank, so he mounted his direct appeal.

Bill's reason for selecting a Marine Corps career was understandable. So was that of the few who had been enlisted Marines before entering the Academy. What of the rest of us? We never took a poll, but undoubtedly in every case there was a more substantial motivation than pique at the Navy. Some of us were attracted by Marine Corps mystique—the tough, elite image. A few really knew something about the Marine Corps beyond the public-relations image and wanted to be a part of this feisty brotherhood. Others preferred fighting on land to fighting at sea.

The Count, I believe, was challenged by the macho, select reputation. As for me, the image was also an attraction, although I knew little about the Marine Corps itself. A mild preference for land over sea warfare was another factor. But what really swayed me was the prospect of attending The Basic School at the Philadelphia Navy Yard, close to home and the wealth of femininity from which I had been forcibly separated for the most part since 1937. Then there was my special girl, Vera Henderson, soon to be a Philadelphia debutante. I might have chosen the Marine Corps without this added inducement, but this was the clincher.

During the fall of 1940, Headquarters, Marine Corps (HQMC) decided that the twenty-six lieutenants soon to be graduated from the Naval Academy did not need to go to The Basic School for indoctrination. The fact that our early graduation made us available at an inconvenient time—The Basic School was in mid course—was probably a factor in the decision. Although no explanation was offered, I surmise that the major reason was the perceived need to accelerate the training of lieutenants for base defense and field artillery duty. To justify an override of the hallowed policy of training all officers as infantrymen before permitting specialization, the need must have been great indeed.

Someone might have even believed that the Naval Academy curriculum provided enough training to allow us to get by. They could not have been more deluded. Throughout my career I felt the absence of this indoctrination, especially during the first five years. It succeeded in saddling me with an inferiority complex and a sense of insecurity alien to my nature. It forced me to compete with contemporaries who had been blessed with either nine months at The Basic School or the slightly shorter Reserve equivalent, Candidates Class, Reserve Officers Course. These fortunates had performed in the field as platoon leaders and platoon sergeants and as machine gunners and mortarmen. They had carried Browning Automatic Rifles and had taken night compass marches. Not only had they been given an infantryman's eye view of the world, they had been initiated into the rites of the Marines by the backbone of the Corps—the tough, professional sergeants who make it run. We received no such indoctrination. It was so monumental a mistake that in later years the thought occurred to me more than once that it had been perpetrated by some headquarters officer who lacked enthusiasm for Naval Academy graduates.

Quantico was a hamlet on the Potomac River about 30 miles south of Washington, D.C., where the Marine Corps had a valuable tract of rolling countryside on which to train embryonic officers. It would soon be transformed into a major officer-training and educational center, but in February 1941 the buildup was just beginning. The first class of officer candidates was graduating at the time of our arrival.

The Base Defense Weapons Course, upon which we now embarked with about thirty recent graduates of The Basic School, was a leisurely four-month effort. The course consisted of one part casual indoctrination into officerlike matters, such as equitation and sword drill, and one part artillery. Since there was no inclination to subject the majority of our class to repetition of what they had received at The Basic School, indoctrination in junior-officer philosophy was almost nonexistent. For the greater part of the course, we were divided into two groups: base defense and field artillery. The Base Defense Section concentrated on the weaponry and tactics of island defense—antiaircraft and coast defense—in preparation for the occupation of islands thought vital to U.S. security. The Field Artillery Section, to which The Count and I were arbitrarily assigned, superficially familiarized us with the 75mm pack howitzer and its employment in direct support of infantry. We were to be assigned duty with the Fleet Marine Force.

Lacking basic infantry training, we were handicapped from the start. The absence of the 5th Marine Regiment and its supporting artillery battalion, then on maneuvers in Cuba, deprived us even of the opportunity of observing infantry and field artillery in action, not to mention the opportunity to actually man the howitzers. The gentlemanly nature and pace of our course and our consequent relaxed attitude surely reflected the myopic national indifference to ominous happenings abroad. Also, after four years of close confinement at Annapolis, we were as much concerned with our new freedom as with our preparedness for war. But I admit to a feeling of foreboding, however slight, that we were not really learning much about our trade.

Two of our more noteworthy instructors were Major John Bemis and Captain Alpha Bowser. Major Bemis was tall, thin, and professorial. He gave the impression that he revealed information to such as us with reluctance. Captain Bowser was stocky, pleasant, soft-spoken, and self-assured.

Together this talented pair introduced us to the so-called black art of field artillery. They revealed how a senior officer at the battalion fire-direction center (FDC) translated the commands of a front-line observer or a hilltop observer within sight of the front lines into commands for the firing batteries. Cumbersome, time-consuming, dependent upon intimate familiarity with the firing tables, this method would soon be replaced by a speedier, more efficient system that employed the simple slide rule. (Why anyone with foresight and persistence had not improved the clumsy method in the years between the world wars defies imagination. Perhaps Marines relied too heavily on the experts at the Army's Field Artillery School in Fort Sill, Oklahoma, to improve the art.) The field artillery brotherhood appeared to be self-conscious about their profession, whose complexity they zealously guarded as if to keep outsiders from learning that their secrets were not that profound.

We also learned how to give commands to the FDC as field artillery forward observers (FOs). Issuing commands as an FO was a tricky business. Often distracted by front-line fire, the FO had to visualize the gun-target line from his position, which was usually on the flank. The process involved consideration of the angle between the FO's line of sight and the target and the gun-target line—an awkward process that was scrapped later in favor of making the conversion in the relative calm of the FDC.

Our introduction to the pack howitzer, the weapon we were being trained to employ, was brief and unfulfilling. In the gun shed one lonely cannon was dramatically, even tenderly, unveiled from its tarpaulin shroud by Major Bemis. Of course, all weapons, particularly artillery pieces, were in short supply in 1941, and this treasured cannon was a spare for the Fleet Marine Force. Apparently the school staff thought it was impractical to train thirty of us individually on one howitzer; we were allowed to inspect its intricacies only fleetingly. Breaking it down into component loads for manhandling or mule-packing was only demonstrated.

Of what we needed most—to learn firsthand the trades of section chief, gunner, and ammunition handler—there was none at all. So what little we picked up about gunnery came from some of our classmates who had previously served in field artillery battalions of the National Guard and had graduated from The Basic School. As a matter of fact, we deferred not a little to The Basic Schoolers, who were almost a year senior to us.

If gunnery was lacking, equitation was not. As an accomplished horseman, Al Bowser was also our equitation instructor. Equitation still held a prominent place in the curriculum of the day, not so much because anyone thought the horse would play a role in future combat but because the officer corps could not bring itself to believe that one could really be an officer and a gentleman without being comfortable in a saddle. One highlight of our riding forays was the proclivity of a broad-beamed student lieutenant, Charles "Shoulders" McLean, to slide quietly out of the saddle and land in a heap on the trail. The betting fraternity would lay odds on where this indignity would occur. A fall was not the worst thing that could happen, however. Even more humiliating was the long walk back to the stables where the scornful grooms awaited after a trailwise steed had unloaded his baggage and bolted home with an empty saddle. The saddle was not my natural milieu, although I had ridden a few times before. I tended to try to force rather than persuade my mount but managed to get by without distinction or distress.

My brother Dick, who had graduated from Harvard in 1938, had joined the 2nd Candidates Class and was seeking a commission. As a private first class, he was not permitted familiarity with officers, even his second-lieutenant brother. One evening he slipped away and visited me at my bachelor quarters in Harry Lee Hall. We discussed the problems he was having with some of his instructors, who were noncommissioned officers (NCOs) and seemed to relish devoting special attention to a Harvard graduate. Dick discounted his chances of gaining his Reserve commission. Evidently, he communicated this conviction to Father, for a few weeks later the judge arrived at Quantico with Congressman Hugh Scott in tow. Scott was in Father's debt—as a fellow Harvard graduate, Father had said a good word for him when he had sought the Republican nomination for a seat from a Philadelphia district. I was ordered to meet Judge Parry at the officers' club, Waller Hall, for lunch. Colonel Lemuel C. Shepherd, officer in charge of the Marine Corps Schools, was in attendance. This was high company for a lowly shavetail, and I spent most of the meal in respectful, attentive silence. It disturbed me, however, that Father kept addressing Colonel Shepherd as "General." Sensitive to such military protocol, I asked him later why he did so. His response: "It never hurts to call an officer by a higher rank." The show of force did not alter Dick's prospects, however, and he soon departed for bluer pastures as an ensign in the Navy.

Lunch at Waller Hall was nourishing and inexpensive, so we lieutenants ate there with some regularity. The luncheon special one noontime was chicken croquettes with cream sauce, rice, and peas—all for 85¢. The waiter brought my plate, which featured just one large croquette. Always looking for ways to augment my diet at minimal expense, I called the head waiter to remonstrate that the menu advertised "croquettes"—plural—and that I had received only one. He pointed out the obvious fact that the single croquette was equal to three normal-sized ones. I persevered. The head waiter, slight of stature but of distinguished poise, treated lieutenants and generals with equal tact. Smiling bleakly, he vanished, returning shortly with a plate groaning under a load of enormous croquettes, which he delivered to my place without comment. My amused lunchmates now demanded that I eat every mouthful of this generous offering. I managed only with some difficulty.

One fine spring day near the end of our four-month course, we were introduced to the hand grenade. The screened windows of our classroom were wide open, and spring fever was in the air. The officer-instructor strove to gain our full attention. He carefully explained that the hand grenade was activated by a simple firing mechanism. He cautioned us not to fool with the pin; it was easily unseated. The grenade was then passed from student to student for closer inspection as the instructor repeated his admonitions about the firing pin. By now the grenade was in the center of the room in the hands of 2nd Lieutenant Hensley Williams, the top man of the Naval Academy contingent whose inquiring mind had earned him high academic rank. Apparently, he could not resist determining exactly how difficult it was to separate the pin from its lodgment. He gingerly tested it. The ensuing hiss sent future combat commanders diving under desks and toward exits. Hensley cradled the grenade for a second or two before deciding to drop it under a desk.

When the smoke cleared and we had reconvened outside the classroom, our instructor confidently assured us that the tear gas would clear the room in a day or two since it was "nonpersistent." Two weeks later we were still wiping tears from our eyes during class. As for Hensley, he spent many weeks in the hospital. He had to repeat the next course and reached the Fleet Marine Force four months after the rest of us.

Parris Island

Upon graduation from Quantico in June 1941, many of us were ordered to Parris Island, South Carolina. Parris Island was a flat, marshy training camp on the coast midway between Charleston, South Carolina, and Savannah, Georgia. Some of us would join the 11th Marine Regiment (11th Marines), the artillery unit of the newly activated 1st Marine Division. Most of the 11th Marines was on amphibious maneuvers off North Carolina. For administrative purposes, those of us destined for the 1st Battalion, 11th (1/11) were assigned to Headquarters and Service Battery, 2/11, while we awaited the arrival of our battalion later in the summer. Inasmuch as there was little for us to do, we were loaned out temporarily to the firing batteries for training. I drew E Battery. As an officer-observer, I accompanied the battery on training exercises such as RSOPs (Reconnaissance, Selection, Occupation of Position) and gun drills. It was a lot better than idly perusing field manuals but still a far cry from actually manning the howitzers or performing as a full-time battery officer. Understandably, the battery commander concentrated his attention on his newly assigned officers, so the observers were just that—we picked up what we could vicariously. Then I got lucky, both literally and figuratively. I was assigned as assistant to Captain Robert B. Luckey, the battalion operations officer.

Bob Luckey was a very senior captain from the University of Maryland Class of 1927 and a veteran of Nicaragua. A gentlemen of the old school, he was tall, angular, balding, and had a prominent nose. He walked with a slight limp, which was the result of an injury in Peking in 1936 when his polo pony tripped and fell on him. Although far from handsome, he was personable and had a lively sense of humor. He was well liked by seniors, contemporaries, and juniors; he was considered one of the most competent artillerymen in the Marine Corps.

During my few weeks as Captain Luckey's flunky, I began to learn about how a light field artillery battalion positioned itself in the field and fired. More important, I experienced some of the easy, rewarding camaraderie that good officers establish with subordinates—so long as the juniors do not overstep certain invisible lines.

On a survey for a battalion shoot, Captain Luckey was having difficulty sighting in on a small mast, probably once a flagpole, atop an airplane hangar. After a few mild expletives, he said, "Lieutenant Parry, why don't you get off your ass, climb up that monkey-fucker, and tie something to it so that I can see it?"

"To the top of that flimsy pole?" I asked incredulously.

"Can't you do it?" he challenged.

Why I did not break my neck I do not know, but I shinnied most of the way up the mast and attached a red pennant.

Bob Luckey must have recognized some well-hidden potential in the raw lieutenant trailing around at his side for those few weeks in the late summer of 1941 because he took a fatherly interest in me from then on.

While I was thus engaged in trying to pick up the artillery-man's trade, my brother George called from Philadelphia to tell me of Mother's sudden collapse and death. Weakened by a stroke in the winter of 1940, she had lived longer than my Uncle Morrie, her doctor, a well-known surgeon, had thought likely. We gathered in late July in Philadelphia for the funeral, her six sons and stepson serving as pallbearers. It was the end of a family era, one to which she had lent grace, compassion, and warmth. One result of her passing was the thought of matrimony, which soon bestirred her sons.

My social life that first summer in the Corps was almost nonexistent. The senior officers, even first lieutenants and second lieutenants with only two years of duty under their belts, ignored the new shavetails. So we were thrown on our own devices for entertainment during off hours. Billeted in tents for the first few days, we then moved into an old wooden barracks too decrepit for troop habitation. Dubiously described as "adequate" bachelor officers' quarters, it was a modest improvement on a tent and saved the Marine Corps the inconvenience of paying us a quarters allowance. From this rickety base we sallied forth into the quiet charm of Beaufort and the backcountry, where sturdy live oaks gracefully festooned with Spanish moss abounded.

Our favorite place in Beaufort was the Golden Eagle Restaurant, whose philanthropic owner served lavish dinners nightly for an affordable $1. His guests would assemble ahead of the appointed hour in the living room, decorously awaiting summons to the dining room below. We would try to predict when the entree would be steaks and lamb chops and were often successful. You could eat all you wanted, there was a wide variety of vegetables, desserts, and—invariably—grits, or "Georgia ice cream" as the waiter would smilingly remind us. We went only once a week because in those days a dollar really was a dollar, and we did not have many. Another diversion was The Count's motorcycle, which he would ferry on and off the base in his station wagon. Officers on motorcycles were frowned on in those days. Sometimes I would accompany him on vigorous rides around the hinterland. Another diversion was a visit to the home of one of our married classmates. A few had married quietly and were living in cottages well off the beaten track. Newly commissioned officers were not supposed to get married until they had been in the service for two years, and because discovery could well lead to dismissal they laid low. But for any sort of real action, we had to travel at least to Charleston or Savannah.

One weekend Bill McReynolds and I ventured to Savannah. Saturday night found us on the outskirts of town at a roadhouse called Duggers. We soon found that it was a hangout of a notorious gang which, among other things, preyed on Yankee servicemen. We had been imbibing for most of the day but without determination. Standing at the bar with beer in hand, we saw a local tough baiting an army enlisted man. Abruptly, as if by signal, the bar emptied into the parking lot, where the soldier attempted to square off with his larger civilian adversary. It was no contest. The thug beat the soldier to the ground and continued to pummel him. Beer in hand, I sought to stop the fight by pulling the bully off the soldier by the scruff of his neck. Almost simultaneously, I was hit by three gang members, two from behind. Every time I would go after the tough in front of me, I would be hit from behind by two or three others—obviously a well-rehearsed scenario. Then I noticed something wet and sticky on my hands and face. I was covered with blood. In the initial encounter my beer glass had been smashed to my face, and it had cut my head and hand. The soldier had long been forgotten; I was now center stage. Several policemen were in the crowd of some one hundred spectators, but neither they nor anyone else moved to intervene. Bill, who had belatedly followed me out of the bar, raised his voice in remonstrance on seeing my plight—he earned a fist in the face for his outburst. A man and wife nearby urged me to give it up, pointing out that the odds were hopeless and that my wounds needed attention. Although reluctant to leave the field to the scum, better judgment finally prevailed. Bill and I got directions to the nearest hospital from the sympathetic strangers. A few hours later, our wounds attended to, we left the hospital and returned to Parris Island. It had taken eighteen stitches to close the gash above my eye, but my alcohol content had been high enough to preclude the need for anesthetic.

Back at base some sergeants from C Battery, 1/11 (which I had joined a few days before) offered to round up a platoon of batterymates to accompany me back to Duggers the next weekend to clean the joint out. Before I decided on the merit of involving myself further in so risky an adventure or on how much the reputation of the Marine Corps demanded retribution (even though Bill and I had been in mufti), I ran into Captain Luckey. After soundly admonishing me, he gave me a direct order to carry this matter no further.

By early autumn I had another matter to occupy my thoughts. I had saved enough money to fly from Charleston to Washington, D.C., to meet Vera, who had been driven there by her grandmother. I had invited Vera to a Navy football game in Baltimore. At first she declined because of an invitation from someone at Princeton. I suggested that if she could not see her way clear to meet me as proposed, she could return my engagement ring. She recanted. William M. Miller, an Academy classmate who lived near us in the condemned barracks we called home, had observed the success of my display of bravado and decided to test the same strategy on his intended. His ring arrived in the return mail. Bill would not speak with The Count or me for several days, blaming us for his ignominy. It turned out all right in the end, however, for the quick-tempered, independent beauty eventually became his wife.

It was during the summer that The Count and I became increasingly fascinated with the idea of going into action by jumping out of an airplane behind enemy lines. Neither our gentlemanly stint at Quantico nor our training at Parris Island as orphans of the 11th Marines had done much to interest us in field artillery. We were both athletically inclined and attracted to the glamor of parachute jumping. We convinced each other that we were for the paratroops.

During those summer days officers were filtering into Parris Island from many sources. One was Lieutenant Harold "Izzie" Schwartz, a short, physically unimpressive doctor from the Bronx. Izzie moved in with The Count and me. We immediately went to work on him. Although no one's idea of what a paratrooper should be, Izzie eventually succumbed to our blandishments and together we volunteered.

Favorably endorsed by our battalion and regimental commanders, we happily awaited our orders to paratroop school. Weeks passed. Finally, the word came down through the chain of command that our requests had been disapproved because the Corps was short of junior artillery officers. At the same time our reluctant medical

compatriot's request was approved, and he received orders to Lake-
hurst, New Jersey. Justifiably, he heaped abuse on his robust Marine bunkies who had talked him into this hazardous adventure. We
bade Izzie a painful goodbye. (We never saw him again, but I
learned at Guadalcanal that Izzie successfully negotiated Lake-
hurst and joined the 1st Parachute Battalion. He was wounded as
he attempted to disembark from a landing boat off Gavutu.)

Wedding Bells

A few days before the 11th Marines departed for the new Marine
training base near New River, North Carolina, I reported in to the
U.S. Naval Hospital at Parris Island with a bad case of catarrhal
fever. According to procedure, a hospital corpsman took a sample of
my blood for routine testing. The next day he returned for more
blood, saying that additional tests were required. The following day
two doctors entered my room, carefully closed the door, and with
grim seriousness informed me that I had syphilis. In my mind's eye
I hastily reviewed possible instances of exposure. I told them that I
did not believe it. The doctors persisted. The first Kahn test had
shown a strong positive result. The second had not only verified the
first reading but had been even more positive. They said that there
was no doubt that I had contracted the disease and treatment
should begin immediately. I insisted that I could not have syphilis.
Faced with my intransigence, one of the doctors acknowledged that
the test was not absolutely foolproof; there was such a thing as a
"biological positive," but it was extremely rare. In view of my conviction, he ordered another blood test. That afternoon a corpsman
drew a pint of blood for dispatch to the doctor who had developed
the test, Dr. R. L. Kahn, in Washington, D.C.

The next ten days while I awaited my fate were lonely indeed.
Dismissal from the service was possible, ruination of my career at
its outset was even more certain. All my friends had left for New
River. I called Vera in Philadelphia to ask her to come to Charleston
for a weekend as soon as I was released from the hospital. (I neglected to divulge my current dilemma.) She said that she would try
to arrange it. I observed the painful treatment then in vogue for the
handful of syphilis patients—periodic massive doses of mercury in
the posterior. I prayed a lot.

Finally, the doctors returned, but this time they wore smiles
instead of frowns. My blood did indeed test positive, but the result

was caused by biological factors and not the disease. With a huge sigh of relief, I asked the doctor what the odds were for a biological positive. He replied, "About 80,000 to one." Long over my fever, I put in for a delay of ten days before reporting to the 11th Marines at New River. Vera was advised by telephone of my impending release from the hospital, and I repeated my invitation to Charleston. She agreed, advising that she and her grandmother would soon be on their way to the Pennsylvania Railroad's 30th Street Station in Philadelphia. With some dismay I inquired why her grandmother was accompanying her, to which she responded that Mrs. Corey insisted upon doing so. This had not been my plan at all—I had anticipated a romantic adventure, and Mrs. Corey's chaperonage had not been part of it. Now fate intervened dramatically in the person of Judge Parry.

Mrs. Corey and Vera had proceeded to the station. The judge was somehow alerted to the impending departure and believed that it could result in an elopement. He rushed to the station from his City Hall chambers and sighted Vera and Mrs. Corey in the act of buying their tickets to Charleston. He approached and with his ever present cane scooped the proferred cash from out of the startled ticket salesman's hands. Many a lady would have been intimidated by this forceful, masculine action. But Mrs. A. A. Corey, Jr. was not easily cowed. Her husband had been president of the Vanadium Corporation and several steel companies before that; her brother-in-law had been president of United States Steel in its heyday as the largest U.S. corporation. She was used to being deferred to, not deferring. So a standoff developed in the vast hall of the station. Somehow these formidable characters reached accommodation. They scheduled a wedding for three days later, ditched the Charleston junket, and summoned me north for the ceremony. The action had been seized right out of our hands. Neither Vera nor I was prepared; nor was either of us, evidently, reluctant enough to call it off. From those initial moments of hesitation, we were irreversibly propelled by events.

On the afternoon of November 20, 1941, we were married in All Saints Church, Wynnewood, Pennsylvania. There had been no time for the bride to be fitted for a wedding dress. The leather Sam Browne belt in which I was married actually belonged to 2nd Lieutenant Emile P. Moses, Jr., who was stationed at the Philadelphia Navy Yard. My brother George arranged the loan so that I could be wed in uniform. Events had moved along so rapidly that I had not even been able to track down The Count, who was on temporary duty at some school in Quantico. In fact, the wedding had all the characteristics of a hurry-up affair, so even noncynics must have wondered at the reason for such speed. Mrs. Corey brought off the whole event brilliantly, and the reception was in her Bryn Mawr home immediately following the church vows. The only delay in proceedings was engineered by Vera herself. The church was overflowing as the time for the ceremony came and went. Minutes ticked by. One emotional dowager remarked to me that "the poor dear probably had a long way to come." I nodded nervously. Vera's house was no more than three blocks from the church. She eventually arrived, twenty-five minutes late. Perhaps she was having second thoughts.

That no serious effort was mounted to talk Vera or me out of such a precipitate action is, in retrospect, puzzling. I was hardly in a position to embark on matrimony—I had saved only enough money for a weekend in Charleston. And though none of us knew how close war really was, there was little question that 1st Marine Division was preparing for commitment overseas in the not-distant future. How long would the groom be Stateside? As for Vera, she was in the midst of an exciting debutante year, with her photograph gracing newspaper pages with regularity. She was the acknowledged Glamor Girl of Philadelphia with innumerable suitors. Further, she had a significant role in *Rigoletto,* which was scheduled to open with her name in lights on the marquee at a downtown theater.

So therein lies the wonder: that two powerful manipulators—Judge Parry and Mrs. Corey—who could without doubt have arranged an indefinite delay, did not see fit to do so. Perhaps each believed that there was more cause for alacrity than there was.

After a night in the Bellevue Stratford Hotel, we flew to Charleston, retrieved my car, and motored to The Cloisters at Sea Island, Georgia. One result of our hasty union was that we had to wire for funds to pay the hotel bill. For better or worse this teenage goddess and I, who only a week before were contemplating no more than a romantic weekend together, were now man and wife.

New River

In the autumn of 1941, 1st Marine Division was assembled in a coastal area bordering both sides of New River, North Carolina. This vast tract of flatland, water, and swamp had been recently acquired by the Marine Corps. (Later it would become the largest East Coast training base, Camp Lejeune.) From Quantico came the 5th Marines and from Parris Island came the 7th and 11th Marines. The 5th and 7th were billeted in a tent camp near the main north-south coastal highway. The 11th Marines opted to fend for themselves and pitched their tents several miles down the highway and up a dirt road from the hamlet of Verona. All went well for a few weeks as the regiment erected the tent camp and pieced together mess halls from scrap lumber "requisitioned" from abandoned houses, barns, and shacks. But then the rains came, and the dirt road from Verona to the camp became a quagmire. Undaunted, the regiment formed itself into an all-hands working party, chopped down pines by the hundreds and built a corduroy road that became the regiment's lifeline in the bitter winter ahead. The experiences of this frigid sojourn would mold these Marines into a resourceful, hardy breed and serve the veterans of that Verona winter of 1941–42 in good stead for the demanding years to come.

When I reported in for duty at the Verona tent camp in late November, I was naively hopeful that news of the wedding had not penetrated the boondocks of coastal Carolina. Perhaps it would not have if a "friendly" agent with a singular lack of discretion had not posted on the 2/11 bulletin board a Philadelphia newspaper's front-page photograph of Vera and me leaving the church. Despite this act of sabotage, my only punishment came from Major Bob Luckey, the new executive officer of 2/11, who administered a scathing tongue-lashing.

Inasmuch as I had checked into the hospital only days after joining C Battery at Parris Island, my integration into the unit began now in the sandy pine barrens south of New River. The Marine Corps light field artillery battery of 1941 was not robust. With only four 75mm pack howitzers, it delivered about half the firepower of the six 105mm howitzer batteries of a few years later. But the pack howitzer was a sturdy, accurate weapon and could be man-handled almost anywhere. It would do yeoman service in the Pacific Island campaigns. The other major element of the battery was the battery detail: the communications section (which tied the firing battery in with the front-line FOs, the battalion FDC, and headquarters) and a survey section (which positioned the firing battery with reference to a battalion control point and a battery observation post). The battery first sergeant and his clerks, the truck drivers and mechanics, the mess sergeant, and the cooks rounded out the 140-man unit.

The battery's mission was straightforward: Move into firing position as quickly and quietly as possible, sight the four pieces parallel, position the battery with respect to a battalion-known point, register a piece (usually number two gun) on some observable point near the center of the expected zone of fire, and then stand by to support the infantry. We were also to dig in and camouflage the position and prepare to defend ourselves if necessary. Above all, we were never to lose sight of our raison d'être: Support the infantry to the best of our ability.

When I finally became a full-fledged member of C Battery in December 1941, the officers and key NCOs who ran it were an amalgam of Regulars and Reserves. The battery commander, Captain Harry Zimmer, slight and unprepossessing, had come on active duty with the Philadelphia Reserve field artillery battalion a year earlier, when it had been redesignated the 1st Battalion, 11th Marines. The executive officer, 1st Lieutenant Elliott Wilson, was a quiet, dependable Regular. His assistant, 2nd Lieutenant John Chaisson, had received one of the few regular commissions awarded to graduates of the 4th Reserve Officer Course (ROC) that summer. Second Lieutenant Tom Jolly, the reconnaissance officer, was a mild southerner from the 3rd ROC. The senior NCOs were 1st Sergeant Baker, a slipshod Reserve and two old-line Regulars, Gunnery Sergeant Lewis H. "Hermie" Howard and Platoon Sergeant "Buddha" Suffern. I shared a tent with Elliott Wilson.

Unsure of myself, I watched the executive officer put the four howitzer sections through their paces at every opportunity. As FO, I would move to an observation point some 2,000 yards to the front, see that wire and radio contact were established with the firing battery, and prepare to adjust the battery's fire on a recognizable point of woods, or hilltop, or a prominent tree in our target area. In the meantime the surveyors were plying their trade, positioning the firing battery and observation post. Day in, day out we would work toward competence in these areas. One aspect was lacking in our training, however: working with and shooting over infantry. Both infantry and artillery had a long way to go in sharpening skills before joint exercises would be practical or safe.

As the nation clumsily began to gear up for the long struggle ahead, it became apparent that few troops were ready for any sort of action. As always, the most ready were the Marines, and awareness of our position added a sense of urgency to all the activities of 1st Marine Division. It seemed inevitable that if any troops were to stop this sweep of the Japanese across the Pacific, it would be the collection of old jungle fighters and new volunteers that were being welded into a fighting team.

For a newlywed the rugged regimen of New River presented monumental problems. The nearest sizable town not swarming with Marine officers was Kinston, North Carolina, a tobacco center about 50 miles west of New River. A few "illegally" married second lieutenants, which I joined, made this drive daily, leaving camp after dark and returning before predawn reveille. Together with the $35 monthly car-mortgage payment, the gas for this 100-mile round trip was a real strain on the pocketbook for two trying to live on $125 per month. Our nightly trips to the Caswell Cafeteria, an inexpensive but relatively wholesome eating establishment a few blocks from "home," emphasized our poverty. Vera and I argued over our respective portions, and it was an eye-opener to me to learn that sweet young things really ate. In our courting days Vera had coyly toyed with dainty portions; later, I learned that she, like many other young ladies, had fortified herself nutritionally before going out in the evening both to spare her escort's frequently limited finances and to avoid the appearance of a trencherman.

In fact, had it not been for the good Lord's guiding hand, which led us to the big old house of Johnny and Helen Sams on the corner of Queen Street and Park, we would have had a far greater struggle. These hospitable people accepted us as their first boarders for the paltry sum of $25 a month. Not only did we have a large room and bath in an empty wing of the house, but they quickly developed an affection for their beautiful teenage tenant. In the ensuing months, they pressed so many breakfasts upon her and occasional drinks and even dinners upon both of us that they were lucky if they broke even. These two of the world's natural nobility were small in stature but giants of thoughtfulness. When Vera suspected her pregnancy in March, it was Helen Sams who took her to the doctor. Later, when our first son was born in Philadelphia, Helen and Johnny Sams, never before north of the Mason–Dixon Line, journeyed to Bryn Mawr to see her. Happily, these good people soon made their mark. Johnny became mayor of Kinston and acquired the major concession for supplying gasoline to Camp Lejeune.

Sunday afternoon, December 7, Vera and I were sitting in our second-floor bedroom when we heard someone calling from the street. It was Bill Miller. He told us of the attack on Pearl Harbor, which we had been unaware of since we had no radio. He knew few details, but we discussed whether we should report for duty immediately—there had been no advice about reporting on the radio. As a newlywed, I was not eager to return to camp unnecessarily and would not have gotten there until dark anyway. So I decided to report in the morning at reveille, as usual. At that time we were not aware of the massive damage to the Pacific Fleet, but I believed that it was about time we became belligerents. In a way I was relieved that now we could get on with the job.

War Comes to New River

In the days after Pearl Harbor, intuitively knowing that our Stateside days were numbered, we worked hard and played hard, bachelors and marrieds alike. War or no war, however, at Christmas many of the officers managed to find their ways to New Bern or other havens where their wives or loved ones were camping out. This left the Verona camp practically depleted of senior officers. Unwilling to leave my bride of a month abandoned on Christmas Eve, when I was duty officer, I arranged for her to be spirited into camp by some of my shavetail friends. Under cover of darkness she made the rounds with me in the one-ton guard truck, and then we repaired to my tent. My tentmate was attending the Artillery School at Fort Sill, Oklahoma, so we put the two cots alongside one another and tried to get comfortable under two blankets apiece. In the damp penetrating cold of that winter such an endeavor was useless. We soon joined forces in my cot with all four blankets. We were not particularly comfortable, but we were reasonably warm. The night passed pleasantly even though it afforded only fitful sleep.

Christmas morning, bright and clear, I stood guard for Vera outside the officers' head (lavatory) when, to my dismay, up strolled Major J. J. Keating, the executive officer of 1/11. Since Major Keating hailed from Philadelphia, I knew that he was aware of my delicate status. We had scarcely exchanged pleasantries when, my gorgeous cotmate, long blonde tresses tumbling over her shoulders, emerged from the "men's" room. The major never flicked an eyelid. After a somewhat embarrassed introduction on my part and a word or two about our mutual hometown, the major proceeded on his way. Neither he nor the battalion commander, Lieutenant Colonel Joe Knowlan, nor my battery commander—all Philadelphians—ever mentioned my marital status.

About the first of the year, the 3rd Battalion, 11th Marines was reactivated with Major J. J. Keating as commander. Captain Zim-

mer moved up to executive officer of 1/11. As new units were
formed, officers and men poured into New River from all over the
Marine Corps to flesh out the division. One unlikely officer found
his way to the 11th Marines and was assigned as the new C Battery
commander. That Captain Frederick Sovereign McKee had reported
in to the 11th Marines at all was puzzling. An Army Reserve officer
who had somehow managed a transfer to the Marines, his experience had been in the infantry. Fat, bald, and singularly unofficerlike, Captain McKee might have fared poorly in the infantry;
that he would do better in the artillery was even less likely. Under
normal conditions he would have been returned to Division for reassignment. But an undeclared war festered between 11th Marines
headquarters and some members of the division staff, and it inhibited normal intercourse. So "Big-Pat-the-Oiler" McKee, as he liked
to refer to himself, was not sent back to Division, and C/1/11 was
the beneficiary. Elliott Wilson was at Fort Sill and Tom Jolly was
reassigned to 3/11, so John Chaisson and I found ourselves with the
battery on our hands.

John Robert Chaisson, almost 6 feet tall, solidly built, and
handsome, was a "black Irishman" from Swampscott, Massachusetts. A 1939 Harvard graduate and sometime semipro footballer,
John was smart and dynamic, exuding a natural charm irresistible
to men and women alike. Pat McKee was shrewd enough to let John
run the firing battery without interference; John, still inexperienced, was smart enough to rely heavily on Gunnery Sergeant Hermie Howard and the section chiefs. With Jolly gone I took over as
reconnaissance officer and busied myself with learning about survey and communications. Pat remained in the background.

That Chaisson and McKee would have rapport was inevitable
since both were Irish and had a fondness for drink. So while I would
take off for Kinston as soon as it was dark when there was no night-
training exercise or I did not have the duty, Pat and John became
drinking partners. They periodically toured the handful of dives
strung along the main north-south highway skirting the New River
encampment.

With de facto responsibility for training the battery, John and I
were slowly learning our trade. I was also, finally, absorbing a little
of the real Marine Corps—the feeling of being special, different from
dogfaces (soldiers) and swabbies (sailors), and a little tougher, more
dedicated, and elite.

With the influx of officers and men came some World War I and Banana Wars heroes. Occasionally, we even caught sight of some living legends as they tried to shape up their charges into professional fighting men in the pine woods, sand, and insect-infested swamp of the sprawling training area. For example, two living legends now led battalions of the 7th Marines, which 1/11 was destined to support in the years ahead. Major Lewis B. "Chesty" Puller, renowned jungle fighter of Haiti and Nicaragua, had 1/7; Lieutenant Colonel Herman Henry Hanneken, who had helped bring the Haitian insurrection to an end by capturing and beheading the rebel chieftain Charlemagne Peralta, had 2/7. Their sense of purpose, drive, and professionalism was infectious, even from a distance.

Another Marine Corps characteristic—taking care of its own— was brought home to me in C Battery. In the circumstances that then applied, officers were required to pay for the meals they ate in the field mess. Monthly bills would be from $20 to $30 depending upon the number of evenings you had to remain in camp. Mess Sergeant Leonard A. Maxson was well aware of my marital status and my struggle to retain solvency. Since I was not supposed to be married, I could hardly draw a married officer's allowance. The bill Maxson would present me each month was ludicrous—$4.75, $5.60, and the like. I was embarrassed to pay so little. This monthly gesture enabled me to continue to drive back and forth to Kinston almost nightly to be with my bride. It also touched me deeply and engendered in me the desire to take care of these men who were taking care of me.

Early one Sunday morning in midwinter, Vera and I were awakened by a persistent soft knocking on the front door. I hastened down to see who was causing the disturbance before the Sams responded. Three disheveled lieutenants were encamped on the threshold, still charged up by the events of an apparently memorable night. I ushered them as quietly as possible up the stairs to our quarters, where they unfolded a lurid tale of battle and bloodshed.

It started around midnight, after Vera and I had sensed the steady increase in rowdiness at the roadhouse about 3 miles to the west of town and had excused ourselves. The Count, 2nd Lieutenant Frankie Jenkins, and 2nd Lieutenant Bob Armstrong had lingered on. When they emerged into the night after deciding to seek action elsewhere, two enlisted Marines who were feeling their oats decided to take on the shavetails. The Count and Frankie had come out first, while Bob remained to settle for the drinks. The enlisted Marines across the road started to bait them. They had made a poor selection. The Count, still in fair shape from years of football and wrestling, and Frankie, the erstwhile 135-pound southern conference boxing champion, strode across the road to discipline the disrespectful troops. The enlisted Marines were by no means helpless, however, and in the ensuing brawl one of them carved open The Count's head with that lethal weapon, the fair leather belt. Rank won the match, though, and when last seen one enlisted Marine was recuperating by the side of the road with an injured jaw and the other was hightailing it toward Kinston with Frankie, his finest pugilistic instincts aroused, throwing punches from all angles at his retreating foe.

Bob Armstrong appeared on the scene after the fray and attempted to bring order out of chaos. After he had rounded up the aroused young bulls, they took The Count to have his head sewn up and then continued the partying. But Kinston is not the Big Apple, so they finally ran out of places to go. Still slightly smashed and looking for a sympathetic audience to listen to their adventures, they sought out the only ones who would let them in. After a few rounds of our gallon jug of red wine and some urging from Vera and me, who were concerned at what the Sams might think of this nocturnal soiree, the three subdued musketeers disappeared into the early dawn.

As the weeks passed, other activity crowded this night into the background. The officers' club was set up in an old farmhouse between the camp and Verona, and it became the focus of the Marines' exuberance. Frequently, The Count's undistinguished but soon well-known brown two-door Chevrolet sedan, christened the Light Tank, was found somewhere in a ditch on the way back to camp. Its angle of incidence and degree of mire offered a clue to the owner's sobriety of the past evening.

On one memorable occasion, the division provost marshal, who had been tipped off to the rowdiness of the 11th Marines officers' club, paid a surprise visit. He strode into the main room, which was also the bar, at the very moment that The Count, Jenkins, Chaisson, and others were playing catch with a log. His sudden entrance distracted the would-be receiver, and the log smashed through a window. This event was later immortalized at the general court-martial when testimony asserted that, "he [Frankie Jenkins] passed the log through the window."

Although this horseplay was not in itself justification for a court-martial, it provided the final piece to a puzzle that had stumped the military police (MPs) for some weeks. For when the MPs added this bit of physical "violence" to the tale told by an enlisted Marine whose mended jaw finally allowed him to describe an altercation with officers outside a roadhouse near Kinston two months previously, they thought that they had their men.

So on the very day that the 3rd Battalion, 7th Marines, reinforced by C Battery, 1/11, was to depart from a railroad siding near New River, The Count was restricted to quarters awaiting trial by general court-martial. Light tanks are not easily overcome by provost marshals, however, and with an assist from that clever, understanding Philadelphia lawyer, Major Keating, they beat the rap. Although they missed going overseas with their outfits, The Count and Bob later distinguished themselves on Okinawa. The Count served as a torpedo-bomber squadron commander and Bob commanded a light artillery battalion.

A Higher Power

As winter slowly gave way to spring, the small group of "illegally" married second lieutenants that had been making the hundred-mile round trip from camp to Kinston almost nightly dwindled. One morning about 5:00 my Annapolis classmate Roland J. "Dutchie" Spritzen, and I were barreling along the two-lane highway about 10 miles from Kinston when I heard a loud flap, flap, flapping. I came, abruptly awake and discovered to my horror that we were heading straight across a cornfield. The shoulder-high stalks snapped over as we raced along. I had fallen asleep at the wheel and missed a curve in the road. This flirtation with disaster apparently convinced Dutchie of the foolhardiness of our nightly run, and I found myself alone as a nightly commuter. I realized that I was testing my endurance, but I was also aware that we would soon be heading for the war zone—with our return, if ever, in the hands of the Almighty. We had only recently learned of Vera's pregnancy, and I was not about to miss a night with her if I could help it.

In late March I climbed into my undistinguished 1941 Ford coupe and headed down the muddy forest track from the 11th Marines tent camp toward the Coddington estate. We had visited this beautiful old manorial spread on several occasions while on artillery maneuvers. On the southern shore of the New River estuary, the main house boasted among its twenty-odd rooms an enormous ballroom. To the west, beyond the stables, there was an oval race-track at least a half mile in circumference. Although slowly crumbling into disrepair, the estate was still impressive and evoked an intriguing pre-Depression history. I had noticed near the house several imposing magnolia trees. Inasmuch as I had no funds for a traditional going-away present, I thought I might relieve them of some blossoms for my bride. We were scheduled to leave by troop train on March 22.

Just before the final rise to the estate, the track ran across a narrow wooden bridge that spanned a shallow stream. I had approached the bridge too cautiously; the car was soon stuck hub deep in mud just over the bridge. Wheel spinning just dug it in deeper.

Unsure how I would extract myself from this predicament, I decided to proceed on foot to the main house, which was less than a half mile away. Some inner voice suggested that I continue with my mission of gathering flowers and have faith that help would come from some quarter. I picked some blossom-laden branches, found a piece of a shovel and some boards, and headed back for the bridge. I had been absent from the car for no more than twenty minutes. To my astonishment, there sat my automobile—high and dry—at the top of the small hill on my side of the bridge. It was facing back toward camp. I had not heard trucks or troops. I walked down the 50 yards to the bridge. There were no footprints or tire marks to indicate human presence which, in any case, I could scarcely have avoided hearing.

Still without any real understanding, I accepted my providential rescue, crossed the bridge at an appropriate speed, and returned to camp. There I related my experience to my batterymate, John Chaisson. John did not question my veracity, but he advised me to exercise caution in my inquiries relative to troop maneuvers in the area and not to disclose my motivation in asking, lest others wonder about my emotional stability. After a day or two of discreet inquiry, I took John's advice to heart and refrained from further investigation. I related this event to my wife, who appeared to take it all in good faith along with the magnolias.

Why I should have been singled out for this visitation by a higher power, I can only guess. It convinced me that some compassionate force was looking after me—a feeling that remained with me through three wars. I was hardly religious. Besides Sunday School as a boy and church as a young adult, I had made no religious commitment. Since the Naval Academy I had allowed my church attendance to lapse. Nevertheless, after pondering the event through the years, I can come up with no explanation other than the fact that the experience had been a spiritual encounter. Surely it is no less believable than inspirational experiences related by many others. It was my brief brush with the power of faith—even a modest, tentative faith—in the quiet wilds of coastal Carolina before we went to war.

PART II

The Pacific War

5

Faka Uvea*

In early 1942 the Marine Corps was called upon to bolster the island defenses of the Atlantic and Pacific with two reinforced combat
infantry regiments. Predictably, the 6th Marines, encamped in
near-tropical San Diego, was dispatched to Iceland, while the 7th
Marines, training in the frigid swampland near New River, North
Carolina, was moved by troop train and Navy transport through
San Diego and the Panama Canal to the tropical Samoan Islands.
The 3rd Battalion, 7th Marines, with C/1/11 attached, was scheduled for a trooptrain. The remainder of the 7th Regiment and 1/11
were to embark at East Coast ports and proceed by sea.

With The Count under detainment, Bob Armstrong brought
Vera to the secluded railroad siding to see me off. It was an emotional parting; I finally disengaged myself from her embrace and
boarded the train. She was a glorious sight with the brilliant sun-
light in her golden hair and tears welling in her eyes—the epitome
of fair womanhood, which the more romantically inclined among us
believed we were off to war to protect. Only nineteen years old, she
would have her own battle to fight as she returned to Philadelphia
to have her first child with her husband half a world away.

The trooptrains crisscrossing the country in those days were far
from luxurious. We crossed the desert in hundred-degree weather
with the air conditioning invariably out of order. The stubbornly

*A Uvean saying that translates as Uvean Custom. It is an explanatory phrase often
used by Wallisians to justify some action. Uvea is by far the largest and most important of the Wallis Islands.

immovable windows were the subject of endless verbal and sometimes physical abuse. But for troops toughened in the Cuban heat
and Carolina chill, the trains represented just another inconvenience to be tolerated. And if the troops were fulminating about the
unyielding windows, it served to take their minds off other
shortcomings—the seemingly endless, pokey trek south and westward, the dreary food, and the confinement.

Eventually we pulled in to San Diego, in 1942 still a lovely,
quiet Navy town. Here Pat-the-Oiler roused himself and charged
John and me with responsibility for loading C Battery aboard ship
(we had not expected otherwise). He informed us that he could be
located for the remainder of our stay in San Diego at one of the
three bars in the U. S. Grant Hotel. He was as good as his word. He
did not, in fact, sober up until our third day at sea over a week later.
This constituted no problem; instead, his absence provided a learning experience for John and me. The NCOs did practically all the
work anyway.

The sea voyage to Samoa aboard the Navy transport USS *Harris*
(named for my great-uncle) was pleasant and uneventful. For a
while we tied up at the dock in Pago Pago. Mist-shrouded Rain-
maker Mountain brooded some 1,700 feet high above the small enclosed harbor. Tiny, picturesque villages were scattered around the
harbor in the shadow of the mountain. Whenever we could borrow a
jeep, John and I visited the headquarters and some of the battery
positions of the 1st Battalion, 10th Marines, an artillery battalion
identical to 1/11 except that it was armed with 75mm French guns.
Mostly, however, we vegetated aboard ship awaiting orders.

We attempted to exercise the troops daily, but none of us showed
much enthusiasm. Then McKee learned that a captain friend of his
had responsibility for a defense sector at the eastern end of the
island, about 12 miles away. He decided that it would be good for
the battery to hike out there, spend the night, and hike back. We
started out after breakfast, making good time for a while. But, as
the miles mounted, men started to drop out with sore feet or other
assorted ills—six weeks aboard ship had not been conducive to good
physical condition, even though we had worked at it.

We had slogged about nine miles, or three quarters of the distance, when McKee came along in a jeep. Another jeep followed
with dinner in insulated containers. We all assumed that he would
set up a chow line along the road to feed the laboring troops, but
Big Pat had other ideas. He brushed aside our urging and, with a

wave of the hand, took off, promising that dinner would be set up for us when we arrived at our destination.

The troops were not overjoyed by this decision, and as we trudged on they dropped by the wayside in droves. When we topped the last rise overlooking our bit of paradise, the leading group had dwindled to John; Sergeant John Molnar, chief of the first gun section of the firing battery; and I. The rest of the men were strewn out as far as the eye could see. Some of the troops were so tired when they finally reached the chow line that they could take little nourishment. It had been a sad display of leadership on the battery commander's part, most untypical of a Marine officer, who is expected to lead by example.

McKee's captain friend, openly shacked up with a shapely Samoan nurse, had planned a festive occasion with a tropical motif appropriate to the surroundings. Stately coconut palms and widely spaced, open-sided, thatched-roofed *fales* (living quarters) overlaid the manicured white sandy beach of this tropical Eden. Several long dugout canoes had traversed the 2 miles of ocean from the offshore island of Aunuu, bringing a treasure of graceful, voluptuous maidens to dance for our pleasure. As we ogled the undulation of breast, hip, and thigh, our passion mounted.

Now to the fore came Robert M. Sack, a Marine gunner (warrant officer) who had joined us just before we left New River. A burly man in his early thirties, Bob was yet another Philadelphia Reservist. Of Armenian extraction from the blue-collar Frankford area, he could not believe that a well-to-do Chestnut Hiller like me could be anything but a horse's ass. Nonetheless, we were slowly warming to each other.

As the troops drifted off to their sleeping bags and the phalanx of solemn duennas kept a watchful eye on their fair charges to see that none strayed into the night with a persuasive Marine, Bob Sack went into action. He had ridden out in the jeep with McKee, bringing with him, we were soon to discover enviously, a dazzling display of trade goods for bartering with the gullible natives. A few of us, drinking beer, watched Sack ostentatiously lay out his trove of beads, trinkets, colored cloth, cans of sardines, and the like. The bargaining began. Our heightened libido could hardly be disguised as we sighted in on the brown, nubile beauties and selected prospective partners in our minds. But for all his talent as a trader who could talk many out of their eye teeth, Gunner Sack was overmatched. As the bargaining gradually moved toward a climax and

Sack anted up more and more trade goods, I had the disturbing feeling that all was not going according to Hoyle. The trade goods were disappearing into the middle of the semicircle of robust, stone-faced matrons, and we were getting steadily more inebriated and sleepier. Yet no maiden had been nudged forward as their offering of good faith. And, sadly, none ever was. Helplessly, we watched the damsels being quietly herded off to their dugout canoes and whisked away in the moonlight by their more than competent chaperones. Along with them went a healthy share of Sack's much-diminished treasure trove. We were left empty-handed. But, I suppose, we had learned a lesson: If you want a girl, you had better seduce her yourself; her mother is not about to do it for you.

It was in Pago Pago in May 1942, while we vegetated aboard the *Harris* awaiting orders, that I met Bigfoot Brown for the first time. Already a legendary character, Brown was a tall, raw-boned, craggy-faced major of Marines. He dominated any group in which he found himself by the force of his intellect and personality. A compassionate man and gifted storyteller, he would often hold audiences captivated for hours with his wry humor and vivid, earthy rhetoric. Frequently, we would find some excuse to drop in on him, knowing that we would be regaled with fascinating yarns of Nicaragua or France or sea duty.

He told me that we would be embarking that evening aboard a survey ship, the USS *Sumner*, and sailing for Wallis Island, about 400 miles to the west, under the escort of a Free French destroyer. The Wallis Group was a French holding, but there was a possibility that there were Japanese ashore. We were to be members of an advance party consisting primarily of I Company, 3/7. Our mission was to reconnoiter the principal island, Uvea, and prepare for the landing of the main body, the 8th Defense Battalion and the 3rd Battalion, 7th Marines, reinforced. As executive officer of the 8th Defense Battalion, Major Brown would be in command and have the only jeep ashore. I represented C Battery.

After a quiet crossing we steamed warily in trace of the destroyer through the narrow southern pass in the reef that encircled the island. We dropped anchor in the eastern lagoon off the principal village of Mata-Utu about midway up the island. We had been led to anticipate no resistance—the presence of I Company being as much a precaution against potentially hostile islanders as it was against the chance that a handful of Japanese might be in residence.

So, I Company scrambled over the side into Higgins boats for what we assumed would be a peaceful run into the beach. As we watched with interest, the landing party formed up under the guns of the destroyer and then headed in to the beach. It was fortunate that there were no Japanese on hand to greet them because a few of the boats hung up on some reefs some distance short of the beach—a scenario that would prove costly nearly eighteen months later at Tarawa. The men had to wade ashore in chest-deep water. With I Company safely ashore and no indication of danger, the *Sumner* moved into the rickety village pier, and the remainder of the reconnaissance party disembarked.

The next two days of trying to cover the 35-square-mile island on foot were largely uneventful. It turned out to be relatively flat, about 9 miles north to south and 4 miles across, with none of the forbidding mountains so characteristic of Tutuila. The highest point, the cone of a long-extinct volcano, was 475-foot rounded Mount Lulu, roughly in the center of the island. Mount Lulu sloped down gently in all directions. This hospitable terrain was the reason the northern part of Uvea had been chosen as the site for an airstrip.

The weather was mild and there were many bananas and coconuts to augment our C-rations. In fact, only one minor incident is worth noting. On the first day Sergeant Carl Trickey, my reconnaissance NCO, and I were walking down a jungle trail in the southern interior, when a husky native swinging a swordlike machete around his finger came up behind us. He followed us at a very short distance for several hundred yards. Unfamiliar with the temper of the natives but unwilling to betray any visible concern, I called to Trickey that it was time to consult our map. Still swinging his machete in lethal sweeps, the native moved on down the trail. Later we were to learn that the Wallis Islanders were a friendly, peaceable breed.

At dusk of the second day, we assembled at Mata-Utu to compare notes, for the troops were arriving at dawn. Bigfoot suggested to me that the pack howitzers be positioned in the northern part of the island and the French guns down south. C Battery, going into a defensive posture on the island, had been armed with four old 75mm French guns and four 75mm pack howitzers, twice the normal complement of weapons for a light artillery battery of that day. Unaware of Bigfoot's solid and justified reputation as an artillerist, I thought smugly to myself, what does this old buzzard know about positioning light artillery batteries?

The next day I led the battery with the French guns to a position on the slope of Mount Loki, from which the guns could sweep most of the northern part of the island. The pack howitzer battery was emplaced around a volcanic lake whence it could cover much of the key terrain to the south. Captain McKee set himself up as a minibattalion commander. Captain Pat McAlinn headed up the pack howitzer battery and I was in charge of the French guns. My executive officer was Chaisson.

Aided by a veteran crew hardened by almost continuous field duty at Guantanamo Bay and New River, John built a firing battery position that was a thing of beauty. The guns were emplaced on wooden platforms that gave them the maximum lateral range without being relaid. Ammunition was dug in and camouflage was artistically draped. Pat, John, Bob Sack, and I settled down in our command post to enjoy the war with a comfortable supply of beer atop Mount Loki, which overlooked the lovely lagoon and islands to the east.

In the meantime Bigfoot Brown, now a lieutenant colonel, had talked the island commander into giving him operational control of C Battery so that he could coordinate our fires with those of the defense battalion's 155mm guns and other armament. The first we learned of this development was when 3/7 called to tell us to report to Lieutenant Colonel Brown for orders. McKee and I jeeped over to the defense battalion headquarters and proceeded to Bigfoot's tent.

In planning the defense of the island, Lieutenant Colonel Brown was well aware that I had ignored his advice in emplacing the French guns in the northern half of the island and the pack howitzers to the south. My reasoning had been that the guns were more difficult to site effectively and the northern terrain favored their deployment there. The pack howitzers, however, were more maneuverable, and Bigfoot wanted them available for ready displacement throughout the open terrain of the north.

As we entered, he fastened a gimlet eye on me, asking, "Fox, where are the French guns?"

"Up north on the slopes of Mount Loki," I replied.

Never blinking an eye, he instructed, "Move 'em south!"

About two months after we had been rousted from our gardenlike aerie atop Mount Loki, we were well bedded down on Mount Lulu, near the center of the island. Lulu was a few feet higher than Loki but with a view far less inspiring.

Our displacement from the slopes of Mount Loki to the slopes of Mount Lulu had not been effected without some acrimony. With some justification John was aggravated that the exemplary battery position over which he and his men had labored for a month was to be abandoned. He declared that he was going "on a toot." He did, leaving me with the responsibility for exchanging the French guns for the pack howitzers and moving the howitzers into the new position. Aware that ignoring Bigfoot's suggestion in the first place had precipitated the upheaval, I voiced no objection. Anyway, it was good experience for me; I assumed the battery executive's role for the only time in my career, shepherding the gun sections into position and laying the battery. After three days of cleansing his system with alcohol, John returned to duty, bright eyed and bushy tailed.

In those days the prospect of war was still a glamorous adventure, and those of us who had become glutted on the tales of Nicaraguan and Haitian ambushes along jungle trails wanted to get on with it. Even though "we'd never be worth a damn because we'd never coal ship"—as an old boatswain's mate at Annapolis acidly predicted—we were tired of old tales and wanted new action. Since there were no Japanese around, we created a little action of our own.

In those days of rapidly expanding forces, many officers were promoted to exalted ranks while still wet behind the ears. I was a first lieutenant for so short a time—twenty-seven days—that I was unable to acquire silver bars. The order promoting me to captain was dated May 8, 1942 and listed some twelve hundred officers. The list ended with "and Francis Fox Parry"—someone at HQMC had seen fit to end with the last man of the Naval Academy class of 1941. So, suddenly, C Battery was deluged with captains—McAlinn, Phil Weems, and I. McKee was now a major.

Phil Weems was a free spirit. He came from a well-known Annapolis family. His father was a pioneer in navigation—the man my Severn roommate and I had visited in 1936. Phil's younger brother, Bea Weems, was a five striper (top midshipman) of the class of 1942 as well as an eastern intercollegiate wrestling champion. So, although Phil was not exactly the black sheep of the family, he followed a divergent path. In his meanderings as battery liaison officer, Phil had acquired a palomino steed that was the envy of C Battery. As the least restricted member of the officer group, he had more than enough opportunity to roam around the island visiting local chiefs and partaking of the native *kava*. This liquid concoction coaxed from taro, a potatolike root, would paralyze you slowly from the legs up.

One balmy night Pat, John, Bob Sack, and some infantry visitors were trying to reduce our oversupply of beer. This pleasant situation had been caused by the arrival of a freighter with thousands of cases intended for a Seabee battalion that had not yet arrived. The freighter had better things to do than linger at Wallis Island, so a call went out for anyone with trucks to come haul the beer away before it inundated the beach. We had no trouble getting volunteers for that working party. C Battery, as well as some of our infantry friends, were well provided for during the rest of our brief sojourn on that friendly island.

The party was getting a little noisy when someone brought up the subject of promotions. Although Chaisson had kept his feelings pretty much to himself, an ample flow of beer had suspended his inhibitions. He sounded off loud and clear about officers who did not know their asses from deep center field masquerading as captains. At this auspicious moment, Phil Weems, having tethered his horse, strolled up. Inasmuch as the diatribe was aimed at him perhaps more than the rest of us, Phil took exception.

McKee and the others were apparently too sodden to halt the carnage. I had the duty that night, so I was relaxing nearby in the tent I shared with John. Although under conditions of equal sobriety Chaisson and Weems would have been well matched and we might have viewed the battle with equanimity, the handicap of almost a dozen beers was too much for John. I quickly intervened.

Next morning at chow call I asked John if he would like me to bring him back some breakfast. He was a sight—one eye completely closed, his face already a vivid hue. Officers' country was only about 30 yards from the enlisted tents, so there was no question that the troops had heard the battle. If John hesitated at all, it was momentary, and we walked down to the mess line. He could hardly speak out of his swollen lips as he said to me, "They heard the fight; they may as well see how it came out."

As the days turned into weeks and no Japanese appeared on the horizon, it became difficult to keep the troops on their toes. There was little ammunition to fire and few permissible targets. Occasionally, we registered on an opening in the reef. But this, together with gun drills and RSOPs—the staples of artillery training—soon became old hat. And the dual banes of troop life in the tropics—boredom and lassitude—threatened to take away the fine edge that had been honed through a rugged winter in the boondocks of New River. It was up to the officers and NCOs to keep the men sharp. So, toward the end of our third month on Wallis Island, troop schools were held, guard duty was emphasized, and all manner of training in small arms, close-order drill, and the like was instituted.

During this period we were directed to look out for likely officer candidates to fill the rapidly expanding need for junior officers in the burgeoning Marine Corps. Anyone with even a partial college education was to be particularly scrutinized. We had one man who had attended Villanova, Private First Class Murray, about whom battalion headquarters periodically needled us. Murray might well have made a good officer with some seasoning, but he had not impressed any of us to date. In fact, because of the repeated queries from headquarters of which he and the NCOs were aware, he displayed a cocky attitude. With enough imperfect officers to contend with already, the NCOs were not about to add another wet-behind-the-ears shavetail of undemonstrated ability if they could help it.

Early one night when I had the duty, Private First Class James A. D'Agostino, the corporal of the guard, reported that he had apprehended Private First Class Murray asleep on watch. He led me to him. Murray was still dead to the world, flaked out on a mess table. I told the corporal to take his weapon, get the sergeant of the guard, and take Murray into custody. The next morning arrangements were made to take him to the 8th Defense Battalion commander, Lieutenant Colonel Gus Cockrell, for office hours. Cockrell was a crusty character with a reputation for eccentricity and a proclivity for easing the ennui of our garrisonlike duty with frequent visits to the bottle.

On the morning appointed for office hours, Lieutenant Colonel Cockrell was fighting a hangover. He received the delegation of Major McKee, 1st Sergeant Baker, Sergeant McGuire, Private First Class D'Agostino, Private First Class Murray, and me in his undershorts. Before the charges were fully read, Lieutenant Colonel Cockrell interrupted. He asked Sergeant McGuire if he were a corporal. McGuire answered that he was a sergeant. The colonel asked him why he was wearing corporal's chevrons. He had been unable to get any sergeant's chevrons, McGuire responded. "Inasmuch as you seem content to walk around as a corporal, I will make you a corporal," retorted Cockrell. He then addressed D'Agostino. The same sequence followed: D'Agostino protested his inability to acquire private-first-class chevrons and Cockrell reduced him to private. McKee, Baker, and I attempted to intercede, but Gus was having none of it. By the time he reached the cause of the debacle, Private First Class Murray, the military justice system had been reduced to shambles. It was anticlimactic when Murray received the almost ludicrous sentence of "three days bread and water." In a state of shock, the contingent from C Battery beat a disorderly retreat.

When the troops learned of this gross miscarriage of justice, there were threats of violence. Murray was hustled off to the safer custody of the brig of the 3rd Battalion, 7th Marines. (He transferred soon thereafter and never returned to the battery.) Injustice or not, the reductions of McGuire and D'Agostino—two of our best men—stood as out-of-uniform violations. It was months later on Guadalcanal before we were able to redress the wrong and repromote them to their previous ranks. Murray never became an officer, and Lieutenant Colonel Cockrell remained in the island backwaters far from the fighting front.

6

The Canal

Mounting Out

Three days after the Marines hit the beaches of Tulagi and Guadalcanal, C Battery scrambled aboard the small freighter, SS *Hawaiian Merchant* for the one-and-a-half-day run from Wallis Island to Apia, British Samoa, to rejoin the 7th Marine Regimental Combat Team. We all knew that our stay in Apia would be short-lived, and this was confirmed by our assignment to a staging area in a field on the eastern outskirts of town.

Our parent battalion, 1/11, which we had not seen since we left New River in March almost five months earlier, was in position at the airfield some 15 miles to the west of Apia. After seeing the battery bedded down in our bivouac area, Major McKee and I reported to the battalion commander, Lieutenant Colonel Joe Knowlan. It was obvious that Major McKee would soon be transferred to other duties in keeping with his rank. Captains McAlinn and Weems were scheduled for transfer, so I was the heir apparent. Not wanting to shuffle John Chaisson and myself in and out of the job of battery executive, McKee mentioned to Knowlan that I was acting as assistant battery commander. Knowlan laughed, saying "There is no such position." He did, however, call me into his office privately to ask, "How do you and Chaisson get along; would he have any problems working for you?"

I replied, "I don't think there will be any problems; John and I are good friends."

There were grounds for the colonel's query. He had not seen us for many months, and John had been listed as battery executive throughout that time—the muster rolls never reflected our temporary two-battery, minibattalion organization on Wallis Island. Further, John was two years older and more mature than I was. In any case, the question never arose again to my knowledge.

Within two weeks we were embarking aboard the USS *Jackson*, one of the three President liners that had hurried back from the August 7 landings in the Solomon Islands to pick us up. But our fortnight layover had not been dull. Across the road from our bivouac was a prosperous home where a New Zealander, his Samoan wife, and their three lovely girls resided. He entertained McKee, Chaisson, Sack, and me at dinner and was otherwise hospitable to us. Diplomatically, he made it clear to us that his hospitality did not extend to his young daughters. When we moved down to the dock area to board ship we alerted him to the partially empty 55-gallon drum of gasoline that we had left behind—gasoline for civilians was worth its weight in gold. We also attended a few *siva-sivas*, or dances, but the girls were well chaperoned and nothing came of them.

There are few places more beautiful than Samoa, and we did our best to absorb some of the abundant charm—the alternately brooding and sunlit mountains, the vivid flora, and the cool forest pools fed by waterfalls. On occasion, Chaisson, Sack, and I would tour the hinterlands in a jeep, well away from the missionary influence of Apia. We would feast our eyes on the handsome, bare-breasted maidens working in the fields or strolling the byways. One afternoon, after considerable inquiry, Chaisson and I found the path leading up a steep hill to Robert Louis Stevenson's grave. It was a rugged climb, but we were rewarded with an awesome view of Apia, the surrounding hills and mountains, and the sea. We were also privileged to see with our own eyes, carved on a wooden bench, his famous requiem:

Under the wide and starry sky,
Dig the grave and let me lie.
Glad did I live and gladly die,
And I laid me down with a will.
This be the verse you grave for me:
Here he lies where he longed to be;
Home is the sailor, home from the sea,
And the hunter home from the hill.

The approach of the naval amphibious group carrying the 7th Marines to the Solomon Islands was cautious. We proceeded on a southerly course to Tongatabu. While riding at anchor far offshore, we were sobered by the sight of one of the newest, most formidable U.S. battleships, the USS *North Carolina*, listing badly and limping slowly eastward—the victim of a submarine's torpedo. Obviously, she was not to be a factor in the desperate struggle for control of the South Pacific. From then on, nights at sea seemed to breathe danger.

At Espiritu Santo in the northern New Hebrides, we rendezvoused with the covering force that was to escort us to Guadalcanal. As with many of the hilly islands of Melanesia, the shore looked inviting: picture-postcard villages and farms, coconut groves, white beaches, and tree-clad hills alternately brilliant or shaded in the intermittent overcast. But there was no shore liberty. That night, as we swung at anchor in the bay, the destroyer USS *Meredith* tied up alongside. I found a Naval Academy classmate, Lieutenant Ray Penrod, aboard. We spent most of the night talking about old times. At dawn the convoy formed and headed north. I was the last of the Class of 1941 to see Ray alive—the *Meredith* went down a few weeks later.

Turning the Tide

Following a hesitant approach, our small armada finally made a dash for it and arrived off the Lunga beaches of Guadalcanal on the morning of September 18. During this roundabout voyage, which consumed twenty-five days, the situation ashore had altered markedly. What had been advertised in Apia in late August as an "administrative landing" over secure beaches had now become a badly needed transfusion of reinforcements to bolster an undermanned, threatened beachhead. Only four nights earlier a Japanese brigade had been bloodily repulsed on a spiny ridge just short of Henderson Field, the airstrip so vital to U.S. hopes in the Solomons. The 1st Raider and 1st Parachute battalions had been badly mauled in the struggle.

Shortly before the 7th Marines and 1/11 had quit New River in the first week in April 1942, Brigadier General Alexander Archer Vandegrift, then inspector general of the Marine Corps, had conducted an inspection of 1st Marine Division. The result had been a housecleaning centered in the division staff. Noted jungle fighters and World War I heroes had been filtering into New River to man the line regiments for several months, as quickly as they could be extracted from other duties. Now the most talented planners in the Marine Corps moved in to take over key staff roles. General Vandegrift, tenacious, resourceful, decisive, compassionate—a Virginian of the Robert E. Lee mold—was selected to lead the division overseas. The Marine Corps could not have made a better choice.

Eager to see the 7th Marines ashore and in the front lines, the division staff was aghast as mountains of tent poles and other housekeeping paraphernalia piled up steadily on the beach. This resulted from the regimental commander's decision to load the transports administratively—supposedly making better use of limited space—rather than for a combat landing. To add to their discomfiture, the transports departed at dusk with much-needed equipment and supplies still aboard. The Japanese, who had not been advised of the noncombat nature of the debarkation that day, visited the newcomers with the first of the many air bombardments they were to endure over the next two months.

The eagerly awaited arrival of the last of the division's three infantry regiments had not been auspicious. General Vandegrift wasted little time removing the architect of this debacle, and the regiment soon flourished under new leadership.

The transports hove to close inshore to speed up the disembarkation. Since the Navy had little control of the adjacent waters when friendly planes were grounded after dark, it behooved us to get everything possible unloaded before the transports sortied to sea for the night; one never knew whether they would return. The advice of the 7th Marines' staff to the contrary, Chaisson and I decided to "combat load" our vehicles at Apia so that we could get key equipment and ammunition ashore early. Doing so was almost routine anyway and not much more trouble. Intuition is often crucial in combat, and survivors learn not to ignore it.

The day was cloudless, not too hot, with a slight breeze. The sea was almost like a mill pond, the scene disarmingly peaceful. I climbed over the side and down the net into a landing boat to lead the C Battery advance party ashore. No sooner had I stepped onto the beach than Major Lou Ennis, 2/11's operations officer, met me and said that we were attached to 2/11. Ennis led me to a battery position close to the rest of his battalion, about 2 miles inland to the southwest. We would reinforce their fire in support of the 5th Marines, which was facing the Matanikau River to the west. Returning to the beach, I awaited the landing of the battery, contemplating what our embarrassment would have been had we not used our initiative and combat loaded.

Gathered on the fringes of the beach were small clusters of combat veterans who had stopped the Japanese at the Tenaru River and Bloody Ridge, and elsewhere around the defensive perimeter. They looked ragged, even gaunt; many had beards and other facial growths. Proud they certainly were, but they were happy to see their 7th Marines comrades led by such men as Chesty Puller and Herman Hanneken swell their thinned ranks. Occasionally, there would be a call of greeting to a friend or the gibe "It's about time you got here, now that the fighting's over"—typical battle taunts unbelieved by taunted and taunter alike.

C Battery on the move was a collection of jeeps, howitzers, and one-ton trucks. The trucks were laden with ammunition as well as the artilleryman's stock-in-trade—aiming circles, drums of wire, field telephones, aiming stakes, tents, radio batteries, and the rest. As we formed up in the coconut grove in from the beach, some of the veterans drifted off to seek cover. It was high noon. At noon Japanese bombers, we promptly learned, predictably appeared some 20,000 feet up in the cloudless sky to the west on their daily mission to ravage the beachhead with their 250-pound general-purpose bombs. Claxons sounded and the westernmost combatant ships trained their antiaircraft guns skyward, waiting for the planes to come into range. Fighter planes from Henderson Field scrambled, and those of us on the beach prepared to hunker down amidst the coconut palms, there being no more likely alternative. Whether the Japanese were after the transports, the beach area, or Henderson Field, it was difficult to tell from our vantage point.

Few bombs landed near us, and those that did seemed to cough up a harmless spray of sand despite their menacing concussion. As quickly as they had come, they turned west again and headed back toward New Georgia and beyond with white puffs of antiaircraft fire reaching for them and Wildcat fighters giving chase. The raid evidently did little harm, and unloading continued. Were it not for the few bombs that had exploded nearby and the noise of the antiaircraft fire, one might have dismissed it as fantasy. Our baptismal air raid had not been scary; in fact, it gave some of us a false sense of well-being.

By early afternoon the battery was assembled and I led McKee, Chaisson, and the troops to our position as 2/11's third foursome of howitzers. (Her missing battery, E, would not arrive from Tulagi for several days.) Happy to be in action again, all hands hurried the howitzers into position—the French guns had been left on Wallis Island. John laid them on the assigned azimuth, and wire lines were run to the FDC. We were registered by 2/11 front-line observers on our defensive barrages and other checkpoints by dark. We were neither assigned an observation post nor called upon to furnish any FOs to the infantry, presumably because our duty tour with 2/11 would be short-lived.

Our days as 2/11's third battery were not particularly active— our firing was largely of the harassment-and-interdiction variety. But it did serve to shake us down, to iron out such matters as local security, and to otherwise enable us to settle in as members of the artillery team. Our assignment to 2/11 had been logical since we had been on detached duty from 1/11 for six months, three months of which on Wallis Island we had operated independently. We were used to thinking for ourselves and acting on our own. Even after we rejoined 1/11, about a week later, we were often used in the role of a "swing" battery to reinforce 2/11 when action along the Matanikau warmed up.

In those early days of the Pacific War, the field artillery was still in a relatively primitive state. The maps of Guadalcanal were almost useless, and the photomap that replaced them was not much better because large sections were obscured by cloud cover. Practically all firing was done from firing charts created in the FDC from survey and actual firing data. Ammunition was almost as primitive. The variable-time fuze, which would provide reliable air bursts far more effective than high-explosive impact bursts against troops in the open or without overhead cover, had not yet reached the field. We used high-explosive impact almost exclusively, trying to get the effect of air detonation from tree bursts. Rounds of white phosphorus, far easier to locate in the jungle than high explosives, were also not available to us. Four 75mm howitzers could deliver about half the firepower at 8,500 yards (about two thirds the range) of six 105mm howitzers, the battery that would be typical in days to come. Our tactical concepts were also archaic. The battery commander, for example, had little to do in our relatively static defensive role; overseeing the battery executive as he directed the firing did not provide useful employment and could provide needless interference. That the artillery acquitted itself well was because most fighting was defensive, the batteries were surveyed or fired in, the front-line observers were tied into their FDCs by field wire, and the ammunition supply was adequate. All firing was done by battery or battalion; individual batteries did not operate independently or fire by platoon.

On September 29, eleven days after our arrival, Major McKee was flown off the island to a new duty assignment, and I took command of C Battery. John had been promoted to captain in August, but each battery was permitted to have two captains for the time being to provide some measure of experience.

In late September we rejoined 1/11 and took up position facing west-southwest along the edge of a coconut grove just south of Henderson Field. This was to be our home base, so we constructed fairly elaborate dugouts topped by two layers of coconut logs at right angles to each other. Inasmuch as most of the action continued to be over by the Matanikau River, we periodically occupied positions in support of 2/11 just east of the Lunga River. This position was to the northwest of Henderson Field, whose runway ran approximately east to west. On the evening of October 13, we were ordered to occupy the Lunga site and await orders. We made a night displacement without lights and laid the battery on a westerly azimuth. We had neither radio nor telephone communications with 2/11.

We had been in this approximate position at night before, but as a reinforcing unit, we were not dug in—the theory was that the Japanese were not supposed to know that we ever fired from such an exposed position. Our local security had been posted along the bank of the Lunga. It was after midnight, and John and I were wondering when the 2/11 wire team would arrive so that we could get our firing instructions for the night. We were talking in muted tones by the executive's post behind the center of the battery when all hell broke loose.

The shock of huge 14-inch naval shells bursting around us without warning was so unnerving that we were momentarily rooted to the ground. Then we dove for the nearest hole of any sort, about ten of us landing in a crater that had been caused by a 1,000-pound bomb. I felt naked indeed near the top of this pile of humanity as salvo after salvo from the battleships, cruisers, and destroyers of the Japanese fleet standing just offshore pounded us mercilessly. The fury of sound and flash, the convulsing earth, the fragments hissing like freight trains overhead and thumping to the ground around us induced in me a feeling of helplessness such as I have never felt before or since. There was nothing I could do but endure—

no place to run, no place to hide. So we prayed and we wondered when our number would be called.

We spent the remainder of the night in this exposed position as the Japanese raked the beachhead over and over again. Some huge fragments came to rest within feet of us. One man in a nearby crater was burned by a spent fragment that dropped beside him. Lucky for us, the 14-inch shells were armor-piercing (intended to sink other ships)—so they did not break up into the jagged pieces that would have been devastating to troops without overhead cover.

After a seemingly endless night, the dawn found us a haggard, isolated group. Deciding that battery morale would be best served by action, I decided to jeep back to the 1/11 command post (CP) for instructions. As my driver and I started down the northern edge of the field, we saw a lone plane coming in low and heading directly toward us. We could not be sure whether it was friend or foe until it opened up with .30-caliber machine guns. The bullets ricocheted off the runway right at us as we jumped from the jeep and dove behind a conveniently located revetment. A hail of bullets smashed into the sandbags and earth, and then he was gone as quickly as he had come. He had been shooting at us all right—our abandoned jeep was undamaged. We mounted up and continued to the 1/11 CP.

To put it mildly, the CP was in a state of shock, and no one showed the smallest interest in focusing on our plight. I tracked down Major Samuel Wooster, the operations officer, and appealed to him. "Sammy," I said, "the CO and exec seem unapproachable at the moment, so why don't you call Regiment and see if it's all right for us to return to our regular position." After a little more badgering, Sammy called the regimental operations officer and received approval. A battery without communications to either the FDC or a front-line observer is practically useless.

The troops were only too happy to quit our shell-pocked real estate. As we drove past Henderson Field on the way back to our regular position, we did not see a single operational plane, although we later learned that some retaliatory activity had been mounted from the fighter strip nearby. When we debarked at our battery position, our eyes were drawn to a 14-inch baseplate stuck in a coconut tree about 10 feet above our dugout. It resembled a discus in flight. Miraculously, not a single man in the battery in either location had been killed or even badly wounded.

Naval gunfire is a shattering experience. Often you can see the guns firing, and they look like they are aiming directly at you. You know that the ships have an almost inexhaustible supply of ammunition and that they can alter range and deflection at will to run you down. To me, it was far more fearsome than bombing. During bombing you knew that once the planes had dropped their loads, that was it. I would choose bombing over shelling anytime.

Several nights later during another naval bombardment, John, Gunner Sack, and I were huddled in our dugout when we heard a crackling sound. We ventured out and saw that a fire had broken out in the division ammunition dump next door. Although we did not stop to discuss it, we knew that Japanese gunners would use the fire (and exploding ammunition) as an aiming point. The three of us attacked the fire with palm fronds and sand and had it out within a minute. As we started back to our dugout, the officer in charge and an aide came puffing up. Briefly we showed them where the fire still smoldered.

Some months later we learned that the officer in charge had received a Silver Star for putting out a fire in the ammunition dump, thus saving it from possible eruption and loss. We never checked to determine the date of his fire-fighting exploit.

Lieutenant Colonel Joe Knowlan, our easygoing, fatherly commander, had been invalided off the island, and Regiment thought that the old Philadelphia Reserve Battalion could use a little shaping up. In mid October Lieutenant Colonel Manly Lamar Curry arrived from Tulagi, where his 3rd Battalion, 10th Marines had languished since that island had been secured in early August. A graduate of the École de Guerre and one of the intellectuals of the Marine Corps, the new colonel made little effort to hide his superior grasp of the fine art of gunnery. His apparent arrogance was enhanced by a luxuriant, flaming red beard, the equal of which was not to be found on the island. After his enforced idleness of the past months, he seemed intent upon making the most of his opportunity for action; he took command of 1/11 with relish.

A few days after the naval battering of October 13, the battalion moved out to the western sector of the beachhead to support a push to the Matanikau River and beyond, where a threateningly strong Japanese force had massed. The first night the colonel decided to lay the sheaf parallel, a sophisticated artillery technique in which all twelve howitzers are sighted on a star. Each gunner must be coached to fix his cross hair on the same star and then stay on that star. At the command "Mark," all gunners simultaneously record their deflection with respect to their own aiming stakes. That night it took several hours, until about midnight, before this tedious technique was brought to an apparent satisfactory conclusion. Many failed to appreciate the need for such esoteric activity. After all, pack howitzers were not exactly precise weapons. Laying the sheaf parallel was an interesting academic exercise, but many thought it somewhat unsuited to the rigorous situation in which we found ourselves. To troops battered by weeks of air bombardment and naval shelling, the good colonel seemed eccentric, to say the least.

A day or two later, C Battery was in a position near the southern perimeter, on the left flank of the battalion. Bob Sack and I had been at the battalion CP and were on the way back to the battery when we heard several rounds of high explosive bursting in what sounded to us like the immediate vicinity of our battery position. As we came over the hill within sight of the battery, we observed John Chaisson and one or two men using blankets and clothing to smother smoldering fires in the ammunition piled up by each howitzer. The fires were out by the time we arrived on the scene. John explained that several rounds of light artillery or mortar fire had homed in on them, but fortunately, no howitzers were damaged. Had I been a more experienced battery commander, I would have written up John and the men for citations. But in those days we were more concerned with the Japanese and survival, and my first thought was to move the battery to a more tenable position. It was the first counterbattery that we had experienced on the island, and our position was more exposed to enemy observation from the slopes of Mount Austen than it needed to be.

I reconnoitered a position to the rear, where the battery would be in defilade and not under direct observation from outside our lines. I secured permission from Lieutenant Colonel Curry to displace there after dark. We were in position and digging in the next morning when Curry arrived by jeep. When I came forward to greet him, I believed that he had come to inspect our new position, but he had other things in mind.

"Do you mind if I play around awhile with your battery, Captain Parry," he smiled.

We had been up much of the night moving in secrecy to our new position. The star business still rankled. What is more, I did not think that we were playing games; the past five weeks had convinced the officers and men of C Battery that this action was very much for real. So, ill-advisedly, I responded, "Not so long as you don't fuck them up." Chaisson, who was standing nearby, almost choked, and he stared at me in disbelief. Curry did a double take but made no comment about my rudeness, which he could easily have decided was insubordination.

We then proceeded to carry out his orders by conducting a high burst adjustment, another sophisticated artillery procedure that determines what the group of bursts from the four howitzers look like in the air. They are then adjusted to a tighter or looser grouping to gain maximum effectiveness. Whether my implied criticism of Lieutenant Colonel Curry's conduct was taken to heart by him, I do not know. Insofar as I could see, it was not reflected in my Fitness Report for the six weeks that he commanded 1/11.

Toward the end of October, the Japanese made a major assault on the 7th Marines' lines south of the airfield and just east of the Lunga River and the ridge made famous six weeks earlier by Edson's Raiders. Lieutenant Colonel Lewis B. Puller's 1/7 stood directly in the path of the Japanese. 1/11 fired heavily in Puller's support, as did other artillery batteries. During the first night of the battle, a battalion of the American Infantry Division's 164th Infantry Regiment (a Dakota and Minnesota National Guard unit) was ordered to reinforce 1/7.

The Army battalion's march took it directly through our battery position. It was pitch black, well past midnight, and we had been firing steadily since early evening. I was standing in back of the battery executive's post when one of the men diverted my attention to the rear. It was an eerie sight indeed to see GIs with fixed bayonets and deployed for battle, pass in complete silence like wraiths through our camp. We had not been alerted to their coming. But it took no second sight to guess where they were going—the sound of battle had been raging to our immediate front for half the night. We promptly ceased firing. They moved through our suddenly silent cannon and on across the open field to our front and into the woods a few hundred yards away. Not a word passed between us. There, in one of the unique actions of the war, the one thousand fresh GIs were integrated with the remaining five hundred battle-weary Marines of 1/7 into a single fighting force. This combined Army-Marine force threw back the determined Japanese assault; once again, the thinly manned perimeter held.

The Koli Point Offensive

A few days after the night infantry action near Bloody Ridge, Lieutenant Colonel Herman Hanneken, the commanding officer of 2/7, was ordered to move east beyond Koli Point to intercept and trap a freshly landed Japanese battalion. But it soon became apparent that his understrength battalion was outnumbered. After suffering many casualties, Hanneken withdrew to the west of the Nalimbiu River, which bisected Koli Point, and waited for reinforcements. Division responded by dispatching a brigade-sized force under command of Brigadier General William Rupertus, the assistant division commander, who had just been transferred from Tulagi. While Puller's 1/7 took up position inland alongside Hanneken, 2/164 and 3/164 moved upstream along the Nalimbiu to prepare for an encircling movement from the south. The goal was to trap the Japanese against the beach. 1/11 was ordered to a position about 2 miles west of Koli Point to support the operation. For the only time during our stay on the island, we had to break the pack howitzers into their component loads to ford one of the swollen streams enroute to this position.

Soon after arrival, Lieutenant Colonel Curry called me over to the battalion command tent and directed me to report to the commanding officer of 3/164 as artillery liaison and FO. I assembled a small team—a scout sergeant and two radio operators (the TBX radio was a two-man load). Since we were to move rapidly, we made no effort to extend a wire line. We would work on foot.

While 2/7 and 1/7 pressed along the beach, 3/164 and 2/164 swung up through the jungle from inland, with 2/164 on the right, or outside, of the end-around sweep.

The day after joining the Army, my team and I were moving along a jungle trail to the east of the Nalimbiu, when we came to an open field of considerable size. It seemed like a good opportunity to register the battery on some prominent feature on the far side of the field. We set up the radio and I climbed a handy tree. Although I could hear the rounds land somewhere in the jungle, I was unable to maneuver them so I could see one. (A 75mm high-explosive burst in the jungle is difficult to spot even if you know where to look.) So after fruitlessly firing about ten rounds, I gave up. It would have been irresponsible to continue to fire indiscriminately into the jungle through which 2/164 might even then have been moving. As we buttoned up the radio and prepared to move out, an infantry squad came along the trail from our rear. Much to our surprise, they informed us that they were the point of the lead company. We had been out in front of the lines for about half an hour.

After the infantrymen moved along the trail to our front around a bend about 200 yards out, the pointman was killed by one round fired by a Japanese sniper in a tree. The squad soon located the sniper, shot him, and continued on. How we had gotten so far in front of the point I have no idea, but I resolved to be more careful.

We reached the beach that night, but the Japanese had sensed a trap and had fled to the east. We set up our radio on the beach and checked in with the battalion CP, hoping to register along the beach to the east the next morning. About midnight the infantry opened up on some troops moving in toward the beach-anchored perimeter from the south. Tragically, the troops were a U.S. Army patrol. By the time the firing was brought under control, much blood had been spilled. The dying and wounded were delivered to an aid station just up the beach from us. The night was punctuated with their anguish. There is nothing more unnerving in battle than the killing and maiming of your own men by "friendly" fire.

The next morning I was detached from 3/164 and ordered to report to 1/7. The two battalions of the 7th Marines had been directed to move through 3/164 and press eastward along the beach. 2/164 was to swing wide through the jungle and, again, attempt to fix the elusive Japanese between the 7th Marines and the beach. I found Lieutenant Colonel Puller along the trail, about 100 yards in from the beach. He was standing in the gloom of a tropical rain in a spot where every Marine of his battalion would pass within feet of him. He had a green issue blanket around his shoulders and puffed on a pipe clenched upside down in his teeth. Imperturbable in the drenching rain, he made an unforgettable picture.

The next day, as the troops pushed eastward, Puller rang up Lieutenant Colonel Hanneken on the field telephone. As near as I could determine from a few yards away, Puller wanted to coordinate his advance with Hanneken's. But somewhere in the frailty of the jungle-wet wire or in the difficulty that the two tigers had in communicating, something went amiss. Chesty was not getting through. "God damn it, Herman," he croaked, "God damn it!" Then he muttered a stream of unintelligible profanity and threw the field telephone in the mud.

Battery Commander

The following day, only an hour after I was relieved by an artilleryman from 1/10 and had started hiking back down the beach toward the Lunga Perimeter, that indestructible Marine, Chesty Puller, was temporarily felled by fragments from a Japanese 77mm round and two sniper's bullets. My FO team was by then about a mile to the rear. When I heard the noise of the fire fight, I stopped and had my radiomen set up the TBX. I had no idea that Lieutenant Colonel Puller was down, but I called for landing craft to evacuate the casualties I was sure his battalion had suffered during the fire fight.

Upon return to camp I learned that promotions had come in and been delivered to the men. Handing out promotions was customarily the prerogative of the battery commander, and I asked John why he had not withheld the warrants until my return. He responded that he knew that I concurred in the promotions, that he did not know when I would return from the field, and that he thought the men deserved to start getting the increased pay immediately. There was little to disagree with in what John said. Nonetheless, I told him that in the future promotions were to be withheld until I was on hand to deliver them personally.

This minor clash illustrated my concern about being away from the battery while being responsible for it. I did not fault Lieutenant Colonel Curry's view that the most experienced officer should be up with the infantry controlling fire, although his philosophy was unconventional at that time. The fact was that I had been in command of C Battery for only about six weeks, and for half that time I had been away as FO or liaison officer. I felt the need to demonstrate who was in charge. Two developing situations offered me this opportunity.

On October 1 we had joined 2nd Lieutenant Clinton E. "Rosey" Bump, of the Hollywood Marines, as we called the Los Angeles Reserve units. Skinny and about 6 feet 3 inches tall, he reminded me of the comic-strip character, Andy Gump. He could talk anyone out of their eye teeth. During lulls in the fighting, he would take a one-ton truck to scrounge around the beachhead, preying particularly on Army units. Most batteries would have been delighted to have had a scrounger of his competence. The only problem was that I already had an operator of no mean talent in Gunner Sack. The first thing I knew they were in an undeclared competition—Sack would bring in the wherewithal to set up a shower for the battery; Bump would somehow procure an "abandoned" .30-caliber machine gun for our local security. And so it went. I could see trouble brewing; one operator for a 140-man battery was surely enough. So I called in Rosey Bump and confided that I needed a more mature FO to man one of our front-line observation posts (Rosey was a few years older than our other second lieutenants). With a twinkle in his eye, he allowed as how he was my man. In no time the infantry became enamored of this eccentric character. Rosey kept them amused with his repartee, his storklike physique, and omnipresent pith helmet. Even the infantry officers in the front lines felt constrained to let him wear that hat because he was obviously a morale builder. In addition, I guess they thought that as long as Rosey was around he would be the initial target of any self-respecting sniper.

The second incident involved two of the battery's most reliable, praiseworthy NCOs—Mess Sergeant Leonard A. Maxson and Pharmacist's Mate 1st Class Ralph W. Brodie, our senior hospital corpsman. Maxson had been trying his damnedest to serve palatable meals and had shown considerable ingenuity. He and his mess crew were also tireless scroungers and labored long hours. But there were just so many ways one could prepare Spam or corn willy. The bitching about chow had reached epidemic proportions.

Brodie, as devoted to the mental and physical health of the men as Maxson was to their nourishment, had also been the target of abuse due to his insistence that all hands take their daily ration of Atabrine, a malaria suppressant.

I had observed this ingratitude for several days with increasing annoyance, well aware that bitching troops were a healthy sign of combativeness. Although Chaisson and Sack thought that I was making too much of common battlefield gripes, I believed the time ripe to come to the support of Maxson and Brodie. I called a battery formation. In blunt, forceful words I expressed my view of their conduct toward the two men who labored so diligently and effectively for their health and well-being. The talk seemed to do some good; the bitching dropped several decibels, and the battery knew who was in command.

We sometimes sallied forth from our position south of Henderson Field to support infantry actions beyond the perimeter, but we were never gone for more than a few days. One constant annoyance during the period was the handful of artillery rounds that landed on or near the western end of Henderson Field every dusk. Although Pistol Pete—as we called the Japanese 155mm artillery piece—caused little damage, the annoyance he created was significant. Further, with a slight adjustment to the left in deflection, he could have homed in uncomfortably close to the division CP. Several patrols and air spotters had attempted to locate Pistol Pete, but none had succeeded.

It was generally conceded that this persistent cannon was hidden in a cave to the west of the Matanikau River. It apparently was wheeled to the front of the cave at dusk to launch a few shells, then withdrawn from sight. Inasmuch as Pistol Pete was an artillery piece, the division staff concluded that an artillerist might have the best chance of pinpointing and bringing fire to bear on it. 1/11 was requested to provide an FO to accompany an infantry patrol in an attempt to bring this miscreant to heel.

Lieutenant Colonel Curry asked me if Captain Chaisson could be spared. It was not surprising that he should focus on John. John had a macho, gung-ho reputation and was respected for his competence and admired by the men. Further, he was a captain in a lieutenant's job, and we would soon have to learn to get along without him anyway.

Some four days after John took to the jungle with the patrol, Gunner Sack and I picked him up at the perimeter and jeeped back to the battery position. After cleaning up just after nightfall, John set off by jeep to report to the division CP. Although he had been unable to spot Pistol Pete, he reported his route and observations to the division intelligence officer (G-2), Lieutenant Colonel Ed Buckley, a Reserve officer from Philadelphia, where he practiced law.

John returned from Lieutenant Colonel Buckley's tent, and we settled in under our mosquito nets. About an hour later the field telephone rang. It was the battalion commander wanting to know why Chaisson had not reported to the division CP. I replied, "He returned from Colonel Buckley's tent just an hour ago." I was told that the division operations officer (G-3), Lieutenant Colonel Merrill Twining, a hard-nosed Regular officer, was expecting a personal report immediately since this had been a "G-3 patrol."

The G-2 and G-3 tents were no more than 20 yards apart, but this was obviously a matter of principle. So Captain Chaisson recrossed Henderson Field to division headquarters in a blacked-out jeep in a second hazardous trip past bolt-snapping sentries. It was about midnight when he dragged his weary but uncomplaining bones back from headquarters, having made the same report twice within four hours.

After the spirited action east of Koli Point in mid November, the stream of Army and Marine units that poured ashore put island dominance out of Japanese reach. With little action expected for 1st Marine Division, Lieutenant Colonel Curry asked to return to his battalion on Tulagi. He had commanded 1/11 through its most active period, from mid October until almost the end of November. Eccentric, flamboyant, somewhat arrogant, he was clearly competent. He was also innovative. His use of battery commanders as FOs and liaison officers not only took advantage of their greater relative experience but also recognized the fact that in a relatively static defensive situation a battery commander is underemployed. The colonel had arrived on the scene charged with putting 1/11's house in order. He acknowledged that he had expected the firing batteries to be subpar; in fact, over the past weeks they had impressed him as three of the finest batteries he had ever seen.

Lieutenant Colonel Donovan D. Sult had been executive officer and acting commanding officer of 3/10, which was based on Tulagi. He arrived on Guadalcanal on November 27 to take command of 1/11 from the departing Curry—who would be resuming command of 3/10. Though the change of command was to take place the next day, Sult lost no time in summoning the sergeant major and instructing him to have a battalion order prepared for release the next day, after change of command, stating that henceforth no beards or other unsightly facial growths would be tolerated in 1/11.

Sergeant Major Cooksey was a slight Marine of mild manner, but he had not become a top-ranking NCO because he was dumb. It was rumored that Cooksey was not overjoyed by Sult's imminent assumption of command because of a grudge that Cooksey had held against him since the days Sult was in motor transport prior to commissioning. Cooksey did not procrastinate in committing the new colonel's order to paper. Somehow or other, however, he neglected to tell the clerk of the condition that it not be released before noon. So, a few hours before the change-of-command ceremony, the battery commanders were stunned to learn that beards were outlawed in the battalion. Curry and Sult had never been close friends. The official farewell between the two was particularly frigid as the most magnificent beard on Guadalcanal returned to Tulagi.

We saw little of Lieutenant Colonel Sult over the next days. We heard persistent reports, however, that he had brought considerably more than his share of hard liquor with him from the 3/10 officers' wine mess and that he was indulging liberally. Inasmuch as there was no action to speak of, his continued absence from the battery area went largely unnoticed.

Then came rumblings of trouble from battalion headquarters. Rumor had it that Lieutenant Colonel Sult, more than a little under the influence, had verbally abused a staff NCO and that this indiscretion had been reported through senior NCO channels to Lieutenant Colonel J. J. Keating, the CO of 3/11 and senior officer of the 11th Marines still on the island. Reports had it that the

chastised NCO had been the former wire chief of C Battery, a hard-
working, well-respected, soft-spoken, polite Southerner. The alleged
insubordination was so out of keeping with his character and record
that it was unthinkable. Dissatisfied with Sult's explanation of the
affair, Lieutenant Colonel Keating bucked the matter to Brigadier
General Rupertus. Just three weeks after his assumption of command, Sult was transferred off the island, yet another senior military officer who was a victim of demon rum. Major Jeff Fields,
Keating's executive in 3/11, took over—our fourth battalion commander in less than three months.

Toward the end of December most of 1st Marine Division had
departed for Australia. As the last arrivals, the 7th Marines Combat Team would be the last to leave. To pass the time until our ships
appeared, C Battery organized a smoker. Officers and men made
contributions as their varied talents allowed. It was an enjoyable
evening, livened up by spirits from a B Battery bootleg still, of
which officers had taken no official note.

A Harvard graduate and nephew of Harvard football legend,
"Tack" Hardwick, one of C Battery's second lieutenants was Winchester Dana Hardwick. The lieutenant's nickname was Zube,
which derived from his exuberant personality. Zube had been an
actor before joining the Marines, most notably the juvenile lead in
the Broadway show *Babes in Arms*. Relatively small in stature,
Zube was strong, fair-haired, and handsome. His act was the grand
finale of the smoker. After a rousing rendition of "Where or When"
in his best Broadway style, Zube started to bow off the "stage"
amidst loud applause. Abruptly, he disappeared in a foxhole. I am
sure he never brought the house down on Broadway or elsewhere
with an exit like that one in a coconut grove near Henderson Field.

On January 4, 1943 we moved from the battery position, our
home for over three months, to a coconut grove just behind the eastern Lunga beaches. We were to embark from the beach the following morning. As we slept, a Marine from a rifle company
bivouacked beside us was hit and instantly killed in his sleep by a
falling coconut. To survive four months of bloodshed only to be
taken by an unthinking coconut hours before departure is somehow
more difficult to accept than being cut down by enemy fire.

Next morning C Battery boarded assorted landing craft with
little regret, made the short run through a calm sea to the transport
area close inshore and embarked aboard the USS *Jackson*, the same
friendly ship that had brought us to the island in September. I had

donned my only presentable khaki shirt for the occasion, but it was short-sleeved—Bob Sack had cut off the sleeves for me because of a torn elbow and stitched them up with neatness that was almost equal to that of a professional seamstress. Although short-sleeved shirts were acceptable on Guadalcanal, they were not yet in vogue in the Marine Corps. Colonel Amor LeRoy Sims, the CO of 7th Marines and a model of sartorial decorum, ordered me below to get in proper uniform. It gave rise to the only nostalgic thought, albeit fleeting, that I had of the Canal.

Eight days later, after an uneventful voyage, we arrived on a gray, overcast day off the coast of southern Australia, plied through Melbourne's spacious harbor, and tied up to a long wharf. Quickly disembarked, we were marched to waiting trains and whisked off to Ballarat some 70 miles to the west-northwest.

In Retrospect: Guadalcanal

Field artillery batteries, even light ones such as 75mm, were very effective in a defensive situation when they had been fired in ahead of time and could be brought to bear on enemy troops massing for an attack. Wire from the front lines to battery positions remained intact most of the time because few Japanese got through the lines and those who did cut little wire. Except for naval gunfire and air bombardment (which were not well coordinated with ground assaults), counterbattery was almost nonexistent. It interfered in no way with the artillery. It did no appreciable damage to our howitzers, communications, or ammunition, and it caused no diversion of fire support from the infantry. Even the lack of suitable fuses for air bursts was not as critical as it might have been because the jungle approaches to the beachhead provided trees in abundance to help an artillerist simulate air bursts.

The effectiveness of artillery in support of infantry forays outside the perimeter was more suspect. Lacking adequate maps and air photos, the artillery was singularly ineffective. Targets were difficult to locate on the imperfect maps, and we could not depend on our radios. To avoid throwing the initial adjusting round onto our own troops, batteries would add safety factors to compensate for the poor maps and frequently lose the round altogether. Trying to bring rounds near the target when we could not see them was deemed foolhardy and dangerous; maneuvering bursts by sound was an inexact science. The brass was unwilling to endanger artillery by sending batteries outside the perimeter if there was potential for enemy infantry attack; therefore, artillery was often out of range.

The most important lesson I learned from my first battles was the reliability of Marine infantry: They held their ground despite the odds. Beyond protecting ourselves from infiltrators, artillerymen did not have to worry unduly about self-defense. We could devote all our energies to support of the infantry. Being Marines meant hanging together, mutual support, and counting on one another no matter what. It was a good feeling and made me want to contribute my utmost to the team.

It was perhaps a measure of the quality of Marine leadership on the Canal that those of us at the battery level never felt the sense of desperation that our plight counseled. We had some knowledge of the fragility of our supply lines—our food ration gave silent testimony to it. But our leaders never imparted to us any sense of panic, and we were not within range of dismaying broadcasts. To my knowledge at the time, there were no thoughts, much less plans, to take to the hills—though such plans had in fact been drafted. As far as we at the battery level were concerned, we were there to stay until the Army and Navy got it together enough to relieve us.

There is something about a Marine that anticipates hardship, that expects to be shortchanged. After all, the Corps had sucked hind teat since 1775. Most of our leaders were nurtured on the Banana Wars, the thankless shoestring type of operation that always seems to fall to Marines. Marines were accustomed to privation, to accomplishing much with little, to winning somehow. On Guadalcanal Marine esprit de corps—that elusive, priceless element so essential to victory in the darkest of times—had one of its finest hours.

As a twenty-four-year-old captain sizing up our situation from the battery perspective, I was more attentive to the everyday concerns of weapons, ammunition, food and water, sleep, and upcoming actions than the strategic importance of Guadalcanal. But even I knew that it was vital to stop the Japanese—stop them cold. If *we* did not, who would? It did not occur to John Chaisson or me to contemplate the historical significance of this battle. We just wanted to finish the job, whip the Japanese, and turn the island over to the Army.

A few times in October we wondered where in the hell the Navy was. During that time I visited a newly assigned battery observation post on a steep hill on the perimeter about halfway between the

Lunga and the Matanikau. Someone pointed to a ship in the channel between the Canal and Savo Island. As it steamed into view, some of the troops broke into a cheer—our Navy was coming back. As the ship moved in closer, however, we saw the "meatball" on the Japanese flag. Nonchalantly, the Japanese destroyer steamed up to the Lunga beaches and poured broadside after broadside onto Henderson Field and nearby targets. It was discouraging—particularly when we saw the destroyer steam away unmolested. Only one lone dive-bomber gave chase and not until after the enemy ship had disappeared from view. Not for the first time, Bob Sack asked me where my buddies in the Navy were. And not for the last time, I assured him that they would be there. And come they did, not long after, led by their new commander, Admiral Bull Halsey.

Many in the Navy like to think of Midway as the crucial battle in the Pacific. The significance of Midway is hardly contestable. But it was a defensive battle, fought on the approaches to Hawaii. How can it compare with the calculated risk of putting 20,000 Marines ashore on an island in the South Pacific that was twice as far from our West Coast supply bases as from Japan *and* telling them to stay there, to beat off the Japanese while the United States licked its wounds and marshaled its forces? It was a desperate gamble. What if it had failed? What if the Navy had decided that it could not prudently sustain any further losses to maintain this far-removed base? How close were the Navy and our national leaders to accepting this dreary conclusion? If they had lost heart, become cautious— how long before they would have dared to initiate another offensive, to challenge the Japanese again in the distant Pacific? How much more time would the Japanese have had to consolidate and strengthen their vast empire?

As so often in history, a small band of determined men turned the tide. Was it not the heroism and perseverence of the Marines ashore that inspired the Navy *not* to abandon them? The Marines encouraged the national leaders to keep the faith and by so doing rallied the nation. The Battle for Guadalcanal was of enormous significance to our war effort, if not the crucial battle of the Pacific War.

7

In The Rear

Ballarat

About 1,500 feet above sea level, Ballarat owed its start to the finding of gold about a century before. It was now the center of a rich agricultural area. Because the nights were cool (even though it was summer Down Under) we were issued woolen Australian jackets, which were similar to Eisenhower jackets. Our stint in the tropics had debilitated us, so the warmth they provided was welcome. Although we feasted at every opportunity on those two Aussie staples, beer and steak-and-eggs, the daily fare of mutton soon became oppressive. It was a vast improvement over our Guadalcanal diet, but it soon evoked caustic comment from the troops nonetheless—a sure sign that they were well on the road to full recovery.

The officers were given permission to billet outside the camp and those senior officers who were veterans of duty abroad were quick to show the way. Chaisson, Sack, and I found pleasant accommodations above a pub on the outskirts of town across from a large lake. There were four small bedrooms atop our pub. The largest was occupied by a retired Australian Army major, a barmaid had another, Chaisson and I shared one, and Bob Sack took the smaller remaining room. Thus amiably situated, we proceeded to enjoy ourselves. We rowed on the lake, walked the quiet, shady streets, ate, and drank well. Pubs in those austere times were required to close early every evening, but many just locked the front door and the favored patrons moved to the back rooms where socializing continued. John and I decided to attend the Catholic Church or the

Church of England alternately. On the second Sunday we were standing outside the Church of England contemplating how we would amuse ourselves, when an elderly lady asked us if we would like to come to her home for dinner. We accepted gladly. It was a big, comfortable house, and Mrs. Menzies (her nephew had been and would again be prime minister) urged us to make it our home away from home. Had I not been transferred back to the States a few weeks later, I am sure that we would have. As it was, we stopped by for tea on more than one occasion. Mrs. Menzies also took us on rides around town in her charcoal-burning sedan, which could achieve speeds of about 30 miles per hour on the flat. This sponta- neous friendliness was typical of Australians and struck an immedi- ate responsive chord in Americans.

The order of the day was rest, relaxation, and staying out of trouble. With a few exceptions in which Marines overimbibed, there was little difficulty. Officers and men alike appreciated that we were unbelievably well off, and none of us wanted to offend these hospitable people in any way.

With the troops and ourselves well settled in, John and I were granted a three-day leave to visit Melbourne. We took the two-hour train ride through the rolling countryside, which was indistinguish- able from many temperate areas of the States. We soon found our- selves in a large seaport metropolis, only fleetingly glimpsed on our way through ten days earlier. The population of Melbourne was over one million, and the city seemed so much like a comparably sized U.S. city that we felt instantly at home. In fact, the Aussie accent was less daunting than many in the States, such as those in Mem- phis and Boston. Most Aussie men of military age were in the Brit- ish Army of the Middle East, so there were plenty of eligible women. They seemed just as eager to meet us as we were to meet them.

In a pub that night, John and I ran into a classmate of his from the 4th ROC. I knew him too. When I had been assigned to the 1st Marines as artillery liaison officer on the Canal, I had bunked in with him in the regimental communications officer's tent. Now he was wearing major's leaves. Jumping to the conclusion that there had been another massive promotion, we asked him, "When did the promotion list come out?" Self-consciously, he informed us that he had received a spot promotion.

At first this puzzled us, then our puzzlement gave way to annoy- ance. The man's job had not seemed particularly hazardous. Others who had not been spot promoted were in equally vital and more dangerous assignments—in infantry battalions, for example. Spot promotees, who often advanced over hundreds of seniors and contemporaries, later paid a price for their temporary good fortune when they were eventually overtaken by those over whom they had vaulted. Human nature being what it is, some exercised their resentment in various ways. This practice was short-lived in the Marine Corps—it apparently caused more trouble than it was worth.

The second day in Melbourne John and I met attractive girls and parted company. Eventually my date and I found ourselves on one of the spacious beaches. A pretty girl with a tempting figure, we were soon embracing passionately in the moonlight. A nurse, she had the duty that night, and when I delivered her to the hospital she said that she would be off the following weekend and could come up to Ballarat. This suggested intriguing possibilities. But my conscience finally made an appearance. I had been married a little over a year. My first-born son had arrived only two months earlier, on November 7, while I was in the action east of Koli Point. Guilt feelings flooded over me as I fumbled for a picture of my wife. After a few embarrassing moments during which she graciously complimented my wife's good looks, we bid a bittersweet farewell, our brief romance dead aborning.

A few days after John and I had returned to Ballarat, we were dining in the restaurant of a local hotel when I suddenly became inescapably nauseous. Dashing to the nearest exit, which fortunately opened on a back alley, I vomited violently. Ashen, I returned to the table but was unable to face food, so we repaired to the room we had taken for the night. Neither of us had experienced malaria nor did we know much about it. We had stopped taking our daily dose of Atabrine upon reaching Ballarat as had many others, thinking that it was no longer necessary. Now I huddled in front of the fireplace, which was fairly throbbing with warmth, shaking with my first bout of chills. Although we had no way of checking how high the fever climbed, it was high enough to trigger the release of some intimate confessions about Vera and me prior to our marriage. I burdened John with these revelations despite his protestation. He was clearly embarrassed, but I was unable to restrain myself. Neither of us ever referred to the confessions of that fever-ridden night.

Within two weeks of our arrival in Ballarat, the local country club was turned over to us for an officers' club. With about three hundred officers attached to five artillery battalions, the 1st Tank Battalion, and 11th Marines Headquarters, the club soon developed into a popular meeting ground.

One night I hit the sack while John went to the club. When the sun woke me early in the morning, I was horrified to see him stretched out on his bed looking like a disaster victim. There was blood all over his face and clothes. I rolled him over to try to see how beaten up he was and asked him if he were all right. "I'm fine," he mumbled, "this is his blood." I later learned that a careless tanker had made a slighting remark in John's presence about the fighting quality of artillerymen. John had taken him to task with a belt to the nose.

Early in February officers were being selected to return to the States both to infuse the home front (Marine Corps Schools, recruit depots, and HQMC) with a sprinkling of officers with recent combat experience and to relieve the division of many extra captains and field-grade officers. Three officers had been selected from 1/11 and were packed and ready to go. At the last minute, however, it was learned that they would be required as witnesses at a general court-martial.

I have never been sure why I was selected to return. Somewhat to John's surprise, I greeted the news with mixed emotions. I had been a battery commander for only four months, and I was thoroughly enjoying it. Further, it was probable that return to the States would ensure that C Battery would be my only field command as a captain. On the other hand, I had been separated from my beautiful, young bride after only four months of intermittent togetherness, and I had yet to make the acquaintance of my three-month-old son. It was the classic career-versus-family struggle.

Although he never admitted it, I believe John had suggested me as a likely candidate. His motivation was altruistic. He knew Vera, was well aware of my son's birth, and he had witnessed my first clash with malaria. At heart a strong family man, John understood the temptations confronting young men far from home and was aware of my nurse friend in Melbourne. I suspect that he believed that it was a good time for me to visit the home front.

The Home Front

So it was with mixed emotions that I boarded the old transport USS *Rochambeau* at Melbourne and headed across the Pacific. We spent a night in Wellington, New Zealand's spacious harbor and a brief and uneventful liberty ashore in the somnolent town. Then we plodded eastward, well south of the shipping lanes and out of range of Japanese prowlers. It was a restful twenty-four-day voyage, marred only by the breakdown of the ship's evaporators, which relegated us to salt-water showers for the latter half of the trip. We were a relaxed group. We tried to put our recent battle experience behind us and adjust to the more mundane realities before us. We read, played bridge, and just laid around.

Returning home early in a war that has barely begun is an odd experience. The Golden Gate rising out of the mist in the glow of evening was an awesome, welcome sight, but we certainly did not feel like conquering heroes. We knew that most of our buddies were still out there and that we would soon return. So our joy was somewhat constrained. We would have to resume family responsibilities, adjust to the frenetic economy of a nation girding for war, and prepare for our own return overseas with new combat units that were now on the drawing board. The thought of being with Vera again, however, overwhelmed these negative considerations.

The first order of business ashore was to become properly attired. Footlockers with our uniforms had not caught up with us in Australia, so many of us were in khaki and protected from the winter chill only by our woolen Australian jackets. Fortunately, readymade uniforms were available in downtown stores. I purchased and walked away in greens with the new cloth belt—the leather Sam Browne belt had been an early victim of the war. There was little opportunity to explore the fabled city of San Francisco before I was squeezed onto an eastbound military flight.

Met by my wife and some of her family at the Philadelphia airport, we embarked on the first of many adjustment periods following my tours abroad. Vera was nervous and underweight, but in a few weeks she was the relaxed and wholesome beauty to whom I had originally been attracted. With the help of Grandmother Corey, Vera had recently settled into a comfortable apartment in Wynnewood, but four-month-old baby or not, she had no intention of languishing there while I attended the Command and Staff Course in Quantico. This represented a real problem—I soon learned that there was no housing available in the vicinity of Quantico.

I had my doubts about relocating a young, inexperienced mother and her infant from a congenial urban environment close to family and friends to whatever housing I could find in the Virginia countryside. My concerns were reinforced my second afternoon at home, when Vera left me with Stevie, my son, to go shopping for groceries. As I bore witness to the baby's helplessness, the reality of father-hood stunned me. What was I doing with this tiny, utterly depen-dent child when we had a war to fight? Until that moment I had given little thought to parental responsibilities—I had heard almost nothing of Vera's pregnancy and delivery, much less experienced any of it. Now my role as a father struck home and I realized that Vera was justified in wanting to be with the father of her son, re-gardless of the handicaps. And handicaps there were.

With the help of a friend, I was able to rent a slave's cabin on an old estate on a bluff overlooking the Rappahannock River. The tiny cabin consisted of a very small living room, an even smaller attic bedroom in which we had to almost crawl, a bath, and a kitchen. Without a car, the 20 miles to Quantico for class every day were a challenge. Most of the time I hitchhiked. Such fundamentals as provisioning our cabin with food was in itself no minor problem. Vera pushed the baby carriage loaded with baby and food up the steep hill from the local grocery several times a week. Another handicap was the small, wood-burning stove, which struggled man-fully to ward off the March chill. On more than one occasion, Vera and the baby woke up to a freezing cabin because I had not properly fired the stove before taking off in the dark for U.S. Route 1 and the hoped-for ride to school. But we managed, and eventually the local motor vehicle bureaucracy granted my impassioned appeal and is-sued a certificate permitting me to purchase a used car. By then it was May, some classmates had provided periodic assistance in the transportation realm, and life had become reasonably enjoyable.

The war-shortened, four-month Command and Staff Course was not up to usual Marine standards. The staff, mostly untested in battle, had the misfortune of teaching officers who were, for the most part, combat veterans. Much of the material was dull; some almost irrelevant. In one unusually uninspired class about foxholes, a young lieutenant struggled along falteringly. Most of us were en-during the drivel with somnolent indifference, but Major Charlie Rigaud (whose weapons company is immortalized in John Hersey's *Into the Valley*) evidently could stand it no longer. Rising to his feet, he broke up the class with the declaration: "Lieutenant, there are only two dimensions to a foxhole—how fast and how deep!"

With orders in hand for Camp Pendleton, I moved Vera and Stevie in with Father in Chestnut Hill. Considering the less-than-stunning success of my first venture in homemaking, I thought it risky to head across the country to the unknowns of Southern California with wife, baby, and limited resources in a second-hand car. Over Vera's objections I decided to proceed on my own and send for her after I had found accommodations.

At the time Father was on vacation. (A Philadelphia judge was entitled to three months off two out of three years and one month off the other.) He elected to go along and visit relatives on the West Coast. We pushed across the country at a good pace, pausing only for gas, food, and sleep. We were crossing the Utah–Nevada desert when we came upon a small oasis with a service station. Papa thought that we ought to refill the gas tank. Checking the map, I believed that we could easily make the next service station, 30 miles farther. The tickets that the Marine Corps had issued me were for full tanks of gas. We still had about a quarter tank, and I wanted to save as many tickets as I could for use in Southern California. Against Father's better judgment we proceeded to the target oasis only to find that the owner had gone for the day with the key to the gas tank. Fortunately, I was able to nurse the near-empty tank some 20 miles farther until we reached the next service station by coasting down hills and conserving precious fuel in every way I knew. Needless to say, the judge never forgave me for this display of foolhardiness.

I reported to Camp Pendleton for duty. Within a few days I had located an apartment in Laguna Beach and sent for Vera.

The Psycho Ward

Camp Pendleton's 125,000 acres, including 18 miles of Southern California coastline from San Clemente to Oceanside, was surely a real-estate bargain of monumental proportions. In July 1943 the beaches and inland rolling hills were bustling with activity. The camp was the site for training replacements for three active Marine divisions. Fourth Marine Division was there as were all manner of nondivisional troops, such as 155mm howitzer and gun battalions. My initial assignment was as the inspector of training, in the artillery battalion of the Training Regiment. I spent all day in the field observing firing and other training exercises, reporting on good performances and discrepancies. It was during these weeks in July that I ran into Bigfoot Brown again. After returning from Wallis Island with a tropical skin disease that resisted treatment, he attended the Army's Advanced Artillery Course at Fort Sill, Oklahoma, and then reported to the Amphibious Training Command in San Diego. There he helped organize the Troop Training Unit, which assisted in the training of Army and Marine divisions in amphibious warfare. Lieutenant Colonel Brown also pioneered in the coordination of naval gunfire, artillery, and air support. As brash and dominating a personality as I remembered, he devoted a few minutes during our brief meeting in the Pendleton boondocks to bitching lustily about his "rear echelon" role.

Vera and, to my surprise, her sister Corey arrived at Union Station in Los Angeles with the baby and a pair of friendly sailor helpers in tow. They and their infant charge had made a hit with the servicemen during the long, strenuous trek across country and had had plenty of volunteer assistance.

I joined the 4th Battalion, 14th Marines, a 105mm howitzer battalion of 4th Marine Division, on July 29, 1943. I began to settle in as operations officer while the battalion increased in strength prior to launching a training schedule. Savage attacks of malaria continued to beset me. Routinely I would dose myself with quinine and sweat out the fevers in forty-eight-hour episodes. I had had over ten separate sieges since leaving Australia and was determined to find a cure before it seriously affected my duty performance. So, following a particularly bad weekend malarial visitation, I went to the main camp dispensary seeking relief. The Navy doctor, a lieutenant recently ashore from an oil tanker and not experienced in the treatment of malaria, prescribed nine Atabrine pills a day for three days, then six pills a day for three days, and finally three pills a day for three more days. After the second day of this enormous dosage, I was on cloud nine. I delivered myself of such pronouncements as "I am the greatest man since Jesus Christ" and "Roosevelt, Churchill, Stalin, and I are going to solve the world's problems." My wife and Annapolis classmate Captain Bill McReynolds hustled me down to the San Diego Naval Hospital. There, after a few more gaudy declarations, I was promptly tossed into the pyschiatric ward.

I soon discovered that the ward was run more like a prison than a hospital. As the Atabrine overdose dissipated, the euphoria slowly subsided, and I approached normalcy again. What was I doing in a ward with sixty-odd enlisted men, most of whom were obviously psychotics? For example, one young sailor was known as Swan because he would dive under his pillow at the approach of a doctor or corpsman. I started to ask questions. The second or third night I was talking quietly to a sailor in an adjacent bunk when the hospital goon squad rushed in. They promptly grabbed us, manhandled us for "talking after lights-out," and shot me in the ass with some serum. In my brief protest and the subsequent assault, I had become bloodied. They threw me in a padded cell. These terror tactics were commonplace in the ward at that time.

On his rounds the next day, the doctor inquired as to why I had torn the legs of my pajamas. "To have something to wipe the blood out of my eyes and mouth," I rejoined. He did not query me further; he apparently accepted the senior NCO's version of the previous night's action. I asked him for writing material. Pen, paper, and envelope were subsequently provided. I promptly penned an emotional appeal to Father, outlining my predicament. Then, I waited until I saw a Marine with a 1st Marine Division patch on his shoulder. I called to him to gain his attention, then floated my letter down from the barred window of my third-story cell. He retrieved the letter, saw that the sender was a captain of Marines, and waved to indicate that he would mail it.

Father did receive the letter and immediately called my uncle, Dr. George Dorrance, a noted surgeon. He forthwith got in touch with Admiral Ross McIntyre, chief of the Bureau of Medicine and Surgery, to whom all naval hospitals reported. Ultimately, the officer in charge of the hospital paid me a visit, and I was treated with kid gloves from then on. By that time I had already been transferred to the officers' ward after repeatedly badgering the doctors responsible for the psycho ward.

Soon after my incarceration in the psycho ward, Vera, Corey, and Stevie descended upon my sister-in-law, Suzie, in her one-bedroom apartment in Coronado. My brother John, a lieutenant and communications officer aboard a Navy transport in Alaskan waters, was at sea. Even so, the apartment was crowded, and sleeping arrangements were primitive. But Vera could not see trying to commute from Laguna Beach to the naval hospital, and no other solution seemed within reach. Despite the considerable discomfiture of all—Suzie's pleasant routine rudely shattered; Vera's life in shambles with an eight-month-old baby and younger sister in tow 3,000 miles from home; and a husband who apparently needed institutional care—they survived. Vera visited me on every possible opportunity, adding her persuasiveness to my urging to transfer me to the officers' ward.

During my stay at the hospital from August 15 to September 22, not a single Marine visited me—a matter I have never forgotten. Apparently, the battalion executive officer made a telephone inquiry, and he was satisfied with the information he received. The Report of Medical Survey dated August 28, 1943 and signed by a panel of three doctors was persuasive, if absurd:

> The psychiatric findings are those of a manic-like reaction in an individual who is fatigued, had malaria, and was under treatment with Atabrine. He has increased psychomotor activity, flights of ideas, circumstantiality, delusions, and poor judgment. It is the opinion of the board that this patient is psychotic and in need of institutional care.

My complaints about the psycho ward and the personal interest of Admiral McIntyre resulted in a trip in a hospital train to Bethesda Naval Hospital, where I was scheduled for reevaluation. The admiral's interest must have led to some personnel reassignments, too, because the NCO in charge was transferred to Bethesda and travelled east on the same train. After an interview with a senior Bethesda psychiatrist, I was recommended for immediate return to duty. I later learned that this was most unusual for it meant that the recommendation of the San Diego Naval Hospital's three-doctor board had been overturned. Of the eight officer-patients on the hospital train, I was the only one returned to duty. The Bethesda Report of Medical Survey dated October 5, 1943 and signed by three Navy psychiatrists concludes:

> It is the opinion of this Board that this officer went through a psychotic episode following the administration of relatively massive doses of Atabrine, that he is now completely recovered and that, with the avoidance of this drug in the future, there is no likelihood of recurrence. No further hospitalization is necessary. He is considered to be fully competent and capable of performing all duties required of his rank.

Following my interview, I was granted indefinite leave and hurried to Bryn Mawr, where Vera and Stevie had bedded down in Grandmother Corey's spacious home. Once again I was visited by a malarial attack, but this time I stuck with quinine. It was also during these weeks that Mrs. Corey introduced me to the system of ration coupons—I accompanied her to the local authorities so that she could get her fair share of meat, butter, and other staples with which to feed her boarders.

Finally, in November, a call from Bethesda informed me that my orders for duty at Quantico had arrived. In a corridor of the hospital to which I returned to pick up my orders and check out, I nearly bumped into my erstwhile nemesis—the hospital corpsman from the San Diego Naval Hospital psycho ward. We were both in uniform and he faced me with some surprise and a hint of alarm. I told him in words that he could not misunderstand that he had better pray to God that he never serve under my command in the future.

FAT Battery

Upon returning to Quantico I was promoted to major (my commission had been withheld while I was a hospital patient). I was assigned as executive officer of the Field Artillery Training Battery. The FAT Battery, as it was inevitably called, was indeed fat. It had been steadily augmented with personnel as its responsibilities grew until it numbered about four hundred men, the size of a small battalion. It was organized like a battalion, too, with two firing batteries and a Headquarters-and-Service (H&S) Battery. The officer complement varied but averaged less than ten officers available for duty, including the battery commander and battery executive. Many of the battery officers also had additional duties of the sort that usually fall to a battalion staff—such as personnel, logistics, and motor transport. Further, the schedule of the Artillery School, to which we provided extensive support, called for considerable field training—the type my compatriots and I never received but sorely needed in 1941. Three courses for field artillery officers were in progress at any one time. Added to this were requirements for support of survey courses and training exercises staged by the Infantry Training Battalion, of which we were a part. So the handful of officers were almost continuously in the field with the two firing batteries and much of H&S Battery. We had practically no time to attend to administrative chores.

The commanding officer, Major Charles O. Rogers, was an attractive, easygoing man who presided over the administrative nightmare without undue concern or boat rocking. His unflappability was perhaps because of his scheduled detachment in early January. He was somewhat of a charmer, causing more than one local feminine heart to flutter. As had many before him and since, he made a pass at Vera, who attracted men like flies. Charlie made no progress, but as my CO he was in a position to keep trying.

Along with our one-year-old son, Vera and I moved into comfortable apartment quarters on the hill overlooking the main part of the base in late November. One early evening in a bar in Quantico, Vera, Charlie, and I were having a drink when a nondescript character at the bar started using loud, offensive language. I was inclined to ignore him, but Charlie, apparently viewing this as an opportunity to impress Vera with his qualities as an officer and gentleman, strode to the bar and verbally chastised the offender. Instead of quieting down, the loudmouth told Charlie to go to hell and continued his uncouth monologue. More politician than roughhouse, Charlie was visibly embarrassed. Because he was my CO, I walked to the bar and grabbed the miscreant by the arm. Using leverage against his elbow, I propelled him out of the bar and headlong into the gutter. Although I achieved the result more by luck than skill or strength, the Marine observers were nonetheless impressed. My stock rose in direct proportion to the fall in Charlie's.

Although officially on six months of "limited duty," on January 12, 1944 I took command of FAT Battery. Now the administrative and logistic chaos was indisputably my problem. The "battery" was armed with most of the Marine's field artillery arsenal—75mm pack howitzers, 105mm howitzers, and 155mm howitzers—which we rolled out as the training schedule called for. This demanded versatility. We even boasted two 75mm-gun halftracks. We had the truck complement of a battalion and needed every one of them to haul the batteries into position; to displace them from one position to another during the two-day and three-day "wars"; and to maintain the supply of ammunition, food, and all the rest. The troops spent most of their time in the field, having almost no opportunity to attend to such basics as laundry and haircuts (we had no battery barber). Unbelievably, the battery was quartered in seven different barracks on both sides of the railroad tracks (which bisected the base and had few crossings) and ate in three separate mess halls, which served at three different times.

To compound this situation, the Artillery School had developed into a first-rate training organization, at least the equivalent of the Army's Basic Artillery Course at Fort Sill. It had an extensive, demanding field-training schedule, and we could not be found wanting often if I expected to prosper in the Marine Corps. Managing this outstanding school were two Marine heavyweights—Colonel Bob Luckey and Lieutenant Colonel Leonard Chapman. I had not run into Bob Luckey on Guadalcanal, where he commanded the 1st

Special Weapons Battalion and later served as the executive officer of the 11th Marines. I had seen him, however, at Ballarat. He had returned from overseas after the Cape Gloucester campaign in February and taken over the Artillery School. His executive, Lieutenant Colonel "Chappie" Chapman, was an organizer and manager par excellence. This was no tandem to let down. And yet my command situation was impossible.

Sometime during March Brigadier General Clifton Cates, the commandant of the Marine Corps Schools, stopped by one of our field messes during an inspection and made some scathing remarks about the appearance of the troops. This was duly reported to me by the Infantry Training Battalion hierarchy. Unwilling to take this criticism lying down, even though I knew it was justified, I bearded the battalion executive in his den. He was aghast when I apprised him of the realities of my situation and suggested that I discuss my plight with the directorship of the Artillery School without delay. Colonel Luckey and Lieutenant Colonel Chapman were instantly receptive. They advised me to propose a table of organization for a battalion-sized unit and submit it with a letter to the commandant that outlined the FAT Battery's predicament.

When I had finished cataloging our monumental problems—two officers for every 125 men instead of five, a backbreaking field schedule, dispersion of barracks and mess halls, and the rest—and committed the list to paper, a strange thing happened. The chain of command could not act quickly enough. My multipage missive sped through the Infantry Training Battalion, the Artillery School, and the Marine Corps Schools almost at the speed of sound. Each command attached a strongly favorable endorsement. Now painfully aware of the tenuous condition of this major training unit, those in responsible positions could not be indifferent. Within a month the Commandant of the Marine Corps approved the organization of a Field Artillery Training Battalion and new officers were on orders to join us. An entire empty barracks building was suddenly discovered, and it became available to us. The FAT Battalion had arrived!

When I inspected the barracks with Lieutenant Dick Havens, my battalion logistics officer, we discovered that it was not completely empty. By the window of a spacious room assigned as the logistics office was a large desk with the nameplate of Master Sergeant Bartley. Dick wanted to place his desk by that window but was reluctant to move Bartley in the top's absence. Who was he, and what was his desk doing there?

A little research uncovered the fascinating information that Master Sergeant Bartley went with the barracks. The oldest Marine on active duty and a confidant of generals, Bartley had quarters just up the hill. There were even steps cut out in the grass-covered bank to facilitate his progress from quarters to office. When the previous barracks occupant decamped, Bartley remained; he would now bestow his services on the FAT Battalion. After some hesitation, Dick displayed the acumen that later took him to the top of the financial world. He moved in near the venerable master sergeant and left Bartley's desk where it stood. Bartley demonstrated that he was worth his weight in gold when the battalion somehow misplaced a jeep. Advising his young boss not to worry, Bartley collected a handful of nuts and bolts and, without any questions then or later, surveyed the jeep—he just wrote it off.

Ensconced in our own barracks with our own mess hall and with officers and men gradually swelling the ranks, morale soared. Of course, there was always a percentage of the command who overindulged on liberty or overstayed leave or otherwise managed to get out of line. So when we received orders to send a cadre of seventy men to provide the nucleus of Pack Howitzer Battalion, 29th Marines, which was then forming at Camp Lejeune, I gleefully cleaned out the battalion by sending all the troublemakers. When I advised Colonel Luckey that the battalion was now in excellent shape, his laugh was diabolical. "Fox," he said, "you recall that table of organization we submitted? Remember that a major was to be the commanding officer? Well, headquarters changed it to a lieutenant colonel and ordered one here to take over. You can either remain as his exec or follow the troublemakers to Camp Lejeune as exec of the Pack Howitzer Battalion." Considering the hardly career-enhancing San Diego Naval Hospital fiasco and the fact that I had been home for over a year, it was clearly time for me to get back to the shooting war.

Tying up loose ends prior to turning over the battalion to the new lieutenant colonel, I was disturbed to see that for the first time in months we had exceeded our fuel allowance. With a demanding field schedule, we were the Marine Corps Schools' major user of motor fuel and, as such, were monitored closely. Exceeding our limit for two consecutive months would surely bring unfavorable comment. Summoning the lieutenant who had recently taken over as motor transport officer, I chided him on his poor first month's performance, citing the enviable record of his predecessor, Marine Gunner Benjamin Hornstein. Promising to do better in the future, the lieutenant explained that his record should be viewed with some open-mindedness—if not sympathy—inasmuch as Gunner Hornstein had handed over the fleet to him so low on gas that his first action had necessarily been to fill up all the vehicles. So much for lieutenants and Marine gunners.

The six weeks at Camp Lejeune were busy ones as we molded veterans, recruits, officers, and men who had not yet tasted combat into battle-ready condition. Much of the 29th Marines, reinforced, had seen action, so the task went well. With respect to artillery there had been notable improvement in gunnery techniques since the 11th Marines had shipped out more than two years earlier. And with the Pacific War moving relentlessly westward, we were a confident group.

Vera came down by train to spend the last weeks with me. She was now almost seven months pregnant and becoming increasingly uncomfortable. I could not suppress a feeling of guilt over leaving her to have her second child without her husband. Guilt aside, I was feeling fit, having had no recurrence of malaria since November. Perhaps a Quantico doctor's recommendation in December that I put on 10 pounds did the trick. In any case, 1943 proved to be the end of my battle with that persistent disease.

8

Back to the War

Return to Guadalcanal

We left Camp Lejeune by troop train July 22 and, after a week at Camp Elliot near San Diego, shipped out on the USS *Morton*. There was strong indication that we would land on Saipan, where the 1st Battalion, 29th Marines was in action. But before we could get there, the situation ashore had taken a turn for the better, and we proceeded directly to Guadalcanal, now a training and staging area for the western Pacific. We landed August 17, twenty-three months to the day since I had first set foot on the island.

Lieutenant Colonel Joe C. McHaney, the battalion commander, was a small, slender, bouncy officer who had never quite gotten over being cadet captain at Texas A&M, the largest cadet corps in the country. Our personalities and values had a tendency to clash, but we got along well enough. Occasionally some brash action on my part would annoy him. He was not pleased, for example, when a tree we were felling to give us additional room in the motor park landed afield from our calculations and smashed onto the bed of a one-ton truck. But then Joe was not perfect either. His Texan drinking buddy, Major Angus M. "Tiny" Fraser, the 29th Marines operations officer, frequently had to deposit Joe in an unconscious condition on the floor of our tent. Most of the time I would lift him onto his cot and tuck the mosquito netting around him, but at least on one occasion I let him lie on the wooden deck of the tent until he sobered up enough to hoist himself into the sack. Joe was a good officer and a competent commander, albeit conservative. When I proposed hewing a softball field out of the edge of the adjoining jungle, he pooh-poohed the scheme as impractical, but he finally gave a reluctant OK. We rerouted a stream across the outfield, covered it with steel matting, and soon had a playing diamond that was the envy of the regiment. Although the colonel never went so far as to applaud our efforts, he did bring higher-ups around to admire the ball field.

A few weeks after our arrival on the Canal, word passed that recommendations would be entertained for observers to accompany 1st Marine Division on the impending assault on Peleliu. With McHaney's approval I volunteered and was scheduled to be the artillery observer. I attended the preassault briefing with the operations officer of 1/11, Major John Chaisson, who looked as energetic and upbeat as ever and who relished the prospect of going home as soon as the operation was over. At the last moment, however, the number of observers was cut to the bone, and my name was stricken from the list.

The 1st Provisional Marine Brigade returned from the reconquest of Guam in September. Now the 4th, 22nd, and 29th Marines (whose 1st Battalion had joined us from Saipan) were formed into 6th Marine Division. The pack howitzer battalions were detached from the infantry regiments and formed into the 15th Marines. When Colonel Bob Luckey arrived in November 1944 to assume command, he too had caught up with the troublemakers.

Before Bob Luckey's intrusion on the scene, however, we had had an intriguing game of musical chairs involving four prominent Marine Corps figures—two of its foremost artillery practitioners, Colonels Bob Luckey and Bigfoot Brown, and two powerful major generals, Pedro del Valle and Lem Shepherd. Bigfoot had made his appearance on the Canal first, ostensibly to organize and command the 15th Marines. As the senior major without a battalion command, I was slated to have the 4th Battalion when formed and was so advised by Colonel Brown. We had hardly made arrangements for the battalion campsite, the aggregation of the battalion staff, and the method by which its batteries would be formed, when Bigfoot seemed to become a sort of nonpresence. For Bigfoot to be on the island and not make his presence felt was uncharacteristic, to say the least. Then, as suddenly as Bigfoot faded away, Bob Luckey materialized, taking command of the new regiment.

Apparently, it all happened with no bloodshed. The trade presumably was engineered by General Shepherd and his influential

G-3, Lieutenant Colonel Victor H. "Brute" Krulak, who might have felt that Bigfoot's style was a little too salty. That General del Valle would have initiated the exchange seems scarcely credible since Bob Luckey had been his trusted executive on the Canal and in Australia, and Bob was set, by all appearances, to take command of the 11th Marines in 1st Marine Division. So Pedro del Valle, the Puerto Rican patrician, and Lem Shepherd, the Virginia gentleman, swapped division artillery commanders while we at the lower levels wondered what was going on. It made no difference to me—I had worked for both and admired both enormously. I also found intrigue at the higher Marine Corps levels fascinating.

The 4th Battalion, 15th Marines, was formed the way a battalion should be. Each of the three pack howitzer battalions was directed to put together four firing batteries of equal strength. Then straws were drawn to select one battery from each battalion to constitute the new battalion. It gave 4/15 three firing batteries ready for action. The key people for H&S Battery were accumulated in much the same way, with all battalions contributing. For all practical purposes, 4/15 was as ready for action as the other three from the day it was assembled.

During this period I met and was impressed by the battery commander of A/1/15. Well over 6 feet and handsome, Captain Benjamin S. Read was a William and Mary footballer and a 1942 graduate who had already distinguished himself in battle at Bougainville and Guam. Later he would be selected by General Shepherd as his senior aide; I made a mental note to keep an eye on him.

My perch at the top of 4/15 was short-lived. Colonel Luckey called me to his headquarters across the cove from us to tell me that two lieutenant colonels were joining the division and that he was slated to get one of them. With three of four battalions commanded by majors, he had to give the new lieutenant colonel 4/15. He offered me the regimental operations job, a tempting assignment. But, on reflection, I decided to stay on as battalion executive of 4/15. I had formed the battalion and felt an obligation to remain with it, particularly because the new CO had no field artillery experience.

Fortunately, Lieutenant Colonel Bruce T. Hemphill, one-time Naval Academy sprinter (Class of 1935), antiaircraft artilleryman, and recent commander of Johnston Island, was a smart, delightful person and a fine officer. Despite his lack of field artillery background, he quickly earned the battalion's respect. We settled down to a full-time training routine. Our camp on a cove near Kokumbona, cooled by the prevailing sea breeze, had been built by a Seabee battalion. In finest Seabee tradition, the battalion had taken good care of itself. Among the amenities were an outdoor theater and an officers' club erected on pilings out over the water.

Soon after we moved to this near-ideal, tropical setting, I was felled by a mysterious malady that robbed me of appetite and forced me to turn into the division hospital, a collection of unscreened, unfloored tents uncooled by sea breezes or anything else. My illness was mysterious because the division doctors were too inexperienced or indifferent to determine what I was suffering from. For days I just rotted on a cot in a steamy tent unable to take any sustenance other than canned fruit juice, with which my faithful 4/15 driver kept me supplied. After about five days of this nondiagnosis and nontreatment, I insisted that the doctor transfer me to the fleet hospital in the eastern part of the island (Admiral Halsey's old headquarters), where proper medical treatment was available.

By the time I was removed to Fleet Hospital 108, I was down to 150 pounds, about 30 pounds below normal. The internist who examined me upon arrival just shook his head in disbelief at the notation "DU" (Diagnosis Unknown) on my health record. He held a mirror in front of me and told me to look at the "whites" of my eyes. There were none. Instead, my brown pupils were surrounded by an almost equally deep yellowish brown. The doctor said that it was obvious that I was a victim of yellow jaundice or hepatitis. My bile count concurred—it was more than ten times normal. In those early days of the wonder drug penicillin, doctors were experimenting with it on many diseases; he asked me if I would object to his trying it on me. To his knowledge, it had not been used before. He had no idea whether it would help. He assured me that it could not hurt. So for three days and nights, every four hours, first one posterior cheek and then the other was shot with penicillin. Either the drug was helpful or the disease had just run its course because soon thereafter I was able to start taking solid food again. With a ravenous appetite to appease and three square meals plus snacks to do it with, my recovery was phenomenal. Of the twenty-seven patients in my ward, twenty-six returned to the States; in fact, it was so routine for patients from that ward to be shipped home that my battalion had just about written me off.

As I gained weight and swam in the ocean, my physical vigor returned. With it came a renewed interest in the fair sex, some of whom disported themselves periodically on the beach. One nurse was a knockout but was seemingly well escorted by doctors. Nonetheless, I discreetly inquired as to her availability. The going rate for this scarce, tempting commodity was $65 and rising, I learned— a sum well beyond my means. Reputedly, she was setting aside a nest egg for the postwar future.

I returned to the battalion on January 15, 1945, having been gone exactly a month. Training was going on full blast as the division geared up for action. We had heard for some time that there was to be a "big one" and a "little one." Clearly, the "little one" was Iwo Jima. Some of us thought the "big one" would be Formosa or the China coast. Few of us guessed our real destination.

Okinawa

The field training and waiting finally came to an end on March 12, 1945. For the second time I shipped out of Guadalcanal, but this time we headed north. From the beginning life aboard *LST 704* was beset with irritations—some minor, some otherwise. To start with, a temporary wooden partition had been erected near the after end of the tank deck, thereby denying 4/15 about 15 feet of cargo space. Although unauthorized, this was not uncommon for LSTs that had been in the Pacific for a while. The unavailable space, however, was larger than usual and fractured our loading plan. Once at sea the skipper, a disagreeable Reserve lieutenant from New Orleans in his late thirties (who probably resented twenty-six-year-old majors), informed me that there would be only two meals a day. Although two meals were customary in combat, we had always had three squares a day while aboard ship. As CO of troops, I protested but not vigorously. The men were not expending much energy lying around the decks, and I was striving to maintain reasonably harmonious relations.

The convoy proceeded to the vast anchorage at Ulithi Atoll, where it formed up with other troop convoys and combatant ships for the final run to Okinawa. During the twenty days we were aboard, there were many rain squalls and the main deck was frequently awash. Inasmuch as many of the men had to live on deck— there was inadequate bunk space below—this represented a continuing problem. The troops' shoes were rotting from the almost continuous water. The main culprit was the 2-inch lip that encircled the main deck and prevented runoff. I appealed to the skipper to cut slots at strategic intervals in the lip (as many other LSTs had done).

He refused, hiding behind the Navy regulation that forbade ship alterations at sea. By now we were barely on speaking terms.

Dawn of April 1, 1945 revealed an awesome sight. For as far as the eye could see, a mighty armada blanketed the sea. It was the largest war fleet that ever sailed, some 1,200 ships. Were it not for the thunder of the warships' guns and the roar of planes overhead, one might have thought we were watching the massive amphibious assault on television, a less stormy reenactment of D-Day off Normandy. Then, as the waves of landing craft and vehicles swept to and over the beaches of Okinawa and the naval and air bombardments shifted inland, a strange quiet settled on the beach areas. Where was the enemy? Easter gift or April fool, the Army and Marines did not tarry to wonder but moved rapidly, if cautiously, inland. The last thing many of us had expected was an unopposed landing on an enemy-held island close to the heart of the Japanese Empire.

Finally focusing on our own small role in this great drama, we had the urge to get ashore, to take up our mission supporting the infantry advance, and to disembark from this ferry boat that had been so uncharacteristically inhospitable. About noon the message came from Lieutenant Colonel Hemphill to land the battalion. He met us at the shoreline and led us to a position on the left flank of the beachhead, about 2 miles in from the beach. After the batteries had taken up position, I returned to the LST to check on the final stages of unloading. Now that the LSTs had moved close in offshore, disembarkation was proceeding rapidly. It was almost dark when I was accosted by the captain, who asked me if the shakedown of 4/15 had resulted in the retrieval of his missing Tommy gun. Each LST had a small complement of Tommy guns, presumably to repel underwater swimmers and such. He was most unhappy when I responded in the negative, and he implied that I had not pressed the search vigorously enough. I eyed him coolly and moved toward the bow and departure for the beach. One of our officers responsible for seeing that unloading was completed suggested that I have chow before debarking, mentioning that the ship was serving steaks. This infuriated me. After short-changing us on food for three weeks, the miserable ship had swindled us out of the traditional steak breakfast before hitting the beach. They had kept the steaks for themselves. I settled for C-rations with the battalion on the beach.

The infantry advanced so rapidly across the island from the East China Sea to the Pacific Ocean that the artillery never really got into action. Then the division continued up the Ishikawa Isthmus with the mission of subjugating the northern two thirds of the island. It had become clear that the Japanese had concentrated their strength to the south. This lack of opposition called for displacement north from one bivouac to another without even occupying firing positions. As the infantry deployed westward onto the Motobu Peninsula, the troops finally made serious contact with the enemy. We were ordered to take position at the neck of the peninsula with primary direction of fire to the west. We were to be prepared, if necessary, to fire to the north. Bruce Hemphill went on ahead to confer with Colonel Luckey, leaving me to take the battalion forward and select and occupy a position. Considering the requirement to fire both west and north and the lack of significant air or counterbattery threat, I selected a position along a low ridgeline running northwest to southeast. This permitted the batteries to have alternate west and north gun positions in the same location without firing over each other's heads. Further, it was easily defensible against what I considered the main threat—harassment by small enemy patrols or infiltrators.

When Colonel Luckey visited the battalion a day or two later, he questioned me on the unusual battery positions. Why had I forsaken the customary site—in defilade, along a tree line? I explained my rationale, which he accepted with a smile. Then he asked about "our troublemakers." No doubt he was well aware that men who sometimes get into trouble while assigned to barracks duty become excellent troops in combat. And so they had, without exception.

The 15th Marines now unlimbered their howitzers and pounded away as the infantry gradually surrounded and wore down the defenders of Mount Yaetake. It was our only real firing of the northern campaign and served as a warm-up for what lay ahead to the south. While we were supporting the final mop-up of Motobu Peninsula, I watched our scout-sniper platoon head off into the boondocks on one of its regular sweeps around the battalion position area— with no infantry within miles it was prudent to do some patrolling on our own. Suddenly I realized that the sergeant major, who liked to accompany the patrol periodically, was carrying a Tommy gun. Marine field artillery battalions did not rate Tommy guns. Ships did! Troops have a way of getting even.

By latter-day standards the 15th Marines was uniquely organized in that all four battalions were similar, with the exception that 1/15 was armed with 75mm pack howitzers. Presumably, there were not enough 105mm howitzers to go around. It gave the regimental commander considerable flexibility in that any one of the battalions could be assigned the direct-support role since all were light artillery and all had FO teams. There was some reluctance on the part of the three infantry regiments to have the artillery battalion that had been an integral part of the regiment for some time replaced by one that was a relatively unknown quantity. This was particularly true with the 4th and 22nd Marines, which had been through several campaigns with their own artillery battalions. So Colonel Luckey did not tinker with the traditional artillery battalion-infantry regiment relationships in the early going. 4/15, as its designation implied, performed a general-support mission by reinforcing one of the other battalions as needed. But the colonel reserved the right to assign 4/15 as direct support and did so later in the south when the fighting became fierce and FO teams needed respite.

I knew all the battalion commanders. I had served as McHaney's executive in 3/15. Major Bob Armstrong, 1/15, had driven Vera back to Kinston from New River in March 1942 when we had shipped out for Samoa. He had served with the 12th Marines at Bougainville and the 1st Marine Brigade at Guam. Major Nathaniel M. Pace, who had 2/15, was a Naval Academy classmate. I had visited Nat in Samoa, where he was then on the 1/10 staff. After a brief tour in the States, he had joined the 22nd Marines. He and Armstrong were steady, reliable commanders.

As battalion executive, my duties were determined by what the battalion commander wanted. This could encompass any assignment such as liaison with a direct-support battalion or infantry regiment, reconnaissance for new positions, or selecting and moving the battalion to a new position. But the latter two were usually performed by Lieutenant Colonel Hemphill. Routinely, I would concern myself with logistics and local security. Defense of the battalion position against any sort of attack was a logical responsibility because it involved coordination of battery defenses. Ensuring the continuing supply of ammunition, gasoline, food, and water had also become the battalion executive's traditional assignment. Of course, I interested myself in administrative and operational matters too, but the commanding officer attended to the former and the latter was more than adequately managed by Captain Benjamin F. Spencer, our operations officer (S-3) who ran the FDC with aplomb. I had known Spence slightly when he was a gunnery instructor at the Artillery School in Quantico in 1944, and I had spirited him away from Joe McHaney when 4/15 was formed.

4/15 had a mess sergeant who thrived on wheeling and dealing. He frequently visited rear areas in search of dietary innovations. After the division had mopped up northern Okinawa and was awaiting orders to move south alongside 1st Division on the western end of the southern front, the mess sergeant decided to take advantage of the momentary lull to go on a food-hunting expedition. Subsequently, he returned with a truckload of steaks. What he gave the Navy transport in exchange was not announced. The word rapidly circulated that there were enough steaks for about half the battalion. Lieutenant Colonel Hemphill—a well-liked, generous commander—decided that the firing batteries should have priority. Accordingly, the three battery commanders reported to headquarters to claim their steaks.

These hard-bitten fighting men, however, thought that they smelled a rat. Why was headquarters so uncharacteristically magnanimous? They certainly smelled *something*, for the steaks were ripe indeed. So, one after another, their suspicious instincts aroused at this odiferous offering, the battery commanders declined. Not a little taken aback at this ingratitude, the colonel and I conferred with the mess sergeant about the validity of their decision. He assured us that he had served steaks at least this ripe in his restaurant in Anacostia without repercussion. So the colonel directed that H&S Battery be given the steaks.

Throughout the evening the firing-battery commanders hovered around the battalion officers' mess, confidently expecting their judgment to be vindicated. They waited in vain. Not a single officer or man was sick from the succulent, if mature, beef. The battery commanders never lived it down.

After the mop-up of Motobu Peninsula, we moved to a picturesque bivouac on the East China Sea just north of the base of the peninsula. There was a small, uninhabited island a few hundred yards offshore from our camp to which we sent the scout-sniper platoon to ensure that it harbored no belligerent Japanese or Okinawans. Other than that we relaxed, took care of our equipment, reinstituted the officers' poker game we had started on Guadalcanal, and wondered when we would see action. Reports were filtering through to us of the slow going down south and of the imminent commitment of 1st Marine Division to the western flank of the line. We knew that it was just a matter of time before we headed south.

In early May, almost five weeks after we had come ashore, we moved to the vicinity of Chibana a few miles north of the southern front. The front was then a line drawn roughly from just south of the Machinato Airstrip on the west to the northern tip of Yonabaru Airstrip on the east. 4/15 was near Kadena Airfield, a bivouac that caused us to question the foresight of our leaders almost immediately. Every time there was an air raid, which triggered the antiaircraft into action, the spent shrapnel rained down on our bivouac. Our tents were being shredded, and we feared for casualties to our men and equipment from the falling jagged metal. Relief was not long in coming, however. We moved to a position just north of the Machinato Airstrip near the shore. This position, from which we fired throughout the battle for Asakawa and the Sugar Loaf complex, had only one drawback—it was adjacent to the staging area of the armored amtracs. These amphibious tractors, with 75mm howitzers mounted in a forward turret, were churning up the roads in the vicinity with their tracks and making it difficult for us to bring in ammunition. Lieutenant Colonel Hemphill directed me to tell the battalion commander to take his tractors elsewhere. Lieutenant Colonel Lou Metzger was not receptive to that suggestion, a fact I duly reported to my chief. He ordered me to repeat the request with more vigor. With some hesitancy I carried out the colonel's order. Metzger was pleasant but unresponsive. I told the colonel that my appeals were falling on deaf ears and that my inferior rank made it awkward for me to impress on Lieutenant Colonel Metzger the urgency of the problem that his continuing presence gave us. I suggested to Hemphill that he was placing his loyal executive in an embarrassing position and that the only hope of budging Metzger and his brood was personal diplomacy on his part. The matter went no further; we attempted to ignore the noisy, road-crippling neighbors as best we could.

We fired away from this position—mostly at night and sometimes heavily—when sizable enemy formations were spotted in the open. That was when we did our best work, for the variable-time fuse had by then been perfected, and light artillery is most effective when raining high explosive airbursts on troops in the open, especially when they are massing for attack.

But the Japanese on Okinawa spent most of their time in an elaborate defense network extending over a mile in depth from Asakawa through Shuri to Yonabaru. They moved in an intricate complex of tunnels, underground rooms, and caves. All strong points were mutually supporting. Against this type of defense, light artillery is relatively impotent. Direct-fire weapons such as 37mm guns, tanks, and flamethrowers were needed to help the infantry dislodge the tenacious defenders. Medium field artillery—155mm howitzers and guns—and the powerful 8-, 14-, and 16-inch guns of the Fleet—were more appropriate weapons to batter and smash Japanese defenses when they could be reached. By and large it was the infantry, with their close-in direct-support weapons, who conquered the dug-in Japanese.

Our FOs finally saw some action when we took over direct support of the 4th Marines for the Sugar Loaf finale. Our air observers had been flying missions since the commitment of the division to the southern front. With the exception of these observers, 4/15 emerged almost unscathed from Okinawa. Only a few stray rounds of counterbattery ever reached us, and no Japanese ever penetrated to our local defenses. Infantry lines were drawn so tightly across the front that only a few Japanese broke through, and these rarely got as far as artillery positions. So the field artillery—undeterred by infantry attack, counterbattery, or air; heavily stocked with ammunition; and massively augmented by the powerful broadsides of the Fleet offshore—poured seemingly endless tons of high explosives on the outgunned Japanese.

When the Naha–Shuri Line was breached and the battle was winding down, Bigfoot Brown decided to commemorate the occasion with a monumental time-on-target demonstration of artillery might and virtuosity. In addition to his four battalions of the 11th Marines, he secured the participation of battalions from other divisional artillery regiments and the battalions of both corps artillery groups—twenty-two battalions in all. The whole shoot was controlled by Lieutenant Colonel Chappie Chapman, the CO of the 4th Battalion, 11th Marines. Ears must still be ringing of the unfortunate inhabitants of the town near the southern end of the island where this thunderous burst of some 400 shells erupted simultaneously—if there are any still alive. That Colonel Brown neglected to inform the division and corps commanders of this shoot caused some distress, but at least Bigfoot let everyone, friend and foe, know of the artillery's presence.

When the Shuri defenses were finally breached and Naha cleared of enemy troops, 6th Marine Division was sidelined briefly while it prepared for the final overrun of the island by an amphibious end-around south of Naha. During this momentary respite while our guns were silent, I was granted permission by Lieutenant Colonel Hemphill to take the day off and try to track down my Naval Academy roommate, Major Al "The Count" Feldmeier, whom I had learned was commander of a torpedo-bomber squadron.

Last seen, The Count was awaiting trial by general court-martial at New River, North Carolina, in March 1942. He beat the rap but missed going overseas with the 11th Marines. He joined the 3rd Marines and accompanied it to Samoa as a platoon leader in the regimental weapons company. Later he returned to the States for flight training, served as a flight instructor at Fort Lauderdale, attended Command and Staff School at Quantico, and then returned overseas to take command of Marine Torpedo Bomber Squadron 232 at Ulithi.

Leaving early in the morning, I jeeped to the Yontan–Kadena Airfield complex and began the hunt. After numerous inquiries I found his squadron, but by then it was noon and he had already been briefed for an afternoon strike. The target was the Japanese 32nd Army headquarters, reported to be in a cave near the southeastern end of the island. The strike group of eight planes would attempt to skip bomb high explosives into the cave entrance. Inasmuch as the air strike would consume much of the afternoon, there was little time for a reunion. As we put down a little lunch and started to bring each other up to date on the past three years, The Count brightened, asking: "Would you like to go along on the raid? You can ride in the rear gunner's seat."

It took me by surprise. I considered it a challenge, so I answered "I'd like to." Rationalizing, I thought that a little first-hand experience in how the other half of the Marine air-ground team lived would not hurt me. The Count believed it inappropriate for me to ride with him, so I was helped into a parachute and settled into the rear gunner's seat of the assistant flight leader's plane.

The torpedo bomber is sturdily built, sacrificing grace and speed for the virtue of being able to absorb considerable punishment before going down. Of course, the need to carry a big torpedo dictated its design but, on this strike, we were only hauling bombs. After we had become airborne and arrived in the target area about 20 miles away, we circled for some time to identify the specific cave. When other planes had cleared the vicinity and we had dropped to lower altitude, some puffs of flak blossomed around us, but none was close. Since nobody else seemed concerned, I figured that it was just a futile gesture by diehard Japanese. There could not have been more than ten rounds anyway.

Watching the planes go down into their bombing runs one by one as they tried to skip their bombs into the cave entrance was not unlike observing an air demonstration of low-level bombing or strafing at Quantico. One or two bombs appeared to hit the target. But when our turn came and we went into a steep dive, it was like heading down from the top of a roller coaster, except that being airborne, unattached to anything terrestrial, lent an element of danger and excitement. We came in low directly toward the cave entrance, released our bomb, and then pulled up and over the hill. I could not see what happened to our bomb. We climbed to altitude again and made a strafing pass at the same target. It occurred to me that it would be fun to crank off a few bursts from my machine gun, but then I thought that I might shoot off a piece of the tail by mistake. When I related this to The Count later, he laughed, saying that I could have fired away, that there were stops to prevent just such mishaps.

We had been airborne about two hours when we set down at Kadena. Though not airsick, I admit to a touch of uneasiness in my stomach. After the debriefing The Count and I had some time over a drink before I had to head back to reach the battalion position on a hill overlooking Naha before dark. It had been a memorable day and, thoughtlessly, I could not restrain myself from relating my adventure to some of the battalion officers. Inevitably, news of my escapade traveled beyond the battalion. Lieutenant Colonel Hemphill did not chastise me for my indiscretion, but Colonel Luckey, upon hearing of it a few days later, went out of his way to give me a dressing down for "needlessly and without authority endangering my life."

Following the capture of Naha Airfield and the strongly defended high ground at the base of Oroku Peninsula, the division entered the lines again further south alongside 1st Marine Division for the final phase of the occupation of Okinawa. 4/15 went into position in the vicinity of Itoman for the mop-up, but we did little firing. As the last Japanese were slaughtered, rounded up, or committed suicide, we turned to recreational activities, such as touch football, to keep the troops busy. Mostly, however, we relaxed. Our poker game heated up.

It was not long before word was passed that the division was moving to Guam, so Bruce Hemphill decided that the poker game, which had been under way off and on since Guadalcanal, should be closed down. Neither the colonel nor I participated the final night. We had both won respectable sums—in fact I was the third-biggest winner and he the fourth. There was no logic to jeopardizing our hard-earned dollars in one last wild night. And wild it was, we were told, although most of the players were careful not to lose more than they could afford. One first lieutenant, however, played recklessly in a futile attempt to recoup past losses. When the game concluded, he owed almost $3,000, about twice as much as when he had started his final fling. Had the colonel or I been present, we would almost certainly have forced him to withdraw, but the other players were apparently unaware of the extent of his distress and the jeopardy in which it put everyone else's winnings. When we went to settle, he admitted that he could not pay up. The colonel asked me to sit down with him and work out a reasonable pay-back schedule. Divorced and contributing to the support of a child, his discretionary funds were limited. By taking almost all his available cash for six months, he could only pay off at 50 percent. I proposed this solution and the colonel approved. But there was bitterness amongst the officers who had dropped out of the game when they believed they had reached their limits. They complained, with justification, that they would have stayed on had they known that they would have to make good only half of their losses. With a change of luck they could even have recouped everything. Even at this payoff, I raked in $800.

9

North China

VJ Day

As the battle for Okinawa progressed from April to May to June, letters from Vera came at increasingly longer intervals. I had none at all for almost a month. With the fighting at an end and no doubt about the regularity of mail service, my concern over this situation escalated. A disturbing letter from Father added to my concern about my marriage. Someone had brought to Father's attention a newspaper item about the beautiful "thrush" who was singing with Leo Reissman's Orchestra at the Waldorf. He wanted to know what the hell Vera was doing in New York and who was taking care of the kids.

When Vera and I had parted in July 1944, we had agreed that she would live in New York and pursue a modeling career. She had moved to an apartment on East 93rd Street off Park Avenue and given birth to our second son, Nicholas, on September 25. Then she found a reliable Austrian nurse, Mrs. Wilde, in White Plains, and after a few months sent Stevie and Nicky to live with her there. It was a prescription for trouble, one which I might have foreseen had I been less naive. She was barely twenty-two and had received several offers for Hollywood try outs. She joined the Conover agency, one of the two biggest modeling agencies in New York, and they encouraged her by saying that she could be their top model. Then she had somehow been introduced to Leo Reissman, whose orchestra was playing at the Waldorf–Astoria. He had been impressed perhaps more by her looks than her voice, although that was adequate, and had started her on voice lessons while she sang periodically with his band. Illustrative of his interest in his glamorous protégé was the stage name he suggested she adopt: Gloria Goddess. Alone in her own apartment in the big city, with promising careers beckoning as both model and songstress, and with a stag line forming, it is no small wonder that it all went to her head and that she had little time to write her husband on the other side of the world.

As I tried to piece together what might be happening to my marriage from the fragments of information I received from Father and Vera, it dawned on me that if I did not act promptly I might be the recipient of a Dear John letter, of which a fair number arrived in the mails every day for members of the division. As soon as we had made camp on Guam after a routine voyage from Okinawa via Saipan on the USS *Bollinger*, I sought out Colonel Luckey and confided my plight. The colonel, who knew Vera from our time together in Quantico in the spring of 1944, granted me emergency leave without hesitation.

The Naval Air Transport Service (NATS) picked me up on July 17 and by slow stages through Kwajalein, Johnston, Oahu, and San Francisco I finally made New York on July 20. Only minutes after arrival at our apartment, the phone rang. In the taxi on the way from the airport, Vera had leveled with me about some of her pursuers, including an attentive young lawyer from whom she had borrowed $2,500. When he identified himself and asked to speak to Vera, I told him that she was neither available then nor would she be since I was home now and that he would receive his money shortly—to get lost. After a visit with our boys in White Plains, we headed for the Jersey Shore, first to Father's cottage in Stone Harbor and then on to a hotel in Longport, a suburb of Atlantic City. We succeeded in reviving our faltering marriage. I convinced Vera that it was time to abandon her budding career and return to Philadelphia, away from the temptations of the big city and closer to family.

My arguments were reinforced manyfold when the electrifying news of the Japanese surrender burst upon us. We hurried down to the Boardwalk to participate in the pandemonium. The convalescent hospital nearby had just about emptied its wards as nurses and hospital attendants brought the war-wounded out in wheelchairs, on crutches, and with bandaged heads and limbs to join the mingling celebrants. People of all ages cheered and shouted in joyous

riot. Women and men were hugging and kissing everyone, especially the crippled veterans. The Atlantic City Boardwalk on VJ
Day—a sight long to be remembered!

The Occupation

In the euphoria of the VJ Day aftermath, I thought that I might be
reassigned to duty in the States. Mature reflection, however,
warned that there was still a lot of tidying up to do in the western
Pacific and that all Regular Marines would be needed. Besides the
occupation of Japan, there were Japanese-occupied territories—such
as Korea, Formosa, and North China—that would require U.S.
forces to repatriate Japanese troops and stabilize the resulting vola-
tile situation. Particularly in China, the contending forces of
Chiang Kai-shek and Mao Tse-tung posed a dangerous situation.

After returning Vera to New York toward the end of August, our
marriage presumably whole again, I started westward on NATS.
Reaching Oahu was not difficult, but then I was stymied. The rush
of all manner of VIPs to Japan had swamped the civilian and military airlines. While languishing in a tropical island paradise unable to return to one's unit might seem to be a fate to which many
Marines would aspire, I had exhausted my financial and emotional
resources and was in no position to capitalize on the situation. Further, there was a persistent rumor that Marines would soon be on
their way to North China.

After five frustrating days of futility spent trying to board a
plane west, I ran across a boatswain's mate who suggested that I
try the docks whence seaplanes made regular mail runs to the islands. In no time I convinced a Navy pilot of the urgency of my
return to my outfit before its departure for China. He allowed me to
climb on top of the mail sacks in the noisy, uninsulated cargo compartment. When the PB4Y finally landed off Saipan two days later
after intermediate stops at Johnston and Majuro Islands, I thought
the deafening roar of those four powerful engines would remain
with me forever. Once ashore I thumbed a jeep ride to the nearest
airstrip and talked a Marine dive-bomber pilot into taking me to
Guam. As luck would have it, I reported to the 15th Marines the
day before ship loading began. We put to sea four days later. My old
battalion had already left for Japan with the 4th Marines, so I was
reassigned to 3/15 as executive officer to my previous boss, Lieutenant Colonel Joe McHaney.

A typhoon was then stirring in the East China Sea, so after a brief stopover at Okinawa we hightailed it up the Yellow Sea for Taku. The typhoon became so vicious that the skipper decided to jettison the pontoon barges lashed along either side of the LST before their crashing against the sides resulted in serious damage. Eventually we outran the blow (which was later reported to have wreaked much havoc on and around Okinawa) and anchored off Taku.

First Marine Division had already landed and moved on to Tientsin, about 40 miles inland. Our small task force was tentatively scheduled to land at Chefoo rather than with the remainder of the 6th Division at Tsingtao. We vegetated for a few days off Taku, with no indication that our departure would take place any time soon. The skipper, a Navy Reserve lieutenant lawyer from New York (with whom I had excellent rapport) and I decided to put a jeep ashore for a run up to Tientsin. Right after breakfast our fifth day at Taku, we set off with one K-ration apiece and every intention of returning that evening.

Our first impression as we drove past the wheat fields was of the sturdiness of the peasants. Accustomed to the smaller stature of the Chinese who had emigrated to the States and those we had seen in the South Seas islands (many of whom had come from South China), it was a revelation to see so many robust six-footers. It was a pleasant ride in the October coolness, and we soon approached Tientsin. There we stopped at the 11th Marines bivouac on the eastern outskirts of town and collected a colleague of Guadalcanal days, Bob Sack. The erstwhile gunner had, somewhat to his discomfiture, been "promoted" to second lieutenant. After a short tour in the States following the Cape Gloucester campaign, Bob had rejoined the 11th Marines on Okinawa. I had a strong inclination to call on Colonel Bigfoot Brown, the 11th Marines CO, but thought it inappropriate to announce my presence in Tientsin when I had no authority to be there. Technically, the LST skipper and I were absent without leave.

Our second impression was the odd experience of seeing company- and battalion-sized units of the Japanese Army, fully armed, going about their business. It was a testimony to Japanese discipline that there were no incidents of any consequence in those first days before they were disarmed and repatriated. This wise decision to allow them to retain their arms undoubtedly accounted for the sparing of many Japanese lives. Contrast this with the disappearance of hundreds of thousands of Japanese troops in Manchuria following the Russian occupation.

We proceeded into Tientsin, tried out a few bars, and regaled each other with sea stories. In midafternoon we heard that the Russian Embassy was having an open house in celebration of Stalin's birthday, and we found our way over there in short order. It was a fairly rowdy group, well supplied with vodka and even some hors d'oeuvres (meatballs wrapped in cabbage leaves). As the evening wore on, the crowd gradually thinned until there were only five of us. The Russians invited us to dinner. By the time we were seated at a long rectangular table and the broiled chicken was served, it was almost midnight. With little food and much liquor in our stomachs, it was a struggle to remain vertical through the seemingly endless succession of toasts with warm red wine to Premier Stalin, President Truman, the Red Army, the U.S. Marine Corps, the U.S. Navy, and so forth. Finally, around 2:00 A.M., we bid a fraternal goodbye and stumbled out into the frigid night. Someone thought that we should visit a brothel. Sack guided us to a reputedly high-class one in a good part of town. When we finally roused the madam, she admonished us from a second-story window that it was too late, to go home, that we were disturbing the peace. By then the temperature had dipped into the 40s and we were not dressed for it. The chill cooled our ardor, and we decided to seek shelter.

We headed back into town, eventually spotting a multistoried, well-lighted, large building that we took for a hotel. Upon trekking in through the deserted lobby and up a wide staircase to the second floor, we were surrounded by young girls and boys advertising the irresistible charms of their older sisters.

We had stumbled into a giant whorehouse. It took some doing to convince the skeptical madams that all we wanted was a room to lie down in. After much remonstrance we were escorted to a room with a double bed and two easy chairs. The three lucky ones crapped out sidewise on the bed, the other two in the chairs. Soon after dawn and only partially rested but now quite sober, we parted company and went our own ways. The skipper and I decided that we had better return to *LST 862.*

Following an uneventful drive to Taku, we boarded the ship shortly before noon. During our absence sailing orders had arrived, and we got under way at high tide in midafternoon. Fate had smiled on the ship's captain and the CO of troops—our unscheduled leave of absence had ended in the nick of time.

The Chefoo occupation was scrubbed because of the large number of Chinese Communist troops in the area. We disembarked at Tsingtao, and a week later I was reassigned as battalion commander of 4/15. This qualified me to move into the villa that the regimental commander had just been assigned in the western section of town. It was only a short distance from the old German horse-drawn artillery barracks in which the 15th Marines was billeted. The villa turned out to be one of the best accommodations in Tsingtao, second only to the mansion occupied by Generals Shepherd and Clement in the eastern part of town near the coast. Colonel Luckey asked the regimental executive officer, Lieutenant Colonel Jim Brower, the S-3, Lieutenant Colonel Walt Ossipoff, and three battalion commanders (Lieutenant Colonel Joe McHaney of 3/15, Major Nat Pace of 2/15, and me) to move in with him. (Our fourth battalion, 1/15, had accompanied the 4th Marines to Yokosuka after the Japanese surrender and had never rejoined us.) In these most pleasant surroundings, we settled down to enjoy the occupation.

1/15 had turned in its 75mm pack howitzers on Guam and had been re-equipped with the 155mm howitzers of a disbanded artillery battalion. The battalion had also been redesignated 4/15 and organized as a general-support battalion; that is, among other minor adjustments, the unit had no FO teams. Because we were a stabilizing force intended to reassure rather than stir up the natives, we held no firing exercises. Division Headquarters did not disclose defense or firing positions to occupy in contingencies or whether, in fact, any positions had been selected. Rather, after the insignificant Japanese forces thereabout had been repatriated, we concentrated on making the most of our relaxing foreign duty.

We quickly acquired a formidable service staff consisting of a number one boy, number two boy, number three boy, cook, assistant cook, amah (a laundress, the number one boy's wife), furnace boy, and outside boy. The colonel had served with the Embassy guard company in Peking from 1935 to 1937 and McHaney had been with the 4th Marines in Shanghai in the late '30s. So, as old China hands, they knew how to deal with the natives. This was before the Nationalist Chinese government was overtaken by runaway inflation and the local economy distorted by the profligate spending of the Fleet on liberty. (Tsingtao was the major Fleet anchorage in North China.) With beautiful living quarters, eight servants, and plenty of good food and drink, we were well off by most standards.

Marse Robert, one of the affectionate names by which Colonel Luckey was known, presided over a most congenial group.

One of our leisure-time occupations in late 1945 was trying to find presents to take home to our wives and children. With the war over for most Americans, those Regulars still abroad had to come home with a little extra to help mollify their long-neglected loved ones. I had bought a patchwork coat of many colors, a dragon hat, and pig shoes for my three-year-old son. For my wife I had a silk robe, ivory hair ornaments, silks, satins and assorted pieces of antique jewelry.

Nat Pace, a small-of-stature, mild speaking Kentuckian, had decided to take the plunge. In a rash moment, by our reckoning, Nat had bought enough uncured mink pelts to make his wife a coat. Amidst many dire predictions about their quality, he confidently stowed them away in his second-floor room. The colonel henceforth addressed the 2/15 commander as Nat the Furrier.

One night at about 9:00, we drifted off to our rooms. When Nat opened his door, out burst a flood of water upon which his hoard of thirty-odd pelts floated. While the furrier feverishly rescued his dripping treasure, Marse Robert doubled up in laughter. After order had been restored and we had determined the cause of the disaster—an overflowed water tank in the attic—Nat's room was mopped out and put in livable condition again. But what of his drowned pelts? For weeks we prophesied the worst but were unable to detect any deterioration in the furs. Twenty years later Mrs. Pace was reported to be still displaying her gorgeous mink coat on festive occasions.

Tsingtao had been a German enclave during the late nineteenth and early twentieth centuries when many European powers had staked out claims to Chinese territory from which to press their trading and other interests. Even though the architecture and broad boulevards were in many areas distinctly Teutonic, the ambient odor was decidedly Chinese. Human excrement was used as fertilizer, and the smell was pervasive. Contractors prized Marines' sewage because of their relatively rich diet, scooped it up from the heads, and hauled it away on a regular basis in dripping "honey wagons" from the 15th Marines compound. Day or night, it was impossible to forget that you were in China.

As distinctive as the German buildings and Chinese smell was the wild traffic. Chinese drivers rarely slowed down for pedestrians, bicyclists, rickshaws, wagons, or other cars or trucks; they just leaned on their horns, expecting all to scatter before them. Most of the time, miraculously, they did.

The Edgewater, a large, handsome hotel on the coast, had been designated as the division officers' club and was soon heavily patronized. One night at the urinal in the men's room, I mentioned to Nat Pace that Josephine, a much-sought young French beauty, was looking tired—not her usual gorgeous self. A voice from the other side of me refuted this observation, stating pointedly, "She looks lovely to me." It was Brigadier General Clement, the assistant division commander, one of the most renowned ladies' men in the Marine Corps. He had been chasing Josephine, but rumor had it that his sergeant driver had the inside track.

General Shepherd was sensitive to the reputation of officers. While cruising downtown in his command car one evening on a routine inspection tour, the general observed two lieutenants standing in line with enlisted men outside an approved division brothel. He was very disturbed by this unofficerlike, ungentlemanly behavior and sent his aide to apprehend them. They saw the aide coming, however, dashed into the house of ill repute, and escaped out the back. The commanding general was not amused and promised terrible retribution when and if the two were tracked down. (They never were.)

As the winter descended upon us, the stables in which 4/15 was billeted became increasingly difficult to heat. The division hired Chinese artisans to install a false ceiling and floor so that all the warmth generated by the small oil heaters would not rise so quickly to the lofty rafters. The handiwork of the Chinese in fabricating the false roof and laying down the wooden floor over the cobblestones was fascinating. Swarms of carpenters (about fifty) hung an intricate lacework scaffolding from the roof using nothing but bamboo and fiber ties. When they had this vast network within 10 feet of the floor, they pasted a paper ceiling over the framework. The floor, though not as complex, was also interesting—all tongue and groove. The barracks proved as warm and snug as anyone could have wished, and we passed the winter without any serious fire mishap.

In early December the colonel told Nat and I that we could have ten days off to visit either Shanghai or Peking. After due deliberation, we elected Peking. Forthwith we repaired to the Tsingtao Airport and climbed aboard a Marine R4D (DC-3). The flight was uneventful until we reached Tientsin. On the first pass at the short airstrip, bounded on both ends by rice paddies, the pilot apparently wanted a close look before attempting a landing. On the second pass he put the wheels on the ground but evidently thought that he had overshot the runway—he gunned it down the strip and took off again. By the third try Nat and I were apprehensive. This time, however, he got her down and with a screeching of brakes brought the old bird to a shuddering stop just a few feet short of the rice paddy.

As we breathed more easily and the other passengers deplaned, I turned back to Nat and said, "I wonder if this joker has ever flown this plane before?"

At the same time the pilot emerged from the cockpit and, much to my surprise, spoke up from behind me. "This is my first landing in an R4D." He then related to us that he had been a fighter pilot on Peleliu. Because most of the Reserve pilots had gone home from all over the Pacific, he had been sent to Tsingtao as a replacement. Of course, we were well acquainted with this sad situation—we were the only field-grade officers in our respective battalions. Nonetheless, it did not do much for our peace of mind. Our landing on the long airstrip at Peking was routine.

Throughout the autumn and early winter of 1945, Marse Robert and I became fairly close—as close, that is, as a colonel and major usually become. This was partly because we were compatible—we played badminton, took long walks on the beach, and had other interests in common—but also because all but one of the other occupants of the villa had taken up with White Russian or Chinese consorts. So when we took off for Peking, I had in my possession a letter of introduction to Monsieur Jacques Bardac, manager of the French Bank of Peking, an old acquaintance of the colonel. Marse Robert also advised us about which sights to see. After Nat and I checked into the Wagon-Lit Hotel, we proceeded to see some of the landmarks—the Forbidden City, the Temple of Heaven, and Coal Hill. On the third day our interests led us down different paths. It was then that I remembered Marse Robert's letter.

The next morning I presented myself to Monsieur Bardac at the French Bank. He was the soul of courtesy and apparently enjoyed the exchange of pleasantries, but the interview was clearly drawing to a close. At that moment I recalled that a dear friend of Father's and her daughter Ellen had been in Peking during the summer of 1937 on the last leg of a world tour. When he heard Ellen's name, it was as if he had suddenly been aroused from the dead. Ellen Gowen

Hood was beautiful, young, rich, and charming. Jacques had fallen head over heels in love with her. He had even proposed. But Ellen Gowen had not been disposed to any such commitment at that stage of life and duly left him heartbroken. Somewhat on the rebound, he had married a lovely Baltimore girl who worked at the U.S. Embassy. He immediately took me in tow.

For the five remaining days of my stay in Peking, the Bardacs deluged me with attention. Jean Bardac and I hit it off famously. She showed me many fascinating sights and took me shopping for my wife. The high point was a late-evening dinner of Peking duck in a small, private upstairs cafe. The waiter carved the succulent cubes of roasted duck before our eyes, and the warm red wine flowed freely. The return rickshaw ride to their house in the foreign quarter in crystal-clear, cold night air through wide, deserted boulevards is a beautiful memory. They even had a cocktail party for me to which the only Marine guests invited were Major General Keller Rockey (the corps commander) and Brigadier General Willie Worton (the troop commander in Peking). Both had arrived slightly in their cups. An interesting conversation with an aristocratic Chinese merchant still sticks in my mind. He could not understand why well-to-do Americans took up arms for their country—in China only peasants manned the armies. Perhaps this philosophy helped precipitate the Nationalists' early downfall. One final memory of Peking is of standing atop Coal Hill, which was alleged to have been built by an early emperor as a place to walk and survey his surrounding domain. At that time it was the highest point in Peking. On my last afternoon there in mid December, I remember seeing a camel caravan winding in from the desert toward the city, which was then completely enclosed by walls. On the flight back to Tsingtao, our pilot flew over the Great Wall from Peking to the Yellow Sea.

Christmas Eve is a trying time overseas—especially when there is no war to distract you, and your loved ones are half a world away. Bob Luckey and I had enjoyed our customary five martinis before dinner (I was his designated drinking partner). After dinner the others had quietly slipped away to find what comfort they could in other nests. The old man and I had the phonograph doing its best with appropriate melodies while we nursed our highballs. As the evening wore on, the music and the liquor made us morbidly nostalgic. He suggested that we go to church.

We sought out one of the Lutheran churches of the old German enclave. It was approaching midnight. As the preacher droned on, we became drowsy. We were in the third pew from the front and almost directly in front of the minister. Marse Robert, carrying a heavy burden of spirits, slowly slipped into unconsciousness. As he did so, his left arm draped casually over the back of the pew and knocked down about five lighted candles. Localized chaos ensued as the parishioners behind us attempted to avoid flame and hot wax. The colonel, drowsily alert, asked me what had happened. I told him. By now the preacher was visiting us with unspoken but withering wrath. A quick assessment of the situation under lowered, beetling brows caused the colonel to decide upon strategic withdrawal. As we retreated up the aisle followed by disapproving looks on every side, Marse Robert delivered a scathing rebuke to his tormentors. "Monkeyfuckers," he muttered. Fortunately, only I could hear. It was an expression for which he was justly renowned, and it seemed to sum up the frustration of troops far from home and unappreciated.

Home Again

Early in the new year, word came of the breakup of the division—only a brigade would remain in Tsingtao. Colonel Luckey decided that the remaining artillery battalion would have two field-grade officers: A lieutenant colonel and major. Since Nat and I were the only majors and neither of us wanted to revert to battalion executive, to say nothing of our desire to go home, we awaited the colonel's judgment with some trepidation. He determined that Nat should remain. We had served about the same total time overseas during the war, but I had been over longer on the second tour. That was the colonel's announced reason. I suspect that my shaky marital status, which I had confided to him in some detail during our long beach walks, also influenced Marse Robert. How much Nat knew of my problems I do not know; he certainly knew that I had been home on emergency leave only five months earlier. In any case, Nat never gave any indication to me that he resented the colonel's decision.

As to the lieutenant colonels, it was instructive to see the alacrity with which they bailed out. Brower, McHaney, and Ossipoff all seemed to have influential agents in HQMC who saw to it that they were urgently needed for some critical Stateside assignment. Before anyone knew it, all were on orders, and an artillery lieutenant colonel had to be imported from outside the division to take command of the remaining battalion.

So in mid January 1946, I reported to the dock for transportation home on the USS *Bolivar.* Upon boarding I gratefully noted two lieutenant colonels at the rail, my assurance that I would not have to worry about being CO of troops on the voyage home. The next morning at 6:00 A.M., I was rudely disabused of this comforting thought. Word came over the loudspeaker for Major Parry to report to the captain's cabin immediately. Within minutes I learned that I was senior troop officer present—the two lieutenant colonels had disembarked the previous evening.

It was soon clear that I had inherited a situation little short of chaos. Troops had embarked haphazardly at several Far East ports. Even the 6th Marine Division contingent, representing about one fifth of the 2,700 troops had embarked at random. There was no unit integrity with the exception of an Army stevedore company of about 200 men. NCOs did not know the men in their compartments and vice versa. Marines, sailors, and GIs had been marched to compartments as they came aboard. Confronted with this disgraceful mess, I took strong action. I selected another major as my executive and assigned captains to take charge of each compartment. In turn, the captains chose lieutenants and senior staff NCOs as assistants, established watch details, and made other assignments. Nonetheless, we had almost reached Honolulu two weeks later before we had an accurate muster.

Responsibility often has its rewards, however. I was invited by the captain to take over the admiral's suite—a cabin, office, and private bathroom. The large, circular, green felt–covered table became the scene of many spirited poker games, and the trip across the Pacific to San Diego was relatively pleasant. Even more pleasant were my orders to Parris Island, where I headed after my reunion in New York with Vera and our two small sons.

It never occurred to me to resign my Regular commission, as others had done while in China. However, return to a quiet, peacetime Parris Island (whence I had started my service in the Fleet Marine Force almost five years earlier) spawned thoughts about whether I should make the Marine Corps my career. It was no contest. I liked the Marine Corps brotherhood, and I liked working with men. Practically speaking, I had a wife, two children and—almost immediately—another one on the way, and a major's pay was not bad.

My brief flirtation with the thought of becoming a civilian did have a positive effect on me—it alerted me to the obvious fact that if

I intended to have a successful career, I had better stop fooling around. My war service had not been bad, but it had been far from spectacular. I had earned no personal citations. It was time to buckle down—to make my mark.

10

Marines at Peace

Parris Island to Quantico

Beaufort and Port Royal in South Carolina had been busy ports in the days of sailing ships, but Charleston, South Carolina, and Savannah, Georgia, had long since captured all the trade. Now Beaufort languished in the sun, dreaming of past glories. The economy of the town was supported to a significant degree by the Marines stationed at nearby Parris Island, South Carolina. Many Marine families also lived in Beaufort, and it was there that Vera and I found a third-floor apartment and moved in with our two sons. The relaxed duty we anticipated, however, failed to materialize.

Upon reporting to the Recruit Depot Training Office, I was told to organize and direct an officers' school for about one hundred newly commissioned second lieutenants. Although these midterm Naval Reserve Officers' Training Corps graduates had incurred obligated service, the Marine Corps was contracting rapidly and had not decided how many—if any—might be needed in the shrunken peacetime ranks. So until The Basic School was ready to take some of them in the summer and the Marine Corps prepared to discharge the rest, we had to keep them busy for two months doing something beneficial. It was a challenge and one that we would not have met had we not secured the services of three top-notch NCOs. Gunnery Sergeant R. E. Janeway and Platoon Sergeants H. M. Clements and M. M. Cook were awaiting reassignment as drill instructors to recruit platoons. They knew what had to be done and did it. They found an empty barracks, drew bedding and personal equipment, located training aids, and effected a plethora of other details with speed and efficiency. These three stalwarts were so competent that what had seemed an impossible assignment five days earlier suddenly became doable. Together with Major W. T. Shafer and Captain H. M. Kissler, we drew up a five-week training schedule for the embryo officers. The final three weeks of the course included learning how to shoot the M-1 rifle and other small arms at the rifle range. The competence and enthusiasm of the drill instructors (DIs) and the adaptiveness of the students (many from top-notch schools such as Yale) made a worthwhile experience out of what otherwise could have been a waste of time.

In May, with the second lieutenants off our hands, I was reassigned as commanding officer of the 2nd Recruit Battalion. Here I learned something of how the youth of America is converted into Marines. Of course, the DIs did all the training; my role was supervisory and administrative. The sergeant major at that time was struggling doggedly with paperwork, notably the muster roll, because the Woman Marines who had so capably managed this function had returned to civilian life. They had been replaced, if that is the right word, by a squad of Marines—ten men for three women— and the job was not getting done. We discussed the problem and decided that he should try to locate the departed clerks and seduce them back as civil servants—at higher pay if necessary. Two were found and brought aboard promptly, much to the relief of the thick-fingered Marines who were delighted to return to field duty.

In the meantime the Parry family was beginning to savor peacetime station duty. We had moved into spacious quarters on the waterfront only two blocks from the officers' club, which had a swimming pool, tennis courts, and other amenities. Our next-door neighbor, a Navy lieutenant in charge of the boat basin, promised us a fishing trip in one of his launches whenever he could get time off from squiring the commanding general and his guests around the nearby fishing grounds. Two Navy dentists, a Navy chaplain, and I got together a post tennis team and were in the process of developing a schedule of matches with nearby teams. In short, we were just starting to experience some of the attractions of service life when I received orders to the six-week Advanced Naval Gunfire Course at Quantico.

The next three months were brutal. In that time we moved five times and exhausted all our war savings. In all, we moved seven times during Vera's third pregnancy before coming to rest in a summer cottage just in from the shore at Virginia Beach. In six months we had glimpsed both the good and the not-so-good of service life.

Bloodsworth Island

The precipitous dismantling of the U.S. war machine was a painful experience for those of us who had chosen to make the military service a career. It was ominous indeed to those few who comprehended the Communist menace. Nor were the Communists long in moving into the vacuum created by contracting U.S. power. Although a significant Marine presence remained in North China for another two years, the Marine departure became inevitable as Mao Tse-tung gained ascendency throughout China. A modest U.S. Army corps was stationed in South Korea and a small army of occupation was in Japan, but the combat capabilities of both were steadily eroded by a shrinking defense budget and the enervation of occupation duty. Sensing increasing U.S. weakness, the Communists pressed forward in Europe and Asia in hopes of some easy victories on the heels of their massive success in China.

During these danger-filled developments abroad, the U.S. military at home sought to retain as much battle-learned know-how as it could in the straitened circumstances. One valuable lesson that we had learned was the potential of naval gunfire in amphibious operations. To foster this hard-acquired capability, schools were established in fleet commands on the East Coast and West Coast. Shore-bombardment ranges were already available in Hawaii, off the coast of Southern California, and in the Caribbean. The Navy decided to activate another range on the East Coast, which was convenient to the Fleet, and a small, swampy island midway up Chesapeake Bay—Bloodsworth Island—was selected for the purpose.

Colonel Donald M. Weller, U.S. Naval Academy Class of 1930, had already made a place for himself in naval lore before August 1946, when I attended his Advanced Naval Gunfire Course in Quantico. He was small of stature and friendly, and the pipe that was frequently in mouth or hand did nothing to dispel the aura of intellectuality that surrounded him. Don eschewed the Napoleonic characteristics of many small, powerful, military men. Although unpretentious and down-to-earth, he was also no-nonsense when it came to the business at hand. He was the single man in the service

most responsible for the development of the art of naval gunfire
support of amphibious operations, a key ingredient in the success of
the island campaigns of the Pacific and the landings in Europe. It
was for this major contribution that General Holland M. Smith,
senior Marine commander in the Pacific, called him in his book
Coral & Brass, "truly an architect of victory."

About twenty Marine and Navy officers labored for six weeks
under his tutelage. The highlight of the course, in which two weeks
at Anacostia were devoted to naval gunnery, was the individual
development of a fire-support plan for a fictional amphibious assault. It brought home to us the complexities of integrating battleships, cruisers, destroyers, and LSMRs (Landing Ship, Medium,
Rocket) into a single plan where each could deliver fire in the
proper locations at the designated time without interfering with
each other, the landing plan, or close air support. With this grounding in naval gunnery and in planning naval gunfire support, my
Naval Academy training and my experience in adjusting field artillery on a target, I reported to the Amphibious Training Command,
U.S. Atlantic Fleet, at Little Creek, Virginia. There, my first duty
was to establish a shore bombardment range at Bloodsworth Island.

Until then the Amphibious Force had been responsible for the
undeveloped range, so my initial trip to Bloodsworth Island was
with Lieutenant Durborow, USN, from that command. We reached
Adam Island, a tiny outcropping just south of Bloodsworth, by rubber boat from an LST anchored more than a mile offshore. We adjusted the fire of destroyers on the few distinguishing landmarks
ashore from a 30-foot wooden observation tower. Our return to the
ship by rubber boat that night forcefully demonstrated the need for
improvement in this hand-to-mouth operation. Our outboard motor
sputtered to a stop about halfway to the ship. For five hours we
bobbed about in the icy December water as Durborow dismantled
the little machine onto my lap while I held the flashlight. By the
time we got the engine going again, we were in the ship channel
well to the south of the LST. Half-frozen, we climbed aboard at 3:00
A.M., mightily chagrined that no one had evidenced the slightest
concern over our prolonged absence.

Despite this inauspicious introduction to my Chesapeake home
away from home, the ministrations of a Seabee battalion had soon
put together a small empire ashore. They replaced the wooden
tower with a 70-foot steel tower with an enclosed room at the top
that contained four radios and other communications equipment.

They put two 15-kilowatt generators and a water-distillation plant into operation. An abandoned hunting lodge was reconditioned and soon boasted five habitable bedrooms and a functional kitchen. On the firing range itself we emplaced twenty red-and-white targets. These slatted wooden triangles were about 12 feet high and placed in strategic locations. Among other amenities we rustled up a surplus propeller-driven swamp boat from the Portsmouth Shipyard. In it we skimmed at 15 knots through the marshes and surrounding water to repair targets. We also acquired an 81mm mortar whose burst out in the range could simulate a target of opportunity. With word that the admiral was showing interest in his new domain, a helicopter pad made of steel matting as well as some "ground-level observation posts" (duck blinds) were installed. The troops from our gunfire-support training unit vied for the privilege of staying at the range between our frequent trips from Little Creek. There was a rich trove of seafood for the catching and an oyster stew on the stove almost continuously throughout the fall and winter months. My tall, personable, relaxed, and highly competent assistant, 1st Lieutenant John McLaurin, and I made twenty-six trips to the range in 1947. Over the Christmas holidays, however, the high command decided to leave the facility unmanned for two weeks. Fortunately for me, I had warned of the possibility of vandalism but had been overruled. When we returned in early January, our worst fears were realized. Not only had the vandals (later presumed by local authorities to have been boys from Deal Island) cut the lock into the tower room, but they had smashed the radios. They had also done considerable damage to the generators and the water-distillation unit. Nothing was said as we placed this equipment back in order, but from then on the range was continually manned.

Another fracas, this one involving the fleet Underwater Demolition Teams (UDTs), livened up my tour as "mayor" of Bloodsworth. Due to the shallow approaches to Adam Island, we routinely made the trip ashore from the LST in amphibious vehicles (DUKWs). The UDTs proposed a channel dredged with explosives and a dock so that we could come close inshore in small boats. This would give us much greater flexibility since we would no longer require an LST to ferry our DUKWs to the range. Whatever the Fleet had available would do, and almost any small boat or landing craft could carry us to the dock.

During the week in question, the UDTs labored for two days in good weather. During the early afternoon of the third and last day, however, fog started to roll in. I had been caught ashore in fog before and knew the difficulty in locating an LST a mile or two offshore, so I ordered all hands aboard our two DUKWs. The UDT commander protested that they were not finished. I explained that we had to return to base that night and that we would never find the LST in the fog if we did not leave immediately. Unconvinced, he reluctantly rounded up his men and climbed aboard. We headed out into the bay. Halfway there we were engulfed in dense fog.

The ship's bell seemed to be coming from all directions at once. The DUKW compasses were erratic. Staying close together, the DUKWs floundered cautiously ahead with all hands straining to see the elusive LST. Minutes passed as the fog swept by us in opaque waves. By now I felt certain that we had missed the LST and were heading into the ship channel, but I had no way of knowing. Suddenly, providentially, there was a break in the fog. We sighted the ship well off our starboard quarter and were able to return to it safely.

Back at the Amphibious Training Command, the UDT commander complained to the admiral that I had prematurely ordered him off the island before he could complete his mission. Captain Frederick Hilles, USN, the director of the Gunfire Support School, advised me of this criticism and asked for my explanation. I laid out the facts as I saw them. He concurred in my decision and defended my action to the admiral. This argument ended in a standoff and was but one of many small frictions between Navy and Marines.

Responsibility for the Culebra Shore Bombardment Range off Puerto Rico was supposed to be transferred from the Training Command to the Amphibious Training Command. However, the Gunfire Support Training Unit (similar to mine) which was supposed to take over the range in early 1947 still languished at Little Creek. To be more specific, the officer in charge languished since the junior officers and enlisted men pulled their share of duty at Bloodsworth. To be prepared to take over at Culebra when and if we received the word, Captain Hilles had sent the lieutenant colonel and John McLaurin to Culebra to inspect the facilities. In early spring he decided to have a look-see himself and invited me to accompany him along with the lieutenant colonel and McLaurin. We flew to San Juan, motored to Roosevelt Roads, and set out in a small Navy tug to negotiate the 20 miles to the island. Standing in the bow savoring the refreshing breeze, Hilles queried the lieutenant colonel about the observation post, the campsite, and the navigability of the dirt road between. In each instance he gave a vague reply almost devoid of information. I wandered aft to the fantail where John was standing and asked him what was going on. Swearing me to secrecy, he related that their "inspection" had been from a light plane 2,000 feet up—it was all that John could do to pry the the lieutenant colonel loose from San Juan's enticements just to make the flyover.

But Fleet politics stymied the transfer of Culebra. Upon return to Little Creek, Captain Hilles directed the lieutenant colonel to divide responsibility with me for the conduct of the firing exercises at Bloodsworth, inasmuch as it did not appear that we would be assuming control of the Culebra Range anytime soon. When Captain Hilles discovered a few weeks later that the colonel had not bestirred himself, he told him personally that he wanted two officers to go on the shoot at Bloodsworth the next day and that Major Parry was not to be one of them. The following afternoon I ran into the captain in the corridor.

"Well," he smiled, "I guess we finally managed to get the colonel to Bloodsworth."

"He's in his office." I replied, "I just saw him there."

Livid, Captain Hilles called the lieutenant colonel to his office for an explanation. Later I learned that a first lieutenant had reported aboard the previous afternoon, and the lieutenant colonel had sent him out with McLaurin. Technically, he had complied with the captain's order. A few months later the colonel was transferred.

Prior to our reassignment in the late spring of 1949, the Hilleses were our dinner guests, and we fell into a discussion of the earlier days. Believing that my vow of secrecy could now be abandoned, I told the captain of the Culebra inspection trip. He was not overly surprised, saying that he had guessed that something like that had happened. Sensitive to the Navy–Marine squabbling at the time, he had decided against pressing the issue. Instead, he unloaded the lieutenant colonel at the first opportunity.

Midway through my three-year tour, I was reassigned as chief of the gunnery section. I was responsible for teaching our assorted classes conduct of fire on shore targets and the basics of a ship's fire control and armament. My principal assistant was a rugged, self-possessed Army major, Max Morris. A conscientious, capable artilleryman and a graduate of Auburn (where he had been a tackle on their fine football teams a decade earlier), Max was also innovative. He developed a graphic firing aid that simplified the conversion of commands from observers ashore to firing ships. In later, advanced versions it was adopted for Fleet use.

Fort Sill

From my earliest days in the 11th Marines, the rare graduate of the Artillery School in Fort Sill, Oklahoma, had been held in almost reverent regard, if not awe. My first mentor, Bob Luckey, was a Sill graduate. Now, at last, I was to become a certified artilleryman myself. I was to be introduced into the brotherhood at the field artillery Mecca, Fort Sill.

To generate family enthusiasm for the journey to America's heartland, I had advertised Oklahoma as a land of cowboys and Indians. Our three boys, aged two-and-a-half to almost seven, reminded me of this as we rolled across the flatlands of eastern Oklahoma enroute to Lawton. Squeezed into a small apartment downtown that night, they reminded me again that they had yet to see an Indian or a cowboy. Next morning, as I pondered how I would produce a bona fide Indian or a cowboy or both, I heard a marching band in the distance. From the window I could see a parade coming toward us down Main Street. Quickly gathering Vera and the boys, we descended to the pavement. Hundreds of Indians and cowboys, resplendent in their most impressive finery and mounted on magnificent horses bedecked in trappings of silver and gold, passed within feet of us. The boys were wide-eyed. It was an awesome display, and never after that morning did we hear from the children, "Where are the cowboys and Indians?" A good omen, it characterized the interesting, rewarding year we were to spend there.

Considered by many the finest artillery school in the world, Fort Sill cherished its reputation and strove to improve it throughout our ten-month course. Tactics, survey, conduct of fire from ground and air, and many other subjects were well taught. But gunnery—the accurate, speedy delivery of fire—was Sill's strong suit. If one was blessed with a mathematics background, the forte of the military and naval academies, one had a decided advantage in mastering gunnery.

Of the 407 students, most were captains and majors, but there were a goodly number of lieutenant colonels and even a few first lieutenants. Almost all—380, in fact—were Army field or coast artillerymen. Seven were Marines and twenty were officers from allied countries. Since our first meeting on Guadalcanal in the autumn of

1944, I had seen Captain Ben Read only occasionally on Okinawa, at Tsingtao, and Little Creek. For the most part, he had served as Major General Lem Shepherd's aide. My high opinion of him had not changed. Of the other captains—Horace W. Card, Ormand R. Lodge, and Raymond L. Valente—I had met none before and would serve closely only with Card in the future. Major Harvey A. Feehan, senior Marine, and Major James M. Callender, neither of whom I had met before, would bulk large in my future.

A member of the Naval Academy Class of 1942, Jimmy Callender was a Texan of small stature. He had eased through the Academy without academic stress, well within the top 20 percent of the class. His initiation into the Marine Corps had been even more cursory than mine. He had also missed The Basic School and its Reserve equivalent, and had attended only three weeks of Base Defense Weapons at Quantico before being dispatched to Samoa in February 1942. Base-defense duty with 155mm gun batteries and sea duty on the USS *Guam* was followed by tours of duty with Reserve field artillery battalions in the Northeast. Now Jimmy, like me, had an opportunity to become a certified field artilleryman. Relaxed, likeable, and smart, Jimmy was easy to get along with.

Despite good-natured, if tiresome, heckling about the status of the Marines—were we allied officers or not?—we got on well with the Army officers, who welcomed us into the artillery brotherhood. Marines, for our part, did not form a clique. Friendly relations were cemented as we played volleyball and golf and roamed the honky-tonks of Juarez during our two-month stint at the Antiaircraft and Guided Missile School at Fort Bliss (near El Paso). We teamed up as survey partners, formed car pools, and attended section parties. For the most part, Marines did well academically. We all stood in the top half of the class.

During midyear there were two diversions. The first was a promotion exam from major to lieutenant colonel, an exam that had been reinstituted in 1949 for the first time since before the war. There was nothing remarkable about it other than the fact that the two most difficult sets of questions for me were on field artillery and naval gunfire support—the two subjects upon which I could be considered expert. Evidently, the more you know about a subject, the more ambiguous questions seem.

The second major distraction was when our landlord sold the house out from under us without warning. Along with four other houses, it was sacrificed to make way for a Safeway store. Post head-

quarters discouraged me from trying to fight our eviction, despite
the fact that Vera was seven months along with our fourth child.
Several unkind kibitzers thought that we were premature in moving so quickly into a vacant apartment in the Fort Sill Cantonment
Area, but when we saw our house moving down Fort Sill Boulevard
on a huge trailer three weeks before John was born, my judgment
was vindicated.

Toward the end of the course we had a series of exams. Some of
our Army compatriots became almost panicky as exam time approached because of the widespread rumor that only the top 10 percent of the class would go to the Command and General Staff
College at Fort Leavenworth, Kansas. (Attendance at the college
was assumed a necessity for promotion to colonel.) They scrambled
around, ferreting out and scrutinizing old exams and seeking some
advantage in the fiercely competitive environment. We Marines
contemplated this frenzy with amusement.

One of the most important exams was a three-hour brain twister
on tactics. This exam was counted as 10 percent of the final grade.
A significant part of this exam involved selection of the main effort
from three alternatives in an attack—on the right, the left, or
equally from both flanks. I selected the correct main effort, but the
two Army majors in my car pool, both near the top of the class until
then, did not. They were purple with rage. Neither forgave me and
they disbanded the car pool forthwith. It was better for them to lick
their wounds in private, and school was almost over.

General Mark Clark, already a tall, impressive Army legend,
spoke at graduation. With his words ringing in my ears, we left Sill
in late June feeling that it had been a year well spent. Not only had
I learned gunnery, survey, and other tools of the trade from the
masters themselves, but I had been accepted into the artillery
brotherhood.

Midshipman 1st Class Francis Fox Parry.
Annapolis, 1940

2nd Lieutenant Bill McReynolds and 2nd Lieutenant
Fox Parry.
Camp Lejeune, 1941

2nd Lieutenant Francis Fox Parry on
his wedding day.
November 20, 1941

Vera Henderson Parry.

A Marine 75mm pack howitzer in action.
Guadalcanal, 1942

Marine Gunner Bob Sack (l.)
and Captain John Chaisson.
Ballarat, 1943

Five of the seven Parry brothers toast their father, Judge George Gowan Parry, during their first postwar family gathering. Standing (l. to r.) Commander George Parry, Jr., Staff Sergeant Ted Parry, Major Francis Fox Parry, Corporal Steve Parry, and Lieutenant Commander John Parry.
Philadelphia, February 1946

Major Al "The Count" Feldmeier during his service as a torpedo-bomber squadron commander.
Okinawa, 1945

Major Fox Parry with 1st Lieutenant John McLaurin (driving).
Little Creek, 1947

Colonel Homer L. Litzenberg, Jr.
Korea, 1951

One of 3/11's 105mm howitzers laid for high-angle fire.
Chinhung-ni, November 1950

3/11 position area.
Yudam-ni, November 1950

Compliments of Ray Miller

Compliments of Ray Miller

Down From The Reservoir: 3/11 artillerymen during a break along the snow-covered road from Yudam-ni to Hagaru-ri. Note the wounded Marine riding on the fender of the truck.
Chosin Reservoir, December 1950

Major Norman "Reds" Miller, 3/11 executive officer.

Major Jimmy Callender, 3/11 operations officer.

1st Lieutenant Willie Gore and 1st Lieutenant Red Herndon, 3/11 battery executive officers.

Captain Ben Read receives his Navy Cross medal from Lieutenant General
Lemuel C. Shepherd, Jr.

Major Hank Woessner, 7th Marines operations officer, is
congratulated by Colonel Homer Litzenberg during a
regimental awards ceremony.
Masan, 1951

Colonel Wilbert S. "Bigfoot" Brown at a reunion with his son, a Marine corporal, during Bigfoot's tour as 1st Marines commanding officer. *Central Korea, 1951*

Lieutenant Colonel Fox Parry (l.) receives his Bronze Star medal for his part in the Inchon-Seoul Campaign. *Quantico, 1951*

Colonel Fox Parry turns over command of the 11th
Marines to Lieutenant Colonel Tom Randall.
Camp Pendleton, 1962

Colonel Fox Parry, 1st Marine Division
operations officer, during a desert
training exercise.
Twentynine Palms, 1963

Lieutenant General
Robert B. Luckey.
*Headquarters, Marine
Corps, 1962*

Major General Herman Nickerson and Colonel Fox Parry await
the return of major components of 1st Marine Division
following the Cuban Missile Crisis and near invasion of Cuba.
San Diego, 1963

Colonel Jimmy Callender, 12th Marines commanding officer, and Major General
Lew Walt, 3rd Marine Division commander.
Vietnam, 1966

Major General Bill DePuy, U.S. Army.
Vietnam, 1966

Colonel Francis Fox Parry, USMC

PART III

Korea

11

Lejeune to Majon-dong

Assembly

Of the seven Marines who attended the Artillery Officers Advanced Course at Fort Sill in 1949–50, three were ordered to the 2nd Marine Division at Camp Lejeune and four to the 1st Marine Division at Camp Pendleton. With our fourth son only two months old, we proceeded directly to Lejeune upon graduation to have a better chance of landing government quarters promptly.

Learning upon arrival that I was slated to be division naval gunfire officer, a staff job of little distinction in peacetime, I could scarcely contain my disappointment, which soon turned to anger. Had I spent a year at Fort Sill absorbing all the fine points of the field artilleryman's trade to be relegated to low-level division staffer? It made me fighting mad. Providentially, there was help nearby; my friend Colonel Bigfoot Brown held forth as 10th Marines commander no more than a mile away. Without a moment's hesitation, I telephoned him. "Colonel," I said, "this is Fox Parry. I've just come from the Advanced Course at Sill and some idiot has assigned me as naval gunfire officer. I had hoped to get one of your battalions." There was a momentary silence, and then the colonel replied, "I didn't know that you were coming. Stay where you are, I'll be right over." Within minutes he had convinced the division personnel officer and chief of staff that he needed me to command his 2nd Battalion, whose present commander he was reassigning as regimental operations officer, and that he would furnish a field-grade replacement to them with naval gunfire credentials. Such was Bigfoot Brown—decisive, persuasive, and instantly responsive to a friend in need.

Now, at last, I had my hands on a direct-support field artillery battalion. The war in Korea had started two days after our graduation from Sill, while I was enroute to Lejeune. With it moving into high gear, there seemed to be a good chance that we would be called to action soon.

A battalion is men; the more competent, the more responsive, the more resourceful, and the more daring the men, the better the battalion is likely to be. It was obvious that the 2nd Battalion, 10th Marines already had many good men. But you can rarely have too many and, with the prospect that we would soon expand to war strength (more than double in size), we would need all the good men we could get. I knew of two good men who would report to the division momentarily, so I advised Colonel Brown of the imminent arrival of my two Fort Sill classmates, Major Jimmy Callender and Captain Ben Read. I put in my bid for both of them.

Jimmy Callender and I had stood in the top 10 percent of the class—he a few numbers ahead of me—and I knew that he was sharp in gunnery. As soon as appropriate, I installed him as S-3 and fire-direction officer. I had had my eye on Ben Read at Okinawa, Tsingtao, and Little Creek. Having long since proven himself a first-rate troop leader, I assigned him as a firing-battery commander. To my delight another talented officer, Captain John McLaurin, my Bloodsworth Island–Little Creek compatriot, also reported to the regiment, and I was able to have him assigned. The character of the battalion was now taking shape, and I had every confidence that we were going to be able to do any task required of us. It had taken me almost ten years to reach this milestone; I had just the command I wanted and I knew exactly what I wanted to do with it.

The war had already started to look ominous, and the Marine Corps had promised General Douglas MacArthur a full-strength division as soon as possible. The plan was to consolidate most of the 1st and 2nd Marine divisions at Camp Pendleton, excepting only the 2nd Division headquarters and the 6th Marines, reinforced (which included my battalion, 2/10). These would remain at Lejeune as the nucleus for the reconstituted division. In furtherance of this plan, most of the division had moved by troop train to Pendleton. Bigfoot shepherded his two battalions to the West Coast to make his bid to again command the 11th Marines; he had been CO, 11th

Marines, at Okinawa and Tientsin in 1945–46. He left me in command of the 10th Marines with instructions to work closely with Colonel Homer L. Litzenberg, the new commanding officer of the 6th Marines. I was to start an officers' school and otherwise make ready for the task of rebuilding the 10th Marines. This assignment was not made easier by the kibitzing of Lieutenant Colonel Press Wood, prospective executive officer of the 10th Marines, who was still carried on the rolls of Division Headquarters. He advised me not to worry about officers' school or about implementing other suggestions the colonel had made. I politely ignored him. I busied myself and the men by cleaning up the mess the departing battalions had left. Our efforts included swabbing out and oiling the 155mm howitzers, which the 3rd Battalion had fired a few days before leaving and had not properly cleaned.

A disappointed Colonel Brown soon returned. Command of the 11th Marines was retained by Colonel Jim Brower, the incumbent, an officer with whom I had served in the 15th Marines. Hard upon Bigfoot's arrival came word that, even with the Marine Corps Reserves activated, the 6th Marines, reinforced, would be needed to flesh out 1st Marine Division.

This grim reality illustrated the deplorable state to which the Marine Corps had been reduced—to two divisions in name, in actuality to nowhere near even one. First Division was not even a healthy regimental combat team; 2nd Marine Division, including the battalion in the Mediterranean (3/6, which eventually became the nucleus for 3/7) was merely an anemic brigade. For four years the military services had been cut and cut and cut again, until the "peace-strength" battalions were but shadows of their combat equivalents.

The light field artillery battalion of 329 men (instead of about 700) was organized into two firing batteries of four 105mm howitzers each—eight howitzers instead of eighteen. The 10th Marines had two such battalions rather than three, as well as a medium battalion of 155mm howitzers, which was similarly reduced in strength and firepower. The condition of the 10th Marines reflected the sorry state to which all elements of the division—infantry, engineers, tanks, service, and the rest—had been relegated. Our nation's leaders, in a time when the catastrophe of World War II should still have been vivid, had learned nothing about the importance of preparedness. And, as on Guadalcanal, it would be the Corps of Marines that paid the heavy price.

We had been in government quarters one week and had not even laid the rugs yet when Colonel Brown called me to his office to advise me that we would be mounting out in three days. Knowing that my wife and baby had both been in the hospital, he urged me to remain as his S-3 to help him rebuild and train the new regiment. It was the second time that I had been asked to take over staff responsibility for the plans, operations, and training of an artillery regiment—a coveted assignment, especially when the commander was Bob Luckey or Bigfoot Brown. The offer illustrated yet another of Bigfoot's many great qualities—compassion. But my battalion was obviously going to war and the regiment was staying behind.

Bigfoot was not through looking after me yet, however. While on the West Coast, he had viewed firsthand the chaos of Camp Pendleton and the political maneuvering in progress there. Having made a special effort to install me as CO of 2/10, he wanted me to stay there. He urged Colonel Litzenberg to be wary of the Pendleton power brokers who might find a major in command of a battalion too tempting a target. Bigfoot, a master manipulator himself, told me that he would like to fly Major Callender to the coast as an advance man to prepare for our arrival. He briefed Jimmy confidentially on his mission, which was to deliver a letter to Colonel Hope Kirk, senior artilleryman at Camp Pendleton. The letter, according to Jimmy, was an impassioned plea to Colonel Kirk to exert every influence to see that I was not replaced as commanding officer of my battalion. Bigfoot directed Jimmy to deliver this letter in person and to reinforce the message as strongly as possible. After a strenuous effort Jimmy finally tracked down Colonel Kirk at a hideaway off base—Kirk could be reached at a secret number only in emergencies of the direst sort. Despite the heroic efforts of Colonel Brown and Major Callender, my battalion command was, nonetheless, in jeopardy.

I will never forget my leave-taking from my lovely wife on a Sunday morning at a siding at Camp Lejeune. Vera clung to me so passionately that I was just able to disengage myself in time to leap on the last car of the troop train. Once again, Vera was being left behind, this time with four young sons, the baby not yet four months old. Along with many other wives and children, she would also have to pay a price for American shortsightedness.

The 2nd Battalion, 10th Marines was undermanned even for a peace-strength organization because Regiment had ordered us to leave eighteen key NCOs at Lejeune at the last minute. We would absorb enough Reserves at Pendleton, they said, to flesh out the battalion to full strength. On the train we spent many hours piecing together the cadres of eighteen gun sections from eight and organizing the third battery on paper—we had no authority to form this battery until several days after our arrival at Pendleton. Entrusted with command of the new battery was Captain John McLaurin. Captains Ben Read and Samuel A. Hannah, both experienced combat-battery commanders, cooperated fully—that is, to the extent that human nature allowed—in this division of talent. We all realized that the battalion would only be as strong as the weakest battery. My experience in forming 4/15 on Guadalcanal in 1944 was instructive in this horse trading.

Upon arrival in Pendleton I reported to Colonel Litzenberg, whose 6th Marines had by then been redesignated the 7th Marines. We became the 3rd Battalion, 11th Marines, part of the 7th Regimental Combat Team (RCT). The rest of the division was already boarding ship. We were to join officers and men; draw all manner of equipment, motor transport, and howitzers; and in about a week prepare for embarkation as the ships became available. The colonel said we would probably have an opportunity to train for two to three months in Japan. I am not sure whether Litz believed this, for the radio and newspaper did not give much encouragement to this view. Whether the post staffers did or not, they used it as an excuse to assign us several nonfield artillery officers, although we had uncovered four field artillery lieutenants buried in the base staff in nonessential jobs; the post staff refused to make these men available.

Despite the colonel's comforting words, intuition told me that we had better do what training we could regardless of the handicaps. A few of the officers were unenthusiastic about trying to conduct training in the midst of the chaos of joining men, drawing equipment, and getting organized. But once I assured them that "we are going to do it," they turned to. That there were no 105mm rounds at Camp Pendleton did not deter us. We insisted that the base staff find them elsewhere. And find them they did, flying rounds in from depots and Army posts. We got all the surveyed rounds—rounds with bent shell cases and other minor defects. The supply people said that we had laid our hands on every 105mm round west of the Mississippi. Jimmy Callender remembers seeing 1st Lieutenant Wilber N. "Red" Herndon, executive officer of How (H) Battery, pounding dents out of a shell case with a hammer so that it would fit into the firing chamber. We fired every round except perhaps a half dozen that were too badly damaged to salvage—about 300 in all. To do this we needed to borrow trucks from Post Motor Transport, and each battery in turn used six of the eight howitzers we had brought with us from Lejeune. These herculean efforts gave each of our eighteen gun-section cadres—we had not yet joined about half our men—rudimentary firing practice that was crucial to our later success. (We were the only field artillery battalion in the division to fire a round.) Training (to the extent possible) and expansion of other key elements of the battalion, such as the FDC and the communications section, went forward simultaneously.

In the midst of this hectic activity, I received blows from two unexpected quarters. The first was a letter of reprimand from Colonel Brown for the condition in which we had left the barracks in Lejeune. Immediately, I smelled a rat. The letter did not sound like Bigfoot, and as one of his protégés I was an unlikely recipient. We held a council of war. Major Norman A. "Reds" Miller, my executive officer, and the battery commanders vowed that they had inspected the barracks just prior to departure and that they were shipshape. Furthermore, we had invited Lieutenant Colonel Wood and the regimental staff to inspect the area the Sunday morning that we shipped out. None had made it. It then dawned on us that the eighteen NCOs that we had left behind at Regiment's direction could have been the culprits. By now my instinct of self-preservation was thoroughly aroused. I asked Major Miller and Captains Read and Hannah to write statements, which I enclosed with my own letter to Colonel Brown. In the letter I outlined my actions from the time he had left me in command of the regiment until our departure. I did not fail to mention our cleanup of the other battalion's mess, my disagreement with Lieutenant Colonel Wood over officers' school, and the absence of regimental staff at our leavetaking. This five-page missive was dispatched air mail special delivery.

A night or so later, I accompanied some of my officers to San Diego on liberty. It was the first time we had been off the base since we had arrived over a week before. Upon return to my room at about 3:00 A.M., I found the door plastered with notes from Colonel Litzenberg, the latest of which was dated 1:00 A.M. They ordered me to report to his office at Tent Camp Two at 5:30 that morning. After an hour's rest, shower, and shave, I sallied forth to meet this latest crisis.

Colonel Homer Litzenberg was stockily built, square-jawed, and steely eyed. Humorless, even ruthless, he was also highly emotional on occasion. A few days before, for example, he had given the RCT a pep talk and become tearful in the process. I would later learn that he was fiercely loyal to those few who made his team. The crusty old man eyed me with coolness as he abruptly stated, "I have decided to replace you as battalion commander with Lieutenant Colonel Rose, who commanded the Los Angeles Reserve howitzer battalion. With the division heavily manned with Reserves, it has been determined to be a politic move to have at least one battalion commanded by a Reserve. Since you are the only battalion commander still at Pendleton who is a major, I have no other choice." He added that Major Miller's background was in antiaircraft artillery and did I not agree that the battalion would be stronger with me as executive and Miller reassigned?

While the colonel had been handing down this gruesome sentence, I was building up a head of steam. I visualized my not-too-well wife and four small sons who would have to move from Camp Lejeune to Philadelphia and fend for themselves. I thought of Bigfoot's offer to be his operations officer, of the four battalions I had already commanded as a major, and of the fact that I was a lieutenant-colonel selectee awaiting a promotion vacancy. When he finished speaking I was ready. Coldly, I launched into vigorous rebuttal. "Colonel," I fired back, "I couldn't disagree with you more. Major Miller has great potential and will be a superb executive. And you can't find an officer better qualified than I am to take this battalion into combat. I have molded it together with my own hands and you'll take it from me only over my dead body!"

Litz had already broken into a broad smile. "You're my artillery commander," he declared.

Had he been testing my guts? In any case we hit it off very well from that moment on, and no artilleryman had better support from his infantry commander throughout the campaign ahead.

As to Litz's old buddy, Bigfoot Brown (they had been corporals together in the '20s), the morning of our late-afternoon sailing a telegram caught up with me: LETTER RECEIVED DISREGARD MINE. BEST REGARDS TO ALL. EXCELLENT REPORT REACHING ME ABOUT YOU. COLONEL BROWN. Bigfoot saw to it that it reached me before I went off to war—another measure of his thoughtfulness. Apparently, Lieutenant Colonel Wood and his cohorts on the regimental staff had some difficult explaining to do.

Crossing the Han

Early on the evening of September 1, 1950, we slipped majestically out of San Diego's magnificent harbor and headed into the setting sun. It was an unforgettable experience. As a Marine band played "Goodnight, Irene," a favorite of the moment, the thousands of troops crowding the deck of the USS *Bayfield* broke into song. The families and loved ones swarming on the dock soon joined in. As we eased past Point Loma into the darkening Pacific, the harbor reverberated with that haunting refrain.

Although 3/11 was spread over seven ships, I directed that each battery commander and key staff officer do his best to conduct whatever training was feasible. On the *Bayfield* the FDC and communications section, among others, were able to get in urgently needed drills. In fact, the FDC had to be organized and trained almost from scratch since we had brought only four trained men from Camp Lejeune, or about one third of the needed complement. That the FDC was rendered functional at all in the less than three weeks available and under the crowded conditions aboard ship was commendable. That it was managed with such success was in equal measure due to Major Callender's knowledge and dedication and the quality of the Reserves we received at the last minute at Camp Pendleton. About 170 men, or about 25 percent of our strength, joined the night before we embarked. The Reserves were mostly from the state of Oregon and Houston, Texas. Many were college students or recent graduates of the University of Oregon or Oregon State. Their intellectual capacity was such that they needed to be told the details of their jobs only once. Jimmy's FDC was filled with men who had scored over 140 on the General Classification Test (GCT), high scores even for officers.

The FDC, the three firing-battery executives, the eighteen gun-section chiefs and their gunners, and the communicators that tie them all together make up the gunnery team. The gunnery team is is the heart of the field artillery battalion. It is a heart that must beat powerfully and with precision, promptly converting observer calls for fire into battery fire commands. The fire commands are then quickly translated into range and deflection settings for each howitzer. The speed and accuracy of this operation is the real measure of an artillery battalion. Of course, the battalion must be positioned and repositioned tactically so that it can do its gunnery job most effectively. The battalion must also be protected from interfering forces and supplied with ammunition. The FOs, the communicators, and the service elements are also a vital part of the battalion, but it is the gunnery team that must deliver the battalion's firepower in appropriate quantity where and when needed. This takes knowledge, training, teamwork, and dedication to the fine points of gunnery at every level. That proficiency in this critical area was attained despite the handicaps (not the least of which was the cold fact that the FDC had not controlled a single round of the battalion's fire in training) speaks volumes about the caliber of 3/11 personnel.

After a calm crossing we steamed into Kobe harbor the afternoon of September 16 only to learn that our stay in Japan would be hours, not months. I was able to assemble the battery commanders and staff from their several ships and formulate a landing plan. This consisted primarily of every unit commander using his initiative to gather his people and equipment as rapidly as possible and move to the assembly area. We were scheduled to get under way for Inchon at first light, so there was no troop liberty. A few officers did go ashore for dinner and visited a geisha house, but our hearts were not in it.

On September 21 we landed at Inchon, which was by then a rear area. The front lines were well inland, near Kimpo Airfield. For almost three days near the beach and in an assembly area inland, we strove manfully to recover all our equipment, much of which was still crated or in boxes that we had never seen. The most critical shortage was communications gear—radios and field telephones. Some were never found. (We fired our first fire mission with the FDC manning a field telephone borrowed from Item Battery.)

With the 7th Marines across the Han River sweeping almost unopposed toward an investment of Seoul from the north, I requested permission to cross the river so that we could provide more effective support. Regiment concurred, and we made ready to cross at first light. 3/11 Headquarters crossed the tidal Han, at that point about 100 yards wide, in a DUKW. We watched as pontoon barges pushed by LCVPs ferried the eighteen truck-drawn 105mm howitzers across. Then, to my annoyance, tanks began to cross. Much of the FDC and communications section, as well as the ammunition trucks, were left stranded as the tanks monopolized the barges. I DUKWed back across the river to discover why my units had been delayed.

The river crossing was controlled by the 1st Shore Party Battalion, commanded by a colorful, tough hero of the Pacific island campaigns, Colonel Henry P. "Jim" Crowe. I sought him out and pleaded my case. He was unmoved. After agreeing that 3/11 had priority for the river crossing, he explained, "Your battalion has eighteen howitzers, right?"

"That's right, Sir," I replied.

"Well, Major, I ferried eighteen howitzers across the river, so what's your problem?"

"My howitzers are practically useless without our fire-direction center, communications section, and ammunition trucks."

The gnarled old colonel turned away, dismissing me with a wave of the hand. "I took your battalion across as ordered."

Locating the nearest field telephone, I called the division G-3, Colonel Al Bowser, who years before had been my equitation instructor at Quantico. An artilleryman himself, Bowser instantly grasped my dilemma. "Get Colonel Crowe on the line for me, Fox," he directed. Crowe took the phone, listened briefly, fixed me with a withering glare, and issued the necessary orders to complete the delivery of 3/11 to the north bank of the Han on a priority basis.

By the time the last vehicle was across, the day was half over but we were able to move up along the Han about 10 miles and occupy a firing position behind some hills to the west of Seoul. We fired the batteries in before dark.

That 1st Marine Division was capable of creditable action in a matter of weeks after being assembled from two division shells and filled out by Reserve units from around the country is remarkable; that it could successfully execute an assault landing as difficult as that at Inchon in September 1950 was a near miracle. Dedicated Marine Regulars and Reservists with Pacific War experience still fresh had bailed out the nation's political leadership, which did not deserve so kind a fate.

Fire Mission

The 7th RCT's sweep to invest Seoul and the advance on up the valley to Uijongbu was not strongly opposed. The 1st and 5th Marines had broken the back of North Korean resistance; the 7th faced only rear-guard action. It was, nonetheless, a most useful shakedown for the 7th RCT, which was far more heavily weighted with Reserves than the rest of the division. We were aware of the desperate need to hone military skills and round the RCT into top physical condition.

After an active firing period devoted mostly to support of Dog Company, 2/7 (which had strayed into the 5th Marines' sector and encountered a North Korean battalion), 3/11 displaced to the north of Seoul preparatory to the push to Uijongbu. While we were awaiting the arrival of the firing batteries at the selected position, 1/7 came up the road and began to bivouac in "our" field. I found the redoubtable Lieutenant Colonel Raymond G. Davis and advised him that the field was already staked out for our firing batteries.

I had seen little of Ray, who was three years my senior, since we had first met with Colonel Litzenberg at Camp Pendleton. (Both of us had complained to Litz about our battalions being split among so many ships.) But I knew something of his background. A Georgian, he had started out as an artilleryman and had been Bob Luckey's executive officer in the 1st Special Weapons Battalion on the Canal. Later, at Cape Gloucester, Davis took over 1/1 and launched his brilliant career as an infantry commander. He had a cool demeanor, bright blue eyes, and a reputation as a tough, dynamic leader. He had won the Navy Cross as a major commanding 1/1 on Peleliu. He was not a man with whom one sought a confrontation.

I declared respectfully, "Colonel, I'm putting the battalion in position in this field; they'll be coming up the road shortly."

"We've marched 18 miles and the men are exhausted." Ray rejoined, "This is as far as we go."

So 1/7 bivouacked on the edge of the field and in the adjacent woods.

As the batteries arrived minutes later, I emplaced them as planned in the field. An hour or two later when the firing batteries began to register, Ray apparently thought better of his stand and pushed his tired troops on to a quieter rest area. There are better places to relax than cheek-to-jowl with cannonading artillery.

This minor confrontation illuminates what from then on became standard practice in the 7th RCT—3/11 had priority in the selection of firing positions. Although priority was not critical around Seoul, it became so in the more confining mountains of North Korea.

For the drive north, which was supposed to be a 10-mile tank-infantry dash to Uijongbu, a battery of Marine 155mm howitzers and a battery of Army antiaircraft artillery-automatic weapons (AAA-AW) were attached to 3/11. According to accepted tactics, the tracked vehicles that carried the dual-40mm AAA guns and quadruple .50-caliber machine guns, were distributed throughout the motor column. The 155s and my own Item Battery were left in position to support the advance, their fire controlled by Item Battery's battery fire chart beefed up by battalion FDC personnel and communicators. Several tanks, however, were immobilized by mines, thus forming effective roadblocks. Anxious to deploy George and How batteries in a forward position from which we could reach beyond Uijongbu, we were frustrated not only by the tanks but also the tracked AAA. It was necessary to order the AAA to take position on the edge of the road so that we could maneuver the firing batteries through them and on up the road into position. We learned, in fact, that attaching an AAA battery to a field artillery battalion is not a good idea. It is well nigh impossible to site the tracked vehicles so that they do not interfere with artillery displacements, communications, and ammunition resupply; their desire to reposition themselves is frequently disruptive; control of their often indiscriminate fire is difficult; and they attract attention. In short, a field artillery battalion is better off without whatever contribution AAA makes to local security. My recommendations to Colonel Litzenberg on the subject were forthright, and the 7th RCT had no AAA attached thereafter.

That night we fired from both forward and rear positions. As long as we had enemy targets under fire from the rear, it was inadvisable to move Item Battery forward. This was our first experience with a split FDC, a practice that was to become commonplace up north. During this period Captain Ben Read and I visited the front lines atop a hill a few miles north of Seoul. While Ben checked in with his liaison officer and the infantry battalion commander, I went on to see the FO in that sector. Second Lieutenant Donald H. Campbell was a Reserve from Aptos, California, who had never conducted a fire mission. I instructed him in the simplest terms I knew for fifteen minutes. That night, he called in a fire mission and was able, with a little patience and assistance from the FDC, to bring fire to bear on an enemy target.

Don was not unique. Eight of my nine FOs were Reservists, and I suspect that most were at least rusty in firing technique if indeed they had ever fired a live mission at all. These largely untried observers, important keys to 3/11 success, were our major weakness— our only serious one. The light action around Seoul and to Uijongbu was an opportunity to give these officers some urgently needed training. It was not much, but they learned their trade. By the time they were called upon to produce in the Korean northland, they were ready.

Night Displacement

Historians and other commentators have already challenged the advisability of General MacArthur's sudden command to halt 1st Marine Division north of Uijongbu. The division withdrew to Inchon and eventually performed an amphibious end-around to Wonsan. That it removed ground pressure from the retreating North Koreans is indisputable. That it gave the Chinese a few more days to prepare to intervene also seems incontestable. But it is doubtful that MacArthur's sudden command made much difference to the ultimate outcome. At the time some of us at Uijongbu jumped to the parochial and, in retrospect, silly conclusion that General MacArthur wanted a U.S. Army division to be the first to cross the 38th parallel into North Korea. Our cynicism was not without some foundation, however. For example, we had learned that despite the fact that supplies of all kinds were needed by front-line troops, the first pontoon bridge across the Han had remained unused for many hours until MacArthur arrived to cut the ribbon to inaugurate its use.

At Inchon we boarded the USS *Aiken Victory* and the USS *Titania* and ships of the Supreme Command, Allied Powers, Japan (SCAJAP)—*LST QO44* and *LST QO92*. We voyaged down the Yellow Sea, through the Korea Strait, and up the Sea of Japan to cruise off Wonsan while the Navy painstakingly swept the harbor of mines. It was an eerie experience, sharing the LST with a Japanese crew who only five years earlier had been our mortal enemies. For each of the three meals every day, the Japanese would eat first. The crew cleaned up the kitchen, mess hall, and wardroom swiftly and efficiently and then turned them over to our cooks and messmen. We ate entirely different meals. One afternoon we even had pizzas—a morale booster even though only a modest culinary success. We languished from October 15 to October 26 on the LST, most of the time boring holes in the water off Wonsan. There were no unpleasant incidents between Marines and Japanese.

About a week before we landed at Wonsan, we suffered our first officer casualty. Captain Robert A. Thompson, our logistics officer and CO of Service Battery, had developed an eye infection so serious that he had to be transferred in open sea by breeches buoy to a destroyer for further delivery to a hospital ship. Bob had done a superior job under the most adverse conditions from rounding up ammunition at Camp Pendleton to outfitting the battalion with vehicles and equipment, to providing logistic support from Inchon to Uijongbu, to embarkation aboard ship at Inchon. To say that he was not missed would be untrue. But we had such a wealth of talented officers—the like of which I have never seen before or since in a single battalion—that his replacement did not represent a serious problem.

This was not altogether accidental, for the 3/11 command philosophy stressed the accumulation of talent. Three of my most valuable officers—Major Callender and Captains Read and McLaurin—had been sought and acquired at Camp Lejeune. At Camp Pendleton we had scoured the base for competent officers, artillerymen, and otherwise. At Inchon I discovered Captain Robert T. Patterson languishing in an inconsequential job in 4/11 and talked Major Bill McReynolds into giving him to me on the promise that I would find him a good billet. (As a first lieutenant on Okinawa, Bob had commanded K/4/15, and I knew his worth.) Of course, there are situations when an overabundance of talent will cause you problems, but combat is not likely to be one of them. Officers are killed, wounded, become sick or are transferred to other units, and having a capable replacement on hand may be the difference between giving superior or mediocre support to the infantry.

Once ashore at Wonsan we were somewhat annoyed that Bob Hope and his touring troupe were already entertaining the servicemen in the area. We were soon apprised, however, that there was serious business ahead. On October 27, 3/11 was again attached to the 7th Marines. I reported to Colonel Litzenberg at his CP, a schoolhouse just north of Wonsan, and learned that the 7th RCT would spearhead 1st Marine Division's dash northward to the Yalu River—the border with China. Inasmuch as little resistance was expected, we were to make all haste, with the infantry leapfrogging battalions by truck whenever possible. As soon as new winter clothing could be drawn from Division, we were to get under way. A long winter campaign in the mountains of North Korea was not anticipated, and the skimpy cold-weather gear available was a far cry from the clothing and equipment with which Korean veterans of future winters would be outfitted. Our shoe-pacs presented particular problems. I wore the same paratrooper boots that I had worn on Okinawa because the liners of the shoe-pac tended to freeze to the foot when they became sweaty and then cooled off.

Major Dave Mell, the 7th Marines logistics officer (S-4), was urged to think in terms of "plus 700" for all supplies needed for the trek north. Although surprised at our requirements for gas, communications replacements, and ammunition, he took on this additional burden without complaint.

Stripped down so that all gear and ammunition could be carried in organic transport in one trip, 3/11 covered the 65 miles to Hamhung over steep mountain roads. The roads were well suited to ambush, but we arrived without incident. After a situation briefing at I Republic of Korea (ROK) Army Corps Headquarters, I positioned the battalion facing west in a field about a mile south of the bridge into Hamhung. While awaiting the arrival of the infantry battalions by train, we reconnoitered the broad valley stretching west from Hamhung up to where the ROK lines were drawn. It was a pleasant 30-mile drive up the narrowing valley in the autumn coolness. We drove alongside a clear, swift-running stream. Our 1:250,000 map told us that the stream would accompany us up the mountains to the Chosin Reservoir, which was less than halfway to our objective on the Yalu.

At Majon-dong, a hamlet a mile from the head of the valley, I came upon a U.S. Army major and captain, military advisors to the Republic of Korea (ROK) Army's 26th Infantry Regiment, who informed me that "Chinese volunteers" had met the ROKs head-on and had driven them back from Sudong. They were now trying to regain suitable ground to facilitate the passage of lines by the 7th Marines. Returning to Hamhung, I reported to Colonel Litzenberg and was directed to lead the regimental column to Majon-dong in the morning. Just after Reds Miller, Jimmy Callender, and I had turned in at about 11:00 P.M., there was a rapping at the window of the school building we were using as a CP. There were two Marines with a jack-o'-lantern—a real pumpkin they had scrounged somewhere, complete with a candle inside. The troops were not going to let Halloween slip by without notice.

About midnight Colonel Litzenberg telephoned to order 3/11 to move across the river into Hamhung immediately—reportedly, a Chinese Communist division was moving on us from the southwest. With the 7th Marines north of the river, we were in an untenable position; he wanted us to move within the city and to be prepared to shoot to the southwest. An unplanned night displacement is one thing. Add to this the imponderables of a strange Asian city and a moonless night, and you have the ingredients of a disaster.

My small reconnaissance party, made up chiefly of the three firing-battery commanders, plunged determinedly into the inky night in search of an appropriate battalion position. Reds was to form up the battalion, lead it to a designated site, and wait for us. We probed cautiously through the city in almost total darkness, casting about for a suitable park or open area. After poking down one street after another, careful to maintain our bearings, we came upon a sizable schoolyard. By the time we made our way back to the rendezvous area, Reds was getting a little nervous. He had kept the battalion moving around in a circle several blocks on a side, prefer-ring some movement to sitting in suspenseful waiting. We reached the schoolyard at about 3:00 A.M., put the batteries in position, and did a little digging in. Since our orders for the morning still stood, we moved out again at first light.

As we proceeded slowly up the peaceful valley along a route that was to become famous before the month was out, I had ample oppor-tunity to ponder the lesson of the unpleasant night. The message seemed clear: Reconnoiter positions in all directions, no matter how seemingly improbable the chance of occupation. At 9:00 A.M., we went into position at Majon-dong to await the arrival of the 7th Marines. That night we went to sleep without having fired a round.

12

The Reservoir

High-Angle Fire

After Majon-dong and for the first time in Korea, the terrain and situation imposed critical restrictions on our artillery technique. Because the 7th Marines was miles from the nearest friendly troops, attack of isolated units was a very real problem. Colonel Litzenberg decided, therefore, that all elements of the RCT should be within the defensive perimeter each night, whenever possible. This resulted in our occupying five separate firing positions from Majon-dong to Chinhung-ni (a distance of some 5 miles as the crow flies), although we could have provided fire support, considering only the range factor, without moving at all.

All rounds delivered during the next eight days were high-angle fire. This was necessary not only to enable us to reach the Chinese on the reverse slopes of steep hills, but also, in many cases, to allow us to clear the overshadowing peaks that hemmed us in.

The Marine Corps, to my knowledge, had seldom fired any high-angle fire before, certainly not in any meaningful quantities. If you use a howitzer in this way, you are—in effect—using it as if it were a mortar, with the tube pointing skyward in the upper half of the 90-degree quadrant. To do this, you must be able to dig a pit for the howitzer to recoil into (not a problem unless the ground is frozen). High-angle fire had been covered briefly at Fort Sill, although neither Jimmy nor I could remember having seen a round fired in training.

We discussed trying it for the first time in combat over our own troops. Jimmy had *Field Manual 6–40,* the field artillery bible, which told us how to do it. If we could fire high-angle successfully, it would greatly enhance our effectiveness. Jimmy believed that his FDC could do it. I said, "Go ahead."

Exercising considerable care, the bright Marines in our FDC and the rest of our gunnery team became proficient in a matter of hours. Of course, a high-angle projectile takes much longer to reach the target than low-angle fire, and that bothered the FOs at first. They even chastised us for firing so slowly. They soon became used to it, however, and realized what an invaluable technique it was.

High-angle fire caught the Chinese by surprise on many occasions when they thought they were safe in defilade behind a precipitous hill. Once we tried to fire at a target close in behind an adjacent hill using only the base charge (a 105mm round has seven charges—you utilize only the number of charges you require to attain the desired range). The round left the firing chamber but lodged in the bore before reaching the muzzle. *Field Manual 6–40* had the answer: Use a bigger charge and fire again. It worked!

All through the night of November 2 we poured high-angle variable-time (VT) and impact-fused shells on the attacking 124th Communist Chinese Forces (CCF) Division. At dawn we learned that the road was cut between 1/7 and 2/7, just north of Item Battery, which was in position about 2,000 yards forward of the rest of the battalion. Small arms were periodically raking the battery's position, threatening damage to the precious howitzers. Item Battery was within minimum range for indirect fire and masked from direct-fire targets by the sheer, winding sides of the gorge. The battery was vulnerable and in no position to support the infantry. I had emplaced the battery on this knoll at the entrance to Sudong Gorge to facilitate fire support of the regiment during the anticipated advance that morning. We had not expected that there would be a need to dig in the howitzers, believing that the advance to Sudong would be rapid. Our failure to dig in proved to be a mistake. Heavy fighting developed that night, and some elements of the infantry moved back through the battery position to more favorable lines. Item Battery was now under small-arms fire and unable to service the howitzers in their exposed positions. Captain John McLaurin reported his predicament over the phone. I told him I would be right there. I jeeped up to his position and together we surveyed the situation as bullets whistled overhead. I directed John to withdraw to the rear and squeeze his battery into the battalion position area. Then I repaired to regimental headquarters, on a hillside about a mile to the left rear. I explained the situation to the regimental commander and the action I had taken.

To my consternation, Litz fastened me with a dour look and said, "I want that battery to stay in place. There's to be no hint of retreat in this first meeting of Marines and Chinese!"

"But Colonel," I argued, "our own infantry is moving to the rear through the battery position!"

Without another word, the Old Man spun on his heel and returned to his command tent.

I quickly instructed Captain Steve Pawloski, the 3/11 liaison with headquarters, to run down to the road and halt the battery before it came into view—I would signal him when it was all right for the battery to move out. Determinedly, I sought out the chief in his lair. After some argument Litz begrudgingly succumbed to the logic that it would be irresponsible to allow irreplaceable howitzers to be put out of action at this stage of the campaign.

I stepped out of his tent and signaled Steve. Seconds later the battery came into sight, moving rapidly to the rear. At that moment the colonel's acid words issued forth from the tent opening, "That's a fast battery you have there, Fox!"

Soon after Item Battery had been sandwiched into the crowded battalion position area and added her weight to the cannonade, the shattered Chinese remnants pulled back. 1/7 advanced almost unmolested through Sudong and on into Chinhung-ni. This rapid advance posed knotty support problems for 3/11. The conflicting requirements of moving within the perimeter nightly and providing continuous fire support to rapidly moving infantry by day necessitated aggressive front-line reconnaissance. Positions had to be selected by 2:00 P.M., and they were based on an estimate of where the infantry would halt for the night. By adhering to that schedule, the forward battery (or batteries) could move into position and assume fire-support responsibility, and the rear batteries (or battery) could still make it into the new area by dark. Reconnaissance was frequently hampered by infantry-battalion vehicles, which habitually occupied the middle of the narrow roads. They pulled over to make room for my reconnaissance party to pass only when "asked" individually.

Whether one or two batteries would be displaced in the forward echelon depended on how much firing we were doing—in other words, on how the situation up forward was developing. If only light resistance was being encountered, two batteries were moved forward to allow more time to secure the new position and shoot in defensive fires for the night. If heavy fighting was in progress, it was prudent to retain the greater part of the battalion's firepower in action. In this situation only one battery was displaced forward. Jimmy took the FDC with the two-battery echelon; the odd battery was controlled by its battery fire chart and beefed up by personnel from the FDC—an assistant S-3, a horizontal control operator, and the Marine who computed the fire commands to the battery from the FDC. The FOs and liaison officers with the infantry battalion that comprised the main effort were in radio communication with both forward and rear echelons over their battery fire-direction net. The other FOs and liaison officers were in communication on the battalion fire direction net. With the radios available, this was the best we could do. Besides the FDC personnel, the firing battery designated to go it alone was augmented by communicators and four ammunition trucks from Service Battery. Reds Miller always stayed with the rear battery or batteries.

On one occasion during our leapfrogging advance through the Sudong Gorge, 3/11 occupied a position on a gentle slope extending eastward, just south of Sudong. Due to the exposed nature of this site, 2/7 was ordered to take up positions on the surrounding hills to protect us. This concern for the welfare of the artillery was thoroughly appreciated by the officers and men and inspired us to ensure that we deserved it by our performance. On three occasions in November, infantry companies were directly attached to 3/11 for protection when it was impossible or inadvisable to emplace within the perimeter. Not once on the advance to Yudam-ni were we left to shift for ourselves.

On November 5 we moved into the valley east of Chinhung-ni. Every yard of level ground between the road and the river was given over to the eighteen field pieces. Service Battery was stationed a half mile forward, up against the canyon wall. Often in this mountainous country it proved of tactical advantage to be able to insert only the required headquarters control elements with the firing batteries; Service Battery, with its many trucks, was relegated to some nontactical locale within the regimental perimeter.

Shortly after 6:00 P.M., with dusk settling in, the battalion was still setting up. Counterbattery fire started exploding in the riverbed about 60 yards to our south. The next rounds dropped in closer. Having had no chance to dig in, we all hit the deck.

Apparently, when the Chinese tried to move their fire on top of us, the rounds caught on the ridge to our front (north). The low angle of their shells' trajectory would not permit them to come any closer. A wire line had just been brought in from our liaison officer with 3/7. Jimmy had a phone put on it and called through to the FO with the lead company. He told Lieutenant George G. "Whispering Wilk" Wilkerson that we had some incoming from his direction.

"Oh, is that so?" said Wilk. "How does it feel to get shot at?"

"Stow the bullshit," Jimmy ordered. "Look up there and see if you can see who is shooting at us."

Wilk reported that he could see flashes behind a ridge about 2,000 yards away. Jimmy told him to adjust on the forward slope and then slide the fire for effect over the ridge about 300 yards. It took only one adjusting round. Then we let them have the entire battalion, three volleys. As soon as the volleys hit, Wilk said, "Holy cow, it looks like the Fourth of July up here. We must have hit an ammo dump!" Darkness had fallen, so 3/7 was treated to a real fireworks display. We received no more counterbattery that night. Later, prisoners of war reported that we had put both horse-drawn 122mm howitzer and 76mm batteries out of action and blown up their ammunition.

We did some of our best shooting in this tight position area. The day after the counterbattery, some cannoneers saw flashes on a mountain peak to the west that had a commanding view of our entire RCT perimeter. No patrols were in the vicinity, so we trained one howitzer from How Battery on the target and fired four rounds of VT. Two days later a patrol climbed the peak and found the remains of the CCF observation post—four dead Chinese and some observing instruments. A day later another 3/7 FO, Lieutenant William R. Phillips, fired three missions simultaneously on enemy automatic weapons, mortars, and troops. He reported success on all three. 3/11 had become an effective fire-support machine, with all hands warming to the task.

Of course, we had our troubles as well. Once we had to refuse a fire mission because it was within minimum range. The handicap of trying to cover the 360-degree perimeter inevitably brought delays incident to the shifting of howitzer trails, delays the supported troops deplored. But some advantages also accrued to our cramped place, such as proximity of liaison and observer teams, which meant short wire lines, close liaison, and ready resupply.

The night of November 6, 3/7 staged a planned withdrawal from two key hills after dark. Colonel Litzenberg believed that the Chinese would try to occupy this important terrain, so he ordered me to fire on and behind these hills throughout the night. Later we learned that our heavy concentrations caught the reserve regiment of the 124th CCF Division moving into position, practically annihilating it. The shattered remnants of the division withdrew before dawn.

In the next few days the 7th RCT consolidated its position, dispersed its supporting and supply units to decrease the concentration of forces that invited air attack, and prepared to quit the valley for the Chosin Reservoir plateau. During this time Colonel Litzenberg became concerned with the several canyons that provided covered avenues of approach into the perimeter. He told me that he wanted howitzers placed at the entrances to these canyons and that we should be prepared to fire on any enemy foray from those directions. I tried to conceal my horror. Litz did not take kindly to having his wishes ignored or to being told that his ideas were foolish and would dissipate the battalion's firepower. So I took a calculated risk and planned defensive fires for each canyon, but I kept the eighteen howitzers in position. I was prepared to tell him, if asked, that we could bring fire to bear on any of the canyons "promptly." Fortunately, the issue never came up. It was the only time I know of that Litz's supporting-arms judgment betrayed him.

During this respite Lieutenant General Edward Almond, the commander of the X U.S. Army Corps, of which 1st Marine Division was a part, visited Chinhung-ni to congratulate the 7th RCT on routing the 124th CCF Division, as well as to view our collection of "Chinese volunteer" prisoners. He was startled upon observing 3/11's eighteen dug-in howitzers occupying most of the available level ground, pointing skyward. He remarked to Colonel Litzenberg, "I didn't know that you had antiaircraft artillery up here."

In the six-day Sudong–Chinhung-ni action from November 2 to November 7, 3/11 fired 227 missions and over 7,500 rounds, all but a handful at high angle. We had defeated a 122mm howitzer battery, a 76mm gun battery, and about thirty mortars. We had accounted for about two thousand enemy dead and one thousand wounded. It would be our major offensive action of the campaign.

The Cold Plateau

On November 9, 3/7 advanced to the top of Funchilin Pass, and we prepared to follow suit the next day. The 155mm howitzers of K/4/11

were again attached to 3/11 to give added range and flexibility to
our fire support. Item and King batteries, whose fires were controlled by Item Battery's battery firing chart, were positioned to the
northwest of Chinhung-ni to support the attack to Koto-ri. Most of
the battalion hit the road in trace of 1/7 and by 10 A.M. was in
position just beyond the top of the pass. Item Battery rejoined the
battalion well before dark, as did 1st Lieutenant Howard H.
Harris's H/3/7, which was attached for local security.

Next morning at the regimental CP, Major Henry J. Woessner,
the regimental S-3, showed me the day's operations order; it directed 3/11 to displace Item Battery to our new position. I told Hank
that Item Battery had been up with us since the previous afternoon
and suggested that the regiment would receive the most effective
fire support if I retained a free hand in moving my batteries. Subsequently, regimental operations orders directed only that "3/11 support the attack," no matter to what degree infantry maneuvers were
spelled out. This freedom of movement in rapidly developing situations, and with doubtful communications is essential if the infantry
is to receive the best in fire support.

Major Woessner—stocky, cool-eyed, and unflappable—had been
Litz's S-3 for only a few weeks. In the early days of the Inchon–
Seoul operation, Colonel Litzenberg, who was demanding and sometimes even abusive, had clashed with his previous operations officer.
Lieutenant Colonel Frederick R. Dowsett, the regimental executive,
had suggested that Major Woessner from his old Mediterranean battalion (3/7) would be a suitable replacement. Hank's temperament
was ideally adapted to dealing with the brusque, driving colonel. If
he were ever disturbed by Litz's fulminations, he did not reveal it
publicly. This in itself was interesting because Hank, now the very
essence of imperturbability and cool logic, had been a heller in his
youth. Hank was a Naval Academy classmate of Callender's, who
told us Hank's nickname had been Boozer. In their brief stint at
Quantico after graduation, in January 1943, Hank had hit the big
city seventeen nights running, a performance considered by his
peers as some kind of record. During World War II Hank had served
with the 8th Defense Battalion at Samoa and Wallis Island and
later aboard the USS *Baltimore* off the Philippines, Iwo Jima, and
Okinawa. After the war he had eschewed his former ways and nickname, gotten married, and tread the straight and narrow. (Academy
nicknames, particularly the more unsavory ones, often dog recipi-
ents throughout their careers. Jimmy, Hank, and I had all managed

to prevent ours from surfacing in the Marine Corps. Jimmy's was Moe, as in The Three Stooges. Mine was Stinkfoot, because of an unfortunate, odiferous fungus that during its brief lifetime had caused consternation among the hospital corpsmen who taped our ankles for football practice.) As the situation became more grim in the weeks to come, Hank's steadying influence in the regimental CP would be increasingly noticeable and appreciated.

For two days 3/11 formed a second smaller perimeter to the south of the 7th RCT lines at Koto-ri. This permitted firing to the flanks as well as the front of the regiment without shifting trails. This highly desirable condition had not been possible when crammed into the rear of a 3,000- to 5,000-yard oblong perimeter. One interesting fire mission developed when 1/7 made contact with a delaying force about a mile northwest of Koto-ri. A Marine fighter pilot adjusted our fire through the forward air controller and our liaison officer and we killed forty or fifty Chinese—a striking example of the value of having our own close air support.

On November 12th the regiment's lines were extended to the north of Koto-ri in anticipation of a rapid advance on Hagaru-ri. H/3/7 was detached and 3/11 moved 2,000 yards into the southern end of the perimeter. FOs who remained in position found it hard to understand the need for refiring night defensive concentrations from our new position. This was a typical example of the problems caused by short displacement, which was dictated by the requirement to relocate within the protected circumference.

On the night of November 12, the first icy blasts of winter swirled down from Manchuria. The temperature dipped to -25 degrees, and the wind-chill factor was indescribable. During the interludes of cold weather that followed, the effectiveness of our fire support decreased. The combat effectiveness of the individual Marine, who had to devote an increasing portion of his energies to personal survival, also plummeted. To combat this penetrating chill, each firing battery was allowed about ten tents to serve as havens where gunners could warm their hands from the burn of icy metal. An extra tent and stove added no appreciable weight to the truck's load, but the need to deploy and use the warming tents and the fact that the men were bundled in parkas, shoe-pacs, and mittens greatly decreased mobility. In addition, digging in trails—even with axes—became a heroic task. Shifting them after they had frozen in was almost impossible. These conditions called for an adjustment in time-and-space computations. Instead of being able to displace the advance echelon as late as 2:00 P.M., I had to give the order by noon if the rear echelon was to be in position by dark. To meet this condition, I had to reconnoiter aggressively, often with the infantry point and, on occasion, in front of it.

Equipment as well as men behaved differently in the cold. Howitzers crept back into battery, taking two or three minutes instead of seconds. This significantly retarded the firing. By virtue of having turned over the engines of our vehicles every hour that night, we were able to move out toward Hagaru-ri the next morning without delay, although our bulldozers were temporarily immobilized by the fact that the water in the diesel oil froze. We leapfrogged How Battery, which had gone forward on November 13. How Battery joined us after dark in our new position halfway between Koto-ri and Hagaru-ri. That night we lost wire communications with King Battery in Chinhung-ni.

This computer line, some 18 miles long, was remarkable in that it had worked at all over this distance. This line had been of marginal value after our perimeter had moved beyond 155mm-howitzer range, and no special effort had been expended to keep it open. King Battery continued to fire harassing missions to our flanks and rear. The 155 battery was still attached to 3/11, but Division had not granted permission for the big howitzers to attempt negotiation of the narrow, winding road. For the time being, then, we lost contact with our fourth battery.

Having attained our objective with the occupation of Hagaru-ri, the village by the southern extremity of the Chosin Reservoir, the 7th RCT pulled up. While the 5th Marines passed through on its way up the eastern shore of the reservoir, the 7th spread out to protect the main supply route (MSR). 1/7 and 2/7 deployed around the town, while 3/7 took station at Koto-ri. At this time 3/11 was assigned defensive responsibility for a segment of the perimeter to the south. Captain Walt Phillips' E/2/7 was attached to us and took up defensive positions to our south and west.

For the next few days we had a spell of Indian summer, which we put to good use. 3/11 bulldozers started to level an airstrip for use by the light observation planes; this was later converted into the crucial Hagaru-ri Airstrip. How Battery was relocated about 1,500 yards north of the battalion area, just northeast of the bridge into Hagaru-ri. How Battery's position permitted us to fire up the broad valley to the southwest, a logical avenue of enemy approach. Our two operative bulldozers turned to on How Battery's new position. By the time the freeze revisited us for good, only the muzzles of the six howitzers could be seen above the piled dirt.

During this interlude Lieutenant Colonel Fred Dowsett—the conscientious, level-headed executive officer of the 7th Marines, who was not given to idle flattery—told me that he had been impressed by 3/11's shooting under a variety of conditions. He referred to our work in all kinds of weather with high-angle fire, low-angle fire, and direct fire. He said, "I can't recall a battalion during World War II that had fired over 10,000 rounds without a single shell falling within our own lines."

Fred was not technically correct about our fire. A few days earlier about halfway between Koto-ri and Hagaru-ri, we had fired upon one of our own patrols at the insistence of an infantry battalion commander, who was convinced that the patrol was Chinese. After checking with the liaison officer and FOs, Jimmy was equally convinced that the patrol was our own. Upon the infantry's demand that we fire, he asked me to intervene. I talked on the radio to the battalion commander, citing our near-conviction that the patrol was friendly, but he was adamant. With the assurance that he took full responsibility, I reluctantly gave the order to fire. Several casualties resulted.

Fred Dowsett was right about 3/11's expertise, though. It does not matter how well managed the positioning of batteries, how alert the FOs, and how intimate the liaison with the infantry; if the battalion cannot shoot, all else is for naught. 3/11 could shoot. And we did not have to search long for the reason why—or, rather, the four reasons why. Major Jimmy Callender, trained at the Naval Academy and Fort Sill, was as knowledgeable and precise a gunnery officer as ever managed an FDC. The three firing battery executives—1st Lieutenants Willis L. "Willie" Gore, Wilber N. "Red" Herndon, and Marshall "Soup" Campbell—were unsurpassed as the fire controllers of the three six-howitzer batteries.

Two other matters also bear mention. Item Battery fed E/2/7 hot chow throughout the four days of its attachment, an effort that was enthusiastically received. We had done it before, but hot meals for attached infantry units now became routine whenever practicable. For its part the 7th Marines never wrested a truck from our control throughout the twenty-one-day period of operations from Hamhung to Hagaru-ri but kept us well supplied with ammunition at all times. During the respite at Hagaru-ri, however, with the bulk of the 1st Motor Transport Battalion detached from the 7th's control, two of our trucks were requisitioned daily for the supply run to Hamhung. This was certainly a reasonable request at the time, but when the move to Yudam-ni materialized suddenly, we were four trucks short (about 800 rounds of 105mm ammunition).

The cold now tightened her icy grip upon us, and winter came to stay. On November 22, Item Battery was attached to 1/7 and displaced to a frozen mountainside just below Toktong Pass, halfway between Hagaru-ri and Yudam-ni. On the night of November 23, 1/7, whose mission was to establish a blocking position between these bleak places, reported that Item Battery's defensive fires had kept two thousand Chinese from counterattacking.

The afternoon of November 23, the 7th Marines were on the move again, going westward to join 1/7. Elements of 2/7 and How Battery were required to hold Hagaru-ri until relieved. Most of 3/11 displaced to an icy patch of level ground over the top of the pass from Item Battery, which had been returned to our control. Inasmuch as the rest of the regiment was about 2 miles beyond us and there was with no conceivable position for more than two howitzers anywhere between us, Captain Milt Hull's D/2/7 was attached for our protection.

The 7th Marines moved on into the Yudam-ni area on November 26, seizing the high ground to the north and west, while 3/11 went into firing positions a few hundred yards west of the western arm of the solidly frozen Chosin Reservoir. The regimental CP set up in an abandoned handful of huts—Yudam-ni—about 300 yards to our northwest. Here we waited for the 5th Marines and two battalions of the 11th Marines to join us. Ominous reports of increasing enemy presence in the hills to the north, west, and south proliferated. When two thirds of the combat strength of 1st Marine Division had massed, the Chinese closed the trap.

The Yudam-ni Trap

Our situation on November 27 was not good. How Battery was at Hagaru-ri unable to rejoin us. The fifteen trucks sent back for ammunition—all that were available except for what we needed to move the howitzers—were cut off at Hagaru-ri and had joined How Battery. We had a little over 3,000 rounds. With no radio contact with either How Battery or the 11th Marines CP, we had no knowledge of the status of supply of 105mm ammunition at beleaguered Hagaru-ri. With the mission of protecting the MSR from Yudam-ni to Hagaru-ri, the 7th Marines was spread around most of the perimeter. The 5th Marines, prepared to strike westward, was astride the road and massed to the west of Yudam-ni.

1/11 and 3/11 were deployed to support the infantry regiments to which they were attached. 1/11 ranged behind the 5th Marines and faced west-northwest. 3/11 favored what was then considered to be the directions of greatest danger for the 7th RCT—west-southwest and south-southwest. This left D/2/7 and E/2/7, which manned two key hills to the north only about 2,000 yards from our position without artillery support.

As increasing enemy pressure strongly implied that the 5th Marines' projected westward drive would not materialize, a more adequate manning of the defensive arc became crucial. The 7th Marines was stretched thinly around more than two thirds of the perimeter—occupying high ground to the south, southwest, west, and north—and would have posed a serious support problem for 3/11 in any case. But with one third of our firepower committed elsewhere (How Battery at Hagaru-ri), an adequate solution was beyond our means. With a view to improving this situation, I suggested to Colonel Litzenberg the formation of an artillery groupment of 1/11, most of 3/11, and 4/11. He agreed and, after a brief discussion with Lieutenant Colonel Ray Murray, commander of the 5th Marines, the decision was made to pool the artillery for defense of the perimeter.

Lieutenant Colonel Harvey Feehan, a Fort Sill classmate, was designated as the artillery-groupment commander. We agreed on the direction of fire of the five 105mm batteries—1/11 to the west, northwest, and north and 3/11 to the southwest and south. Major Bill McReynolds's three 155mm howitzer batteries were similarly sited to cover the perimeter. The weakest link in this realignment was the coverage of the two hills to our immediate north, 1282 and 1240, which were occupied by E/2/7 and D/2/7, respectively. I suggested to Harvey that he relocate one battery to the south of the bridge over the stream that fed into the western tip of the reservoir—from there it could support Dog and Easy companies with close-in low-angle fire. High-angle fire was now impractical because recoil pits could not be hewn out of the frozen ground, even if the battery had been proficient at this type of fire, which it was not. In the stress of the moment the battery was never moved.

The artillery groupment nominally controlled our fire for the next three days. Inasmuch as 1/11 batteries were ranged behind elements of 3/7 to the west and Dog and Easy companies—which were under the operational control of 1/7—to the north, our FOs called down the fire and our FDC controlled it. This was a poor arrangement at best but an improvement on our original artillery posture. Many of the difficulties and delays that rendered this system so frustrating were incident to our overall predicament rather than the fault of the artillery groupment. The constricted perimeter forbade really close-in fire support to the north because of minimum range restrictions from the firing position. At other points of the compass, however, this was not a factor. Also, enemy attacks from several quarters simultaneously precluded, for the most part, the massing of two batteries. Overall artillery firing hung the darkening shadow of shrinking ammunition stocks, with no adequate resupply.

On the night of November 27, the Chinese hurled their massed might at the encircled Marines. Striking from the west, northwest, and north, they strained but never broke the thinning ranks of infantry that clung to the bare, foreign hills. Throughout the long, cold night, the artillery spoke and spoke again but not with the authority of days past. Ammunition, life's blood of the field artillery, was in desperately short supply. With plenty of ammunition, artillery—the so-called King of Battle—can overwhelm the relatively defenseless attacker as he masses to strike. He can stop the enemy dead in his tracks before the very eyes of the thankful infantry that waits in relative safety within their holes. But at Yudam-ni many a hero perished because we could not slaughter the Chinese massed to assault our embattled companies. It was heart wrenching to answer our FOs pleas for more fire with a pitifully inadequate "two guns, four rounds, fire for effect." And, although the artillery did its best, it was the rifleman who won at Yudam-ni on the strength of his own courage and stamina. He had less help than he had the right to expect from his anemic fire support.

This bloody night set the tenor of artillery support for the remaining days at Yudam-ni and on the road back to Hagaru-ri. Frustration and determination best epitomize 3/11's actions—frustration at being unable to give the infantry necessary support and determination to make every round count in enemy dead.

Our surgeon, Bob Shoemaker, was a youngster of twenty-five who had not even completed his internship. He and Reds Miller, our compassionate, peripatetic executive, had befriended one another. Each was somewhat new at his job, and they gave each other sup-

port. For his part, Reds had endeavored to instill in the young doctor the confidence to perform in the field when the occasion arose.
Shoemaker had said, "They didn't tell me about battle wounds at
medical school."

The occasion arrived the night of November 27, and the apple-
cheeked surgeon rose to the challenge. Blood-spattered and exhausted, he grew inches in stature that night as the men of 3/11 led
or carried into the tent that was our sick bay many of Dog and Easy
company's wounded. These men had stopped the Chinese from pouring down into our position—but just barely. During the morning of
November 27, over seventy casualties, mostly from D/2/7, were in
3/11's sick bay.

Captain Milt Hill, Dog Company's bull-like commander, was
one of the casualties, with head wounds and a bullet hole clear
through his upper arm. Wounded as he was, Milt had led a counterattack to retake the hill behind us.

On November 28 the three battalions of the 11th Marines were
pared 25 percent in strength to provide replacements to help fill the
depleted ranks of the 5th and 7th Marines. At the same time 3/11
was assigned a small arc of the northern defense sector—an arc
extending from Dog Company to the western arm of the reservoir.

Several airdrops of 105mm ammunition were made by Air Force
C-119s during this period. Shells packaged in wooden boxes were,
for the most part, undamaged; those in steel or cardboard containers were often too crushed or bent to be serviceable. Of some fifteen
hundred rounds dropped, a little over half could be fired. For thirty
howitzers in action, that amount meant only a few minutes of cannonade. But we were glad to have every round. No 155mm ammunition was included in the drops because we decided that more benefit
would be derived from the same payload of 105mm projectiles.

When word came on November 30 that we were to fight our way
back to Hagaru-ri, the artillery groupment was dissolved. 3/11 supported the 7th Marines as it pushed down the deep valley to the
south. 1/11 covered the rear-guard action of the 5th Marines to the
north and west. 4/11, having exhausted its ammunition, had been
formed into infantry platoons for protection of the wounded and
further augmentation of the infantry regiments. Only a skeleton
force remained to take out its guns.

This critical juncture would appear to be an odd time to inten-
tionally switch battery commanders, and I agonized over the decision. Back in the balmier Indian summer at Hagaru-ri in mid
November when we had been naive enough to believe that the war

would soon be over, I had promised some of my staff battery commands at the end of the month. In no way did this reflect on the firing-battery commanders, who were all performing superbly. It was more of a share-the-wealth scheme designed to give each of my trove of talented captains an opportunity at both command and staff assignments in combat. Further, it was not as chancy a matter as it might appear. All our captains were thoroughly indoctrinated in 3/11 command philosophy, and the three battery executives were superior officers who were fully capable of running the batteries by themselves. I rationalized that failure to make the promised switch would not only break my word but also imply a lack of confidence in the prospective battery commanders. So on December 1 in the throes of our Yudam-ni agony, Captains Ernie Payne and Bob Patterson took over George and Item batteries from Sam Hannah and John McLaurin. The 7th Marines, whose bloody occupation inured them to frequent battalion and company command changes, scarcely noticed the difference.

During the next few critical days, the command relations of the Yudam-ni force were left unclarified, and the reason why has always remained a mystery to me. None of the latter-day explanations seems very convincing. If Brigadier General Eddie Craig, assistant division commander, had been at Hagaru-ri rather than home on emergency leave, it is safe to assume that he would have helicoptered in to take command. The division commander, Major General O. P. Smith, could have flown over and assumed direct command. But Smith was not a flamboyant leader, and there were ample justifications, in any case, for his presence at Hagaru-ri, which was located in the center of the division's area of responsibility and from which he was better able to communicate with his three regimental combat teams, his support base in the Hamhung–Hungnam area, and higher headquarters. That Smith was reluctant to send a senior colonel to take command when one of his most senior colonels—Litzenberg—was already there is understandable. Why then was Litzenberg not given overall command of the 5th and 7th Marines and their three artillery battalions? The question became especially significant in the last days of November, when it was clear that the 5th RCT was not going to attempt to push west. From that point the salvation of the 5th and 7th RCTs depended upon their staying together as a unit and acting jointly.

Colonel Litzenberg was controversial. Some regarded him as a bully. Although he was not universally admired, he was respected for his ability as an infantry leader. He demanded performance, to which his reputation as a "lieutenant-colonel breaker" attested. (Around Pohang in January and February 1951 some newly arrived lieutenant colonels assigned as battalion commanders were summarily relieved because they did not measure up to Litz's standards. To those who did, he was strongly loyal.) Litz was a skilled tactician who understood the value of supporting arms better than most infantry commanders. He had conducted a masterful campaign in leading 1st Marine Division to Yudam-ni. To me, it is indefensible that he was denied command of the breakout forces for the push to Hagaru-ri.

Using their own initiative, the 5th and 7th Marines did act jointly with Colonel Litzenberg taking the lead, as befitted his seniority. Joint action, however, is not the same as unified command. Two victims of this ambiguity were 1/11 and 4/11, which were ambushed a few miles out of Hagaru-ri. The ambush resulted in the loss of several howitzers. The battalions of the 5th Marines, individually exercising their own initiative, came to the rescue. With air support they reduced the Chinese strongpoint that had tormented them. Nonetheless, it is debatable that this situation would have developed in the first place if an overall commander had been on the spot. By the time 3/11 reached this battleground, it was strewn with abandoned trucks and howitzers.

The Road Back

Often during December 1 through December 4, we could not fire in support of our troops as they pushed down the rugged hills that rose abruptly from either side of the narrow valley floor. Our troops were within minimum range. Several times our gunners took groups of Chinese under direct fire 1,000 to 3,000 yards from us on the steep slopes. Often as not, however, our Marines were so intimately mingled with the enemy that we could not fire safely.

Before quitting the valley just south of Yudam-ni for good, word came to destroy all equipment that could not be carried in one load of vehicles. Fifteen trucks had been sent to Hagaru-ri on November 26, leaving only their trailers. These trailers and much gear were burned or otherwise mutilated by 3/11 to meet the condition. Ben Read's trailer, which he had left with us expecting to reclaim it when he returned with How Battery the next day, was another victim but only after we had salvaged two bottles of brandy and a wristwatch. There were many wounded who had to ride on the already heavily taxed transport of the fighting force of the 5th and 7th Marines.

As the North Korean winter fastened its icy grip tighter about the throats of the weary combatants, the Marines clawed their way down the ridges to where the narrow road left the valley floor and wound up the side of the mountain to Toktong Pass. It was to be a decisive forty-eight hours, and the Yudam-ni Marines had chosen two of their most trusted, illustrious warriors to lead the way. Lieutenant Colonel Bob Taplett, with his 3rd Battalion, 5th Marines, was to lead the main body up the tortuous road and Lieutenant Colonel Ray Davis, with his 1st Battalion, 7th Marines, was to strike across country behind the Chinese to relieve F/2/7 and secure the top of the pass toward which the main body was slugging its way.

Since our two headquarters were confined to the valley floor near its narrow road, I was able to confer with Litz frequently and exchange information on the developing situation. After dark I had walked across the road and about 30 yards up the side of the hill to his small command tent. By happenstance, I joined Colonels Litzenberg and Davis in the command tent only minutes before Ray took off on his epic trek. Inside Litz and Ray were huddled together discussing Ray's imminent march. Litz motioned me to join them.

My principal recollection of this meeting is of Ray's cool determination and his matter-of-factness. Surely he understood the importance of his crucial mission. Upon his success rested the fate of the 5th and 7th RCTs. If this force bogged down or did not come through to Hagaru-ri as intact fighting units, the fate of the remainder of 1st Marine Division was in extreme doubt. The chances of mishap were everywhere. His map was primitive. Maintaining his companies in close contact and headed toward their objective through snow and ice, darkness, and treacherous mountain slopes would require a heroic effort. He could count on little artillery help if he got in trouble. He was on his own, and not the least test of his leadership would be keeping his exhausted Marines moving forward—steadily, inexorably forward—until they reached Fox Company. But, for all this, Ray was as self-possessed as if he were about to set out on an evening stroll.

The rugged old warrior beside him was also taking a monumental gamble. Litz had augmented Ray's battalion as much as he dared—it was his strongest battalion with his most experienced, most dynamic leader. He was sending it off into the frigid gloom away from the main body, thus splitting the undermanned, tired force already heavily burdened with wounded. It was a dramatic ploy fraught with danger. The stakes were enormous.

Neither man raised his voice nor did a hint of passion insinuate itself into the tiny command tent. They were just two men going about their business. I remember feeling that it was a privilege to be there. With an everyday farewell and a shyly confident smile, Ray got up and headed quietly down the hill to his destiny. Moments later, I left the Old Man to contemplate the loneliness of command.

During the cold death struggle between Marine and Chinese riflemen, artillery played only a minor role. We were almost out of ammunition. Our radios were growing weaker daily from cold and unavoidable misuse. Our men were either in the ranks of the infantry or forced to defend themselves almost continuously. Obviously, we could not perform our close-support mission with anything like normal effectiveness. Further handicaps were the need to move with the column and the almost total lack of howitzer positions. Into this breach stepped the fired-up Marine airmen who flew to our aid time and time again under the most horrendous conditions.

A few isolated skirmishes on the road from Yudam-ni to Sinhung-ni best illustrate 3/11's role. On December 1, as the 5th Marines withdrew from the hills north of Yudam-ni to those dominating the valley to the south, many Chinese streamed over a saddle just above our vacated position area. They appeared to be in pursuit, although later it developed that they were in search of rations. Item Battery reemplaced one piece to fire north and blasted away with direct fire at 2,500 yards. The results were spectacular. On December 2, George Battery came under heavy mortar, machine-gun, and small-arms fire at close range from high ground to the west. Groups of Chinese were taken under direct fire, and several machine guns were silenced. Later, after displacing southward about a mile, George Battery came alongside the regimental motor column, which included many trucks laden with wounded. The column was under machine-gun fire from the cliffs to the west. The hostile gun was immediately taken under fire by George Battery's number 6 gun at about 1,500 yards. It was destroyed by a direct hit on the fourth round.

It was during this period that Colonel Litzenberg confided to me with some emotion that 3/11 would be the last artillery battalion to be converted to infantry. As it happened, 1/11 and 3/11, although depleted by casualties and drafts to strengthen the infantry, continued as field artillery units, but it was heart-warming nonetheless to receive this vote of confidence from the boss.

While George and Item batteries continued to take enemy troops and weapons under fire whenever they could be clearly identified, hip shooting of this sort required special care. For example, a piece from Item Battery unlimbered and fired a round at a suspected enemy patrol from a firing position on the road halfway up the mountainside to Sinhung-ni. I gave immediate orders to refrain from such promiscuous shooting. As it turned out, it was a 5th Marines patrol; fortunately, no casualties resulted.

On the morning of December 2, Colonel Litzenberg ordered 3/11 to take station in the column right behind Bob Taplett's 3/5. The mission was to take up position at Sinhung-ni as soon as possible and to assume support of the rear guard from 1/11. George Battery was left in position at the foot of the mountain road to provide support to either 1/7 or 3/7, as called for. Headquarters, Service, and Item batteries fell in line behind 3/5. 3/5 was at the point of exhaustion after a week of steady fighting and moving. A heavy snow fell at midnight, further retarding 3/5's efforts to attain the top of the pass. Not until 3:30 P.M., December 3, after taking a day and a half to negotiate about 6,000 yards, did Item Battery go into position on the small ice-covered clearing at Sinhung-ni.

As Item Battery was trying to snake her howitzers into position over the slippery footing, one of the men of the FDC spotted some Chinese emplacing a small field piece (probably a 76mm gun) about 2,000 yards away. We managed to raise How Battery on the radio, and Jimmy Callender stood in the doorway of the Korean hut in which we were setting up the FDC and called in a fire mission. The target proved to be just within How Battery's range. Jimmy adjusted on a point about 400 yards away from the gun, then moved to the target calling, "Fire for effect!" They never knew what hit them; the gun and about six Chinese flew in all directions in small pieces. Red Herndon came up on the radio after cease fire to verify that the battalion operations officer had really fired the mission. How often does an S-3 conduct a fire mission? Then again, how often is the FDC over 10,000 yards in front of the firing battery?

Despite this bit of sharpshooting, we were still receiving intermittent small-arms fire in the battery position. To permit the crews to service their pieces, we pulled a prime mover, a 2½-ton 6 by 6 truck, alongside each howitzer. Between the howitzer and the direction of fire from the southwest, each truck acted like a shield. George Battery rejoined us at about 8:00 P.M., going into position about 200 yards east of Item Battery. Minutes later, word was received from Colonel Litzenberg to join the column just ahead of either 1/11 or 4/11. As these units had passed by some time before, this order could not be executed. With 3/11 now the only artillery in position to support the infantry battalions still to our rear, I decided to remain there until the rear guard, 3/7, came within range of How Battery.

At about 11:30 P.M., we learned that 3/7 had broken contact with the Chinese and was approaching our position. With some difficulty, we extracted ourselves from icy Sinhung-ni and joined the column between 2/5 and 3/7 at midnight.

Ben, Red, and the Men of How Battery

Fate picks her executors with care. And so she did on the afternoon of November 26, when she allowed Captain Ben Read, my How Battery commander, to cross over Toktong Pass and return safely to Hagaru-ri. Ben had come to Yudam-ni to familiarize himself with the situation and see the position area that I had selected for his occupation, which we assumed would take place the next day. Another of 3/11's sometime battery commanders, 1st Lieutenant Robert K. Messman of K/4/11 (attached to 3/11 from November 8 until November 22), met Ben on the road, but he was not so favored. Bob waited for some missing supply trucks and was captured, as his smashed jeep and rifled dispatch case bore mute testimony. Ben, his driver, and two passengers from 3/11 were the last to make the trip from Yudam-ni to Hagaru-ri unmolested. That Ben Read was spared was fortunate for 1st Marine Division—his contribution to the Marines' successful withdrawal from the Chosin plateau was, in my opinion, exceeded by few in two weeks of a rich harvest of heroes.

That How Battery had been detained at Hagaru-ri in the first place was interesting, if not unusual. Colonel Litzenberg had assigned 2/7 the mission of holding Hagaru-ri until the 1st Marines could bring up a battalion for its defense. He had then taken Dog and Easy companies with him to Yudam-ni and ordered Fox Company to occupy and defend the crucial terrain dominating Toktong Pass, the high ground about halfway between Hagaru-ri and Yudam-ni. This left 2/7 at Hagaru-ri without its three rifle companies. Perhaps Litz felt uncomfortable about leaving Hagaru-ri so short of defenders. In any event, he hesitated in giving me authority to bring How Battery to Yudam-ni, although he reassured me that he would probably give permission the next day.

So it was that How Battery was stranded at Hagaru-ri—the only rifle company or firing battery of the 7th RCT to be so detained. Could the colonel have had some divine insight that Fox Company would desperately need artillery support, which only How Battery could provide? Could he have guessed that How Battery's deeply dug-in guns north-northeast of the bridge into Hagaru-ri would prove critical to the defense of that place? The fate of many is often hinged on such a decision, which is viewed at the time as relatively inconsequential.

A born leader, Ben was loved and respected by his men and valued by his commanders. His executive officer, 1st Lieutenant Red Herndon, a few years older than Ben, was a wiry redhead from Tennessee who had won a Silver Star as an enlisted man on Iwo Jima. A matchless pair, all their know-how, courage, and leadership would be needed during the two weeks that they and their men held the fort at the southern tip of the Chosin Reservoir.

On November 26, How Battery furnished trucks to transport F/2/7 to Toktong Pass. At the same time 3/11 dispatched fifteen trucks to Hagaru-ri for ammunition. These seemingly unrelated actions significantly influenced How Battery's future conduct. For when the battery prepared to displace to Yudam-ni on November 27, along with our loaded ammunition trucks, Division ordered Ben to stay in position. Fox Company had come under heavy attack, and the road to Yudam-ni was now cut in several places by Chinese blocking positions. As a result, How Battery now had more ammunition than George and Item batteries combined, and the thirty-eight ammunition handlers and truck drivers doubled the number of riflemen, machine gunners, and bazookamen who protected the battery.

Although How Battery would have undoubtedly given a good account of itself under any conditions, the relatively healthy supply of ammunition and the extra thirty-eight men for perimeter defense measurably aided her posture. When Colonel Jim Brower, the 11th Marines CO, left it up to Ben to decide whether to move the battery inside the Hagaru-ri defense perimeter or remain in his exposed position, Ben did not hesitate. He had Fox Company's surrounded redoubt zeroed in, and any move would have necessitated the re-firing of all the vital defense fires from the new location. Communications with Fox Company had become tenuous. Fire commands had to be relayed from the FO, 1st Lieutenant Don Campbell, through Fox Company's radio to How Battery's liaison officer at 2/7 headquarters in Hagaru-ri, whence they were forwarded by wire to the battery. Any move would have jeopardized Fox Company's defense, if not her existence. 3/11 lived by the creed that the artillery's sole reason for existence was to support the infantry, and none followed this more faithfully than Ben Read. Perhaps it was fortunate that Fox Company was under heavy attack at the time for there was no pressure from 11th Marines or Division to tighten up the defensive perimeter. With its howitzers dug in so that only the muzzles were visible, How Battery was ideally sited to perform manifold missions of which support of Fox Company was the foremost.

How Battery also had to defend a segment of Lieutenant Colonel Gus Banks's 1st Service Battalion perimeter and to assist in the defense of East Hill, just beyond. On East Hill Captain Carl Sitter's G/3/1 clung to the dominant height commanding the Hagaru-ri bridge. In her spare time How Battery reinforced the fires of D/2/11 in keeping the vital Hagaru-ri Airstrip operational. Failure to successfully perform any of these important missions could have seriously disrupted plans for the defense of Hagaru-ri and withdrawal from the plateau. Firing both direct and indirect fire, often simultaneously, How Battery laid and relaid her six guns to the west, southwest, east, and northeast. The battery responded to emergencies with precision, spirit, and deadly effect.

How Battery mauled the nearby hills to her northeast, east, and southeast with direct fire day and night from November 28 to December 2. The battery accounted for at least one thousand Chinese dead with never more than three of her guns—the other three howitzers were needed for almost continuous support of Fox Company and occasional reinforcement of D/2/11.

There can be no more eloquent tribute to the vital nature of How Battery's fire than that of Colonel—then Captain—William E. Barber, the commander of F/2/7. (Barber won the Medal of Honor for his part in the company's heroic defense of Toktong Pass against two Chinese regiments from November 26 to December 3, 1950.) At the reunion of the Chosin Few in San Diego in December 1985, Bill said to Jimmy Callender, "I would not be here today if it had not been for Don Campbell and How Battery!"

On December 1, How Battery's exposed position was the closest to the reservoir, to the road, and to the railroad skirting the reservoir to the east. This position enabled her to assist in the rescue of U.S. Army troops withdrawing from the east shore of the reservoir. How Battery fired in their support, organized rescue parties to bring in survivors, and provided food, first aid, shelter, and transport. It was a busy week for How Battery, and it was called upon for all the firing virtuosity the men could muster, along with courage, perseverance, and good old Marine esprit de corps.

Field Artillery Epic

Upon arrival in Hagaru-ri just ahead of the 3/7 rear guard, I reported to Lieutenant Colonel Carl Youngdale, the new 11th Marines CO. (Colonel Jim Brower had been flown out a few days earlier due to sickness.) The colonel indicated an area in which he wished me to bivouac my battalion. My memory must have been affected by fatigue. (Except for catnaps in the jeep, none of us had slept since leaving the valley floor two days earlier, and we had slept very little since November 27, when the Chinese had launched their offensive.) Upon return to the battalion I was unable to remember the location. Major Reds Miller said, "Boss, for God's sake take a nap. I'll find out where to go." He did, while I fell into much needed sleep.

The next day Lieutenant Colonel Youngdale told me that he would like to reapportion the 105mm howitzers between 1/11 and 3/11 in order to even up our firepower. I objected and suggested that 1/11 go back and retrieve her guns from the valley a few miles north of Hagaru-ri. A rescue effort was attempted, but it bore no fruit. In any event, we were allowed to retain all of our eighteen howitzers— How Battery having returned to 3/11 control.

Hot food, warmth, and rest went a long way toward restoring the troops' strength. Little of a restorative nature could be done for our badly spent radios, however, by which all indirect fire was of necessity conducted from Yudam-ni to Koto-ri. Welcome as this day and a half of rest was, the division, now largely reassembled, had little inclination to prolong her mission on this inhospitable plateau. So on December 6, 1st Marine Division, with the 7th Marines in the vanguard, struck southward toward Koto-ri.

To support the attack, 3/11, now resupplied with ammunition, was formed into three self-contained firing units—that is, three firing batteries augmented by fire direction, communications, and ammunition personnel. This appeared to be the most logical tactical plan for supporting the advance because there would be no opportunity to execute normal displacements along the narrow vehicle-glutted road from Hagaru-ri to Koto-ri. How Battery remained in position to support the attack, while the rest of the battalion fell into the column behind 3/7.

The advance moved slowly and, by nightfall, we were only about 3,000 yards south of Hagaru-ri. Inasmuch as How Battery's position was under heavy pressure from the Chinese and rapidly becoming untenable, I ordered George Battery off the road at 6:00 P.M. When George Battery was in position and ready to take over fire support of the 7th Marines, How Battery was ordered by radio to pull into the column as best it could. My intention was that How Battery remain in this position in the division column until reaching Koto-ri, where it would rejoin the battalion. George Battery would follow suit after Item Battery had gone into firing position within range of Koto-ri.

About 1,500 yards south of George Battery's position, the creeping column halted for an unhealthy length of time. Upon investigation in the now near-total darkness, Reds Miller and I learned that machine-gun fire had persuaded several jeep drivers of 3/7 to disembark and seek cover in the ditch alongside the road. Fortunately, there was a tank standing idly by about 50 yards off the road to the west, and the tankers were motivated after some effort to fire in the direction from which the Chinese machine-gun fire had presumably emanated. Then, fueled by a little profanity, the column started up again.

3/11 (minus George and How batteries) ran by this Chinese machine gun and perhaps another. After we had gotten clear, I mentioned to Reds, who was in the rear seat of my jeep, that we had had a close shave. Matter-of-factly he responded, "Yes, Boss, I'd say so." He held up his right hand, which had been holding onto the bar above my head. There was a clean hole through the flesh between his thumb and forefinger. Headquarters, Service, and Item batteries plus a battery of 4/11 ran the gauntlet with only minor casualties. The division trains failed to follow, however, and a menacing situation soon developed.

Taking advantage of the break in the column, the Chinese reinforced their machine guns with infantry and mortars until they had developed a formidable roadblock. The Chinese used mortars to set several vehicles at the head of the stalled column afire, and these became a major obstacle to further advance.

In the meantime, How Battery had joined the column at about 7:00 P.M., and had advanced slowly about 1,000 yards south of Hagaru-ri. At that point How Battery came under small-arms and mortar attack. With the assistance of some tanks, the battery fought off this attack but was halted again after another 1,000-yard advance. Movement was so slow that Ben Read sent Red Herndon and Sergeant Herbert E. Blizard out on foot to lead a tank to the roadblock, where they hoped it could help get the column under way again. It was slow going in the gray-black night. The men maneuvered the tank around and through the stalled vehicles, across fields, and through ravines. By the time they arrived at George Battery, Major Callender, who had remained with the attached FDC increment, and Captain Ernie Payne had been up to the roadblock to assess the ominous situation. They could see little in the darkness and, not knowing how far south the friendlies were, thought it irresponsible to fire George Battery indiscriminately in the direction of possible enemy positions. Besides, they were close to minimum range for indirect fire. They sent an FO team forward to prepare to fire at first light, when identification of enemy targets would be surer. Also, a bulldozer driven by Private First Class Dave Long was sent to clear the road of damaged vehicles, which it did. Soon after Jimmy and Ernie, returned to the battery, Red Herndon showed up with the tank, which subsequently made it to the head of the column. Like Jimmy and Ernie. however, it had no luck finding enemy targets in the dark. Red and Sergeant Blizard returned to How Battery, which was tediously working its way south through the stalled vehicular column.

Jimmy reported the dangerous situation to me by radio. It was well past midnight as I groped my way along on foot through the 7th Marines motor column searching for Colonel Litzenberg. After about half an hour, perhaps around 2:00 A.M., I found Litz and reported on the roadblock and the plight of the division trains. Litz directed 3/7 to send a company back to clear the road, and I advised Jimmy of this action. It was also during the early morning hours that the roadbound 7th Marines CP was hit. The Chinese killed Captain Don France, the regimental intelligence officer, and wounded Lieutenant Colonel Fred Dowsett, the regimental executive officer. Finally, when Koto-ri had been won at dawn and several miles separated the 7th Marines from the crucial break in the column, the entire regiment was about-faced and started back to clear the road.

It was now about 6:00 A.M., and the first flush of daybreak was beginning to penetrate the inky blackness. With herculean effort, Ben and Red maneuvered How Battery through and around the dormant column and reached George Battery. Ben asked Jimmy if he were assuming command of the two batteries, to which Jimmy replied, "Affirmative!" But before Ben could squeeze his battery into position beside George Battery, the Chinese launched a heavy mortar barrage. The barrage increased in accuracy and intensity as light began to break and caused a considerable number of casualties in both batteries. One of the wounded was Jimmy's FDC section chief, Staff Sergeant Jim King, who died on the way to Koto-ri despite the best efforts of two corpsmen to save him.

By now it was abundantly clear that the Chinese were about to assault the division trains directly opposite George and How batteries. Major Callender, Captain Read, and Captain Payne wasted no time getting ready for action. Trucks were jockeyed back and forth so that the muzzles of nine howitzers could be thrust between them. Inasmuch as 3/11 still had the mission of direct support of the 7th Marines, Jimmy and Ernie decided that three of George Battery's pieces should be retained in position facing south. These three howitzers could also defend the flanks and rear of the batteries if necessary.

The stage was now set for a battlefield drama that is perhaps unique in the annals of war, and certainly in the history of this century: the fight-to-the-finish struggle between an infantry battalion and the better part of two light field artillery batteries at point-blank range. An infantry battalion of from 500 to 800 Chinese had approached under cover of darkness to a defiladed position behind the railroad embankment from 50 to 75 yards from the road upon which the division trains languished helplessly. The Chinese had every right to expect that they could carve this centipede into bloody segments at will. Instead, two field artillery batteries—battle hardened, superbly led—equalized the contest. In a frenzied burst of activity, the six howitzers of How Battery and the three howitzers of George Battery of the 3rd Battalion, 11th Marines were hastily formed into a firing line between the trucks of the division trains.

As the first streaks of dawn lit the eastern sky, the men of George and How batteries feverishly unloaded ammunition from the gun and ammunition trucks. Into this controlled chaos the Chinese poured artillery, mortars, small arms, and grenades.

Sergeant Russell R. Rune's local security team of How Battery had set its light machine gun near the railroad tracks. At about 6:00 A.M. Rune and his men began to have some visibility. To their astonishment they saw hundreds of Chinese on the other side of the tracks massing for an attack. "Here they are!" yelled Rune. His team started firing into the Chinese and were themselves subjected to a hail of bullets. Captain Read ordered Rune and his men back to the truck line, where he and Ernie Payne were organizing the truck drivers into a firing line that included about ten machine guns.

It was none too soon. Individual Chinese were already sticking their heads above the embankment or jumping up for a better look. Now they were flattened by our small-arms fire. Although the howitzers were so close to the railroad that Jimmy thought they were well inside the bore-safe range, a few rounds fired at the tracks with minimum charge exploded on impact and lofted lethal fragments behind the embankment. Urged on by their leaders, the men of George and How batteries knew their task well. They fired at the tracks as rapidly as possible and prevented the Chinese from scrambling up and over the railroad embankment and closing the last 40 yards to the Marines.

The nine howitzers blazed away. There was no time to dig in the trails in the frozen ground. Each gun section of about eight men braced themselves against the gun shield to absorb the recoil and help keep the gun in position between the trucks. There was no time to sort ammunition; the men threw the rounds into the breeches and fired away. After every fourth or fifth round, each gun section had to push the piece back into position. By now casualties were mounting in the batteries and the truck column, but the cannoneers maneuvered around the wounded and kept every gun in action. High explosive, white phosphorus, and armor-piercing rounds bombarded the railroad embankment and the treeline beyond, spraying deadly fragments on the Chinese.

No artillery textbook would advise firing direct fire at targets 40 yards away for fear of injuring your own gun crew with shell fragments. This was no textbook battle, however. It was a life-or-death struggle between nine howitzers and the men who manned them and an enemy infantry battalion. For an hour or more, as daylight slowly illuminated the killing ground, the dramatic duel emblazoned the sky. The gunners, firing each round with only the base charge, knew what was at stake and never let up, wounds notwithstanding. In one instance a crewman in the passion of action neglected to remove the ammunition charges for longer range. The howitzer recoiled 20 feet, knocking down and running over the entire crew. Ben Read ordered the dazed troopers back to their gun, and they quickly rejoined the fusillade.

Throughout the battle, the two rugged old-timers—1st Sergeants Horace Cline and Red Hopkins—were everywhere encouraging the men to greater effort.

With increasing light and a slackening of enemy fire, the officers and senior NCOs pointed out target areas from which mortar and artillery fire was probably coming. These were brought under fire as steady pressure was kept on the Chinese troops huddled behind the railroad embankment. Jimmy Callender spotted automatic weapons fire coming from a gun in a sort of pigpen made of railroad ties about 200 yards south along the tracks. The target was pointed out to Sergeant Vincent E. "Moose" Mosco, of How Battery. Moose yelled, "Gimme a charge 7," sighted through the open breech, and fired one round for a direct hit. Ben Read spotted an observation team on a hill 3,000 yards to the east. Four well-placed rounds took care of it. All up and down the firing line, officers with field glasses spotted as gunners took under fire any target that showed itself. Soon, forty to fifty Chinese were seen fleeing from behind the railroad embankment. They left from 500 to 800 of their dead and dying on the battlefield. A patrol from the 5th Marines verified the count.

George and How batteries had fired 600 rounds in something over an hour. They had sustained casualties of three dead and thirty-four wounded. But by their initiative, timely action, good shooting, and intrepidity, they had stopped an enemy infantry battalion dead in its tracks 50 yards from our guns and prevented an assault on the division trains. They cleared the way for the resumption of the march to Koto-ri.

To a man they had performed heroically. Ben Read, Red Herndon, and the men of How Battery had sensed the danger and moved to the sound of the guns undaunted by cold, dark, enemy fire or the blocked road. They had arrived at the place of greatest danger just before daybreak, in time to ensure that the desperate action evolved in our favor. Jimmy Callender, Ernie Payne, Willie Gore, and the men of George Battery had stood their ground and never lost sight of their assigned fire-support mission. George Battery had anticipated the mounting danger and joined with How Battery in the point-blank defense of nine blazing howitzers. Has field artillery ever had a grander hour?

To Hungnam

When the roadblock disintegrated and the column started to move again at about 10:00 A.M., George and How batteries were ordered to hook up and join the column. Fire support was taken over by 2/11 from Koto-ri. Carrying their dead and wounded and with only minor harassment from small enemy groups, these two tired batteries moved into an assembly area with the rest of 3/11 at about 2:00 P.M. Headquarters, Service, and Item batteries, 3/11, had reached Koto-ri at about 9:30 A.M., and Item Battery had gone into position with the principal direction of fire to the west. Due to the extreme crowding of troops within the Koto-ri perimeter, the other two batteries did not go into firing positions. Those climactic morning hours of December 7 brought to a close, for all practical purposes, 3/11's contribution to the Chosin Reservoir campaign. Although Item Battery would fire over 1,200 rounds on December 8 and 9 to disperse Chinese forming for counterattacks to the west of the Koto-ri encampment, the rounds were mostly of a harassing nature.

Although our winning through from Yudam-ni to Hagaru-ri had convinced most of us that the division's breakout from Chinese encirclement was no longer in doubt (the Chinese lost their greatest opportunity), our arrival in Koto-ri was further confirmation. The Korean winter was now a greater foe than the half-frozen, starving Chinese. The division would suffer more casualties and crises, but it was going out with all transportable gear, the dead and wounded, and thousands of Korean refugees. The Chinese were not about to stop us.

The momentary layover at Koto-ri permitted a moment of reflection. 3/11, I realized, would never be quite the same again. For one thing, Ben Read would no longer be at the helm of How Battery. A tower of strength, Ben had been felled by a grenade fragment in his knee, which had so stiffened by the time of his arrival in Koto-ri that he could not walk. The doctor ordered him evacuated by air. I bid him an affectionate farewell, kneeling beside his stretcher in a How Battery tent just before he departed on the last DC-3 to take off from snow-swept Koto-ri Airstrip. Although command of How Battery would revert to the more than capable hands of Red Herndon, an era had nonetheless ended. As fine a battery as the Marine Corps has ever fielded was now a part of history.

Colonel Litzenberg called a meeting that night of battalion commanders to outline the plan for 1st Marine Division's exodus from the plateau, which the 7th Marines would lead. As I walked through the eerily quiet starry night on my way to the colonel's command tent, I saw a familiar figure perched atop the three- or four-holer in the center of the town. From this eminence that famous Marine, Colonel Chesty Puller, CO of the 1st Marines and the Koto-ri enclave, was contemplating his bleak command. We exchanged greetings as I passed.

December 8 saw heavy snowfall and a continuation of the attack south from Koto-ri. The Chinese were soon to get their final crushing blow from a winter that convinced us of the foolhardiness of conducting a winter campaign in the North Korean mountains. At 2:00 P.M., December 9, 3/11 joined the 7th RCT motor column as 2/11 took over our fire-support mission.

After a bitter cold night in the windswept pass, 3/11 reached Chinhung-ni at midmorning. At the division regulating point, Colonel Eddie Snedeker, the division deputy chief of staff, ordered us to proceed to the 11th Marines assembly area near Hungnam. For us, this campaign was over.

3/11 had run the gamut of artillery experiences. Firing from thirty positions in forty days (not counting direct-fire missions by individual guns), one quarter of our fire had been high angle. We had come in for our share of direct-fire missions, both in our own defense and offensively, in support of the infantry. We had not only contributed one quarter of our strength to fight as riflemen but had also manned segments of several defense perimeters while keeping our eighteen howitzers in action. We had learned and suffered much.

What was the keynote of this experience? The transcendent feature, as far as the artillery of 3/11 was concerned, was that of being an integral part of an infantry regiment. We became so much a part of the regiment, in fact, that we were frequently referred to as the 4th Battalion, 7th Marines. It was not easy to adapt ourselves to the cramped quarters of an infantry regimental perimeter or to carry the burden of supporting so large a unit alone. It took cooperation and understanding by both combat arms. But intimate liaison, faith in one another's ability, demonstrated performance, and resolution gradually produced the cohesion that highlighted the 7th RCT's operations to Yudam-ni and back.

A Tale of Two Corporals

The story of the Chosin Reservoir was as much the story of the struggle of individuals as the struggle of our military units. A case in point is the story of Marvin Pugh of Item Battery, 3/11. Pugh was returning to Nashville on a hardship discharge. He was one of two corporals who rode from Yudam-ni to Hagaru-ri in the back seat of Ben Read's jeep, the last vehicle to make it through Toktong Pass before the road was cut by the Chinese on the afternoon of November 26. The other corporal, David S. Berger of Headquarters Battery, 3/11 had orders to return to Hungnam to accept a commission as a second lieutenant.

After a night at 11th Marines Headquarters in Hagaru-ri, Berger and Pugh were told to hitch a ride in a 2½-ton truck and a jeep on their way to Koto-ri. They deliberated briefly about who was to ride in the heated, closed cab of the truck. Before Pugh departed from Yudam-ni he had been relieved of his winter gear by buddies who did not think he would need it. Berger had winter clothes, so he took the open jeep. It was a fateful decision.

With the truck in the lead, they came upon a Korean family waving in front of a hut. The truck continued on. The jeep carried two South Koreans who could interpret, so the driver stopped. The Koreans told them that Chinese had been there the previous night. As the jeep continued, the road was interdicted by sporadic fire. The driver pulled up, and everyone hit the ditch. By now the truck was out of sight. The jeep driver thought it prudent to return to Hagaru-ri. Upon reporting back to Regiment, Berger was advised to try to bum a ride at the airstrip. He caught a light plane, which executed a John Wayne take-off with Chinese firing from the end of the runway. The pilot flew to Hamhung, landing in a street. Berger accepted his commission on November 30.

Marvin Pugh was not so lucky. The truck driver had run past the interdiction fire, but as he rounded a bend they ran right into a Chinese machine gun in the middle of the road. The windshield was shattered, but Pugh and the driver miraculously escaped injury. The driver stepped on the gas and ran right over the Chinese. For a few hundred yards there was no fire. Then all hell broke loose.

Chinese swarmed on both sides of the road, peppering them with submachine guns, rifles, and grenades. They couldn't turn around and had no choice but to try to run the gauntlet. Pugh, who had no rifle, grabbed the driver's carbine and tried to load a clip. The bolt was frozen. After kicking the bolt loose on the floor of the truck, he was able to get off a few rounds from each of two clips. It was like a Wild West escape with Pugh firing from the careening truck but soon—with all the tires flat and the engine riddled—they came to a sputtering halt. Pugh and the driver tried to escape, but

Pugh's leg was shattered and he couldn't walk. The driver was shot down trying to run for help. Pugh was then shot in the other leg so that he couldn't attempt escape. A Chinese soldier took his field jacket, dungaree jacket, and cap, leaving him in the subzero weather in only his undershirt. He wouldn't even have had that if he had not fought the soldier when he tried to remove it.

It was now almost dark. Pugh tried to drag himself along the creek bed near the road in hopes of finding pieces of wood to make splints—he could not find a twig. The sand was unfrozen due to the absence of moisture, so he was able to scoop out a shallow foxhole before passing out. In the morning he awoke and was unable to see his surroundings. He was buried in a providential snowfall that had probably saved him from freezing to death.

While he lay in his foxhole covered with snow, he saw American troops contesting for the hills to the west. There was intermittent firing as tanks and trucks moved up the road toward Hagaru-ri. Finally, Pugh was able to attract a soldier's attention. Four men came, laid him on a tarp and transferred him from his foxhole to a jeep trailer. The men covered him with a tarp and assured him that he had been rescued. But the firing continued, and from his observation post flat on his back in the trailer, it soon became clear to Pugh that the Chinese had captured the convoy. Later he heard muffled explosions. The Chinese had tossed grenades into all the trucks and trailers to ensure that no one in the relief convoy was still alive. He felt himself being lifted off the trailer. Then he passed out.

When he regained consciousness, he noticed Chinese moving up and down the road during the day, which was probably December 1. Two Chinese noticed that he was alive, lifted him out of the trailer, and carried him about a quarter of a mile up a hill. He was deposited with several other wounded prisoners. He noticed a Royal Marine, a soldier, and another Marine, all of whom had sleeping bags. The Marine managed to pull off his sleeping bag cover and give it to Pugh, who struggled for days to tug it up around himself.

Days and nights came and went. Planes and artillery fired on the hills around them but never on their hill. They ate snow for moisture. Once the Chinese gave each of them four new potatoes; otherwise, they left the wounded to themselves. They received no medical treatment. The Chinese withdrew the night of December 6; in the morning they were alone.

During the day eight Marines came with stretchers and moved them to trucks. Pugh was alone in a truck stacked with frozen bodies. The next morning he was taken to an aid station in Koto-ri, given a morphine shot, and eventually flown by Piper Cub to Hungnam. Later, in Yokosuka, Japan, he lost his legs—both were eaten with gangrene. Pugh was treated for malnutrition and flown to the States on December 27.

In 1985, thirty-five years later, Berger and Pugh were finally brought together by telephone. It was an emotional conversation. Neither had known whether the other was dead or alive. Marvin Pugh assured Dave Berger that he had no reason to feel guilty about the decision to let Marvin ride in the heated truck; he had enjoyed the warmth while it lasted.

13

Hungnam To Pohang

Rest and Rehabilitation

The drive back through Sudong Gorge, ideally suited to ambush (as we were well aware), invoked a rush of memories. Could it be that only forty days had transpired since we went into position at Majon-dong while heading north? Just east of Majon-dong, a battalion of 155mm self-propelled howitzers from the U.S. Army's freshly committed 3rd Infantry Division loomed out of the mist. Quiet at the moment, their latent power was poised to assist the exit of 1st Marine Division from the Chosin plateau.

At the 11th Marines assembly area near Hungnam, we went into bivouac and finally allowed ourselves to relax. As our physical and emotional systems lowered their defenses, many of us came down with an assortment of minor ailments—fevers, colds, slight cases of pneumonia. Little wonder. But within three or four days most of us were feeling fine again. There was some talk at the time of holding a defensive perimeter around Hungnam and daring the Chinese to try to throw us out, but nothing came of it. Soon, along with thousands of other troops, we were crammed on the USNS *Daniel I. Sultan,* a large luxury liner. We got under way on December 12 and arrived in Pusan the morning of December 14. This voyage was remarkable only because of the behavior of the half-frozen, half-starved troops. Many never left the chow line. They moved through it as many times as the sympathetic mess force allowed and then they slept in line on the floor of the passageways.

Although the cooks and stewards must have been amazed at the troops' insatiable appetites, they persevered. The only modification in the excellent cuisine was the abandonment of some of the frills, such as soup and nuts.

I gained 20 pounds in four days; I went from 150 to 170 pounds, 10 pounds under my normal weight of 180. This was by no means unusual. We had subsisted over the past fortnight mainly on crackers, hard candy, and mouthfuls of snow. It was miraculous what four days of nourishing food, water, and rest accomplished. At Pusan we transshipped on the USS *Catamount* for the 50-mile run westward along the coast to Masan, where we disembarked on December 15.

At Masan, a quiet seaside village, all battalions of the 11th Marines came under direct regimental control for the first time since mid September. Although the school buildings and grounds where the regiment now clustered were somewhat confining, the site provided adequate shelter and an opportunity to benefit from some of the services regimental headquarters could furnish, such as the rehabilitation and resupply of communications equipment and ordnance. There was also plenty of food, particularly turkey, and an opportunity to divert the troops with recreational sports and motion pictures.

Our mail now started to catch up with us. I received a letter from the commandant of the Marine Corps, which my battalion sergeant major, Billy Boynton, was hesitant to deliver. My pay had been docked for failure to reimburse the railroad for my meals on the troop train from Camp Lejeune to Camp Pendleton. My fury could not have been greater. Some Headquarters warrior had jumped to the insulting conclusion that the battalion commander had ridden free because the railroad had claimed an extra fare. (Actually, we had discovered a stowaway a few miles out of Lejeune and had been directed by the executive officer of the 10th Marines to take him with us.) A scorching rebuttal to the section of HQMC responsible resulted in prompt restoration of my pay, albeit without apology.

Morale was a problem with many of the officers and men. They believed that they had earned a rest in a rear area where they could have some real liberty. Japan was the logical and most popular choice. But most of us knew that this was wishful thinking. The situation in the north, where U.S. Army units were in considerable disarray, was anything but stable, and it was predictable that 1st Marine Division would soon be needed to help form a reliable front.

Rehabilitation of weapons, equipment, and transport and rounding the men into reasonably good physical shape were the orders of the day. One of our tasks was to calibrate our tired old World War II howitzers—that is, segregate the long shooters in one battery and the short shooters in another. That they had given such faithful service without calibration was remarkable, for a few even had pronounced muzzle droop. We had scarcely seen ten of the howitzers until they came ashore at Inchon; Masan was our first opportunity to calibrate them.

But significant progress in rebuilding battalion élan was only achieved after replacements began to arrive. It is always difficult to ignite the troops with offensive spirit when they can look around them and see the gaping files that represent their dead, missing, wounded, and evacuated buddies. 3/11 had sustained casualties to about one third of her strength. This percentage was not particularly noteworthy when compared to the ravaged infantry battalions, but it was most unusual for an artillery battalion, where attrition rarely exceeds 10 percent. As crack officer and enlisted replacements were assigned to batteries, morale perked up noticeably. 3/11 policy called for all second lieutenants and scout sergeants to be adept at adjusting fire on enemy targets. With the new second lieutenants well grounded in artillery technique and veteran FOs and scout sergeants to teach them and other new NCOs the combat lessons just learned, we soon had our observer corps in top shape.

Liaison with the 7th Marines also needed revitalization. So many key officers and NCOs had been replaced that intimate liaison, a trademark of 3/11, had to be fostered all over again. Talks to the 7th Marines' officers and men helped in this regard, but there is no substitute for friendly, knowledgeable, aggressive cultivation of the infantry commanders and staffers by battery commanders, liaison officers, and FOs. A good relationship between these two groups is the lubrication that makes the infantry-artillery team work. This initiative must come from the artillery, and it must be pursued with perseverence in the barracks as well as in the field.

To Pohang

On January 15, 1951 the month of rest and rehabilitation ended. We motor-marched to Pohang on the coast about 80 miles north of Pusan. Arriving two days ahead of the 7th Marines, to whom we were now attached again, we had an opportunity to check out the local color. Captain John McLaurin, now our intelligence officer, reconnoitered the surrounding countryside and discovered that we were in an area rich in seafood. He procured enough enormous flounder to feed the officers and most of the staff NCOs for $1. The following day we feasted on fat shrimp for $2. With the coming of the infantry, however, the Koreans quickly sensed what the market would bear, and the price of seafood escalated geometrically.

The 10th Division of the North Korean People's Army (NKPA) was reported to have infiltrated by small units into the rough square bounded by Pohang, Yongchon, Andong, and Yondok. It was 1st Marine Division's mission to embark on an antiguerilla campaign and hunt them down. This called for the utmost versatility for 3/11. As infantry patrols tracked down platoon-sized and smaller groups of NKPA, we had to bring fire on them promptly, although not necessarily in heavy concentrations. The batteries had to be able to fire in any direction on short notice. It was not uncommon to see a battery sited by platoon—two guns to the east, two to the west, and two to the south. Two platoons might be laid for low-angle fire and the other for high-angle fire to enable it to reach over and behind a nearby ridge. This placed a heavy burden on the individual firing battery, even though each was augmented by battalion FDC and communications increments. I doubt if field-artillery batteries anywhere ever surpassed the sophistication and competence that George, How, and Item batteries of 3/11 demonstrated routinely in January and February of 1951.

About February 1, while in the field to the west of Pohang, I received word from Colonel Litzenberg that my promotion to lieutenant colonel had finally arrived. The dispatch announcing my promotion was memorable for me because of the elite company in which I was included—the dispatch promoted Colonel Chesty Puller to brigadier general and Lieutenant Colonel Raymond L. Murray to colonel. I jeeped the few miles to the 7th Marines CP and joined Litz in his small command tent. There, we proceeded to wet down the silver leaves he had just pinned on my collar. The colonel was well supplied with Old Grand Dad, courtesy of the 1st Marine Aircraft Wing, whose commander, Major General Field Harris, was an old drinking buddy of Litz's. (Old Grand Dad was a means of relaxing from the rigors of the northern campaign, and Litz had regrettably come to imbibe a little more than was good for him.)

On this occasion I was well into my second highball when a battalion commander entered the now-crowded tent to report an enemy contact. The lieutenant colonel had just arrived in Korea a few days before and was not familiar with all the regimental commander's policies and foibles. Hard on the heels of the brief action report, Litz bored in. "Where are the North Koreans now?" he asked.

The unwary battalion commander admitted that his patrol had lost contact.

Inwardly I grimaced—losing contact with the enemy after the great efforts we were expending to track him down was a grievous sin. Litz showed no mercy; he castigated the neophyte commander in devastating terms. Soon after the newcomer's red-faced retreat, I requested permission to return to my battalion, embarrassed that I had been witness to the dressing down of a senior officer. I thought at the time that the Marine Corps would be well advised to send Litz home before the gallant, tough old warrior suffered further burnout.

Emergency Leave

I received word in early February from Vera's doctor that she was suffering from persistent anemia. Vera had given birth to four sons, although she was only twenty-eight. The doctor believed that she had never recovered completely from the last baby's birth, and he urged my prompt return. It was a painful decision to request emergency leave for thirty days because I suspected that Vera's condition was not amenable to a month-long cure. I felt deeply about leaving 3/11. That I would never again command so talented and responsive a combat battalion was certain. Difficult also was my leave-taking from the 7th Marines, a great regiment that had taken 3/11 as her own. The 7th Marines considered us her fourth battalion, and it was no empty tribute for this regiment could claim such Marine giants as Chesty Puller, Herman Hanneken, Homer Litzenberg, and Ray Davis among its number.

I thought that I had arranged with Lieutenant Colonel Carl Youngdale, the 11th Marines CO, for Reds Miller to take over 3/11 during my absence, and I had imparted this information to Reds. However, when the helicopter arrived to fly me out, Major Bill McReynolds, until then CO of 4/11, alighted. I could see Reds's face fall as McReynolds announced that he had been sent to take command. I had nothing against Bill, and old friend, but I knew that it was a bitter pill for Reds to swallow. I was depressed that this misunderstanding should cloud my last minutes with my beloved battalion.

The helicopter ferried me to Pohang, whence I was flown by the 1st Marine Aircraft Wing via Pusan to Itami, Japan. I spent a rousing evening at a house in the nearby hills that was favored by officers of the air wing. The next morning, I took a train that departed precisely on time from Kobe. (I almost missed it, not being used to such timely train service.) After a day's stopover at a rest camp at Otsu, we continued by train to Yokosuka. The bunks in the sleeping compartments were designed for Japanese, and the narrow spaces, which were only 5 feet 10 inches long, afforded only fitful sleep. This amounted to small penalty, however, because there was fascination, even in the dark, in watching the lush countryside and villages flash by my window. After a night at the naval base, I was driven to Haneda Airport on the outskirts of Tokyo for an Alaskan Airlines flight via Anchorage to Seattle. Two noteworthy incidents enriched the final stages of my journey home.

While waiting for our flight to be called, military police shepherded all the passengers to the far side of the airport lounge. From that vantage point we saw several long limousines roll up and disgorge top-hatted, swallow-tailed Japanese dignitaries onto the tarmac. There they waited. Finally, John Foster Dulles, at that time minister plenipotentiary preparing for his future assignment as secretary of state, emerged from a limousine and strode to a waiting plane. He mounted partway up the steps and paused with the cluster of Japanese just below. As minutes passed, Dulles evidenced obvious impatience, but the Japanese remained impassive. Then a limousine 2 feet longer than any of the others rolled up. There was an aura of anticipation. Electricity filled the air as General of the Army Douglas MacArthur alighted. In his khaki, open-necked shirt resplendent with the circular five-star insignia and his grommetless gold-encrusted cap at a jaunty angle, he strode to the airplane steps to bid Dulles bon voyage. There was no question in any mind as to who was the real emperor of Japan. Little did we know how short-lived MacArthur's reign would be.

In Seattle I learned that an Air Force B-50 bomber was making a speed run to the East Coast in quest of the transcontinental record. I begged a ride. As we crossed the Mississippi River at a record-setting pace, one of the starboard engines burst into flames. I was in the bombardier's bubble below the pilots' seats. I had no parachute and no way out except up through the pilots' cabin. The minute that it took the crew to extinguish the fire seemed like an eternity. With one engine out of commission, we limped into Savannah an hour or so behind our projected arrival time. The East Coast never looked so good.

In Retrospect: The Early Battles in Korea

It would be difficult to imagine a situation that we did not experience during those relatively brief periods of combat at the Chosin Reservoir and Pohang. Certainly, the conditions under which we fought were unique in my experience and in that of field artillerymen I have known then and since. We learned hard lessons, lessons tested in that most exacting of crucibles—combat. That they are lessons that paid off handsomely in terms of success in battle and lives saved should render them worth consideration by today's infantry and artillery, as well as by all Marines.

The Inchon landing through the breakout at the Chosin Reservoir had some similarities to as well as differences from Guadalcanal. Both were intended to turn the tide against victorious aggressors. Both were chancy. In both cases Marines were rushed from far-flung duty stations to meet the challenge. And, in both cases, they paid a heavy price for U.S. unpreparedness.

There the similarity ends, for the Marines on Guadalcanal rallied the nation to redouble her efforts and to press forward to ultimate, complete victory. With equal heroism the Marines at Inchon and Chosin stirred the nation—but not to the pursuit of complete victory. In contrast, an indifferent nation suspected there was a disparity between a Japanese juggernaut driving for hegemony of East Asia and the Korean Communists seeking to unify their country by force.

Little is to be gained by examining the motives of the North Koreans and what induced them to think they could conquer South Korea while we stood idly by. Nor is there merit in exploring further the reasons why we felt compelled to stop this obvious threat to, among other things, our new and potentially powerful ally, Japan. The fact remains that we were singularly unprepared to meet the challenge militarily. We were even less prepared psychologically. The British had long since relinquished their role as the world's policeman—a role they had played with limited resources and considerable aplomb for a century. We were clearly the heir apparent. Just as clearly, we had done little to prepare ourselves for the part.

We clothed the fighting in the mantle of respectability of the United Nations. We convinced the world that we were carrying out our obligation of police action by punishing the aggressor. We also managed by this subterfuge to convince the nation that this was not a real war. By inference, then, it did not require a real national commitment. The lack of national support did little to inspire the troops in the field.

We did induce other nations to provide token forces for the common defense, and we did eventually achieve a stalemate that restored the status quo ante bellum—a modest success in the new era of the limited war. It is how we went about accomplishing this modest success that bears scrutiny.

Marines are special troops; they are different. They were the only troops ready and reliable enough to be committed to the first offensive action of World War II, at Guadalcanal; they were the only troops capable of successfully bringing off the difficult landing at Inchon on a moment's notice. They were, in my opinion, the only troops who could have overcome the countless handicaps of the ill-starred Chosin Reservoir campaign and come out with flying colors.

The assignment of the 1st Marine Division to the Guadalcanal and Inchon missions were well-considered gambles. The Marines turned the tide, which is the proper use of an elite force. In contrast, 1st Marine Division was pushed up onto the Chosin plateau at the onset of winter in the face of incontrovertible evidence that China had entered the war in force and that the original parameters of the conflict no longer applied. Chosin was not a gamble; it was criminal stupidity. You do not sacrifice your elite force without overpowering justification. What purpose was served by stringing out 1st Marine Division in the mountains of North Korea in winter?

If we are to survive as a world power, we must save our Sunday punch for knockout opportunities—not squander it in a purposeless bloodbath in mountainous wastes where victory or defeat is not likely to influence the outcome of the war.

PART IV

After Korea & the Cuban Missile Crisis

14

The Marine Corps Schools

The Naval Gunfire Section

The Marine Corps Schools mushroomed during World War II to form a major educational and training center for officer candidates, newly commissioned officers, and company- and field-grade officers. Certain specialties that could be accommodated on the Quantico reservation, such as basic field artillery, were also taught. With the shrinking of the Marine Corps to considerably less than 100,000 men and women in the years between the wars, the educational center had been consolidated into three principal schools—The Basic School for newly commissioned second lieutenants, Amphibious Warfare School (the Junior Course) for company-grade officers, and Amphibious Warfare School (the Senior Course) for field-grade officers. But Quantico was a lot more than an officer educational center. Only an hour away from HQMC in Arlington, it had become an important resource upon which HQMC could draw for support in the high-stakes game it now had to play with the bigger services in the Pentagon. To this end, HQMC consciously stocked Quantico with talented officers upon whom it could call for doctrinal development, planning, and reinforcement of one sort or another.

One such officer was Lieutenant Colonel Robert Debs Heinl, Jr. Named partly for the U.S. Socialist hero of the turn of the century, Bob Heinl was unique by any standard, particularly that of the Marine Corps. Of slight build and decidedly nonathletic tastes, Bob sported a small mustache that gave him a Hitler-like appearance.

Some British affectations, such as the handkerchief tucked inside his sleeve, set him even more apart. But his foremost characteristic was brightness—shining, blue eyes, quick mind, and a sparkling personality. A graduate of Yale at nineteen, Bob had interviewed the vice-president of the United States for a school paper while a student at Saint Albans.

Upon return from Korea in the spring of 1951, I was ordered to Quantico to augment the Naval Gunfire Section, which was then gearing up for the 1st Naval Gunfire Officers' Course scheduled for an eight-week run that summer. I was to be Bob Heinl's assistant director. Ultimately, I relieved him as section head during the school year and became school director during the summer, but before that I spent the better part of two enlightening years at his side.

There were some responsibilities that Bob had acquired while on duty at Quantico, however, to which neither I nor anyone else would fall heir. Bob was one of a kind and, in some ways, an enigma. He was as unlike the Marine stereotype as one could be; at the same time he was completely devoted to the Marine Corps. As history will attest, Bob Heinl was as powerful a contributor to the future of the Marine Corps as many of her more conventional heroes.

At that time a good deal of the advanced thinking on amphibious warfare was incorporated in the Advance Base Problem. In 1951 Iceland was the subject of the problem, which dramatically illustrated amphibious-assault strategy and tactics. The Norway problem, its successor, was then in preparation. During my three and a half years at Quantico, I would participate in the last performance of Iceland, in almost all of Norway, and the first few of its successor, Denmark. The Advance Base Problem was an illustrated two-day, eight-hour lecture that we delivered to the top military schools in this country (War colleges, Air University, Armed Forces Staff College, Command and General Staff College, Artillery, Armored and Infantry Schools) as well as in England and occasionally at NATO Headquarters and the Pacific Command in Hawaii. It was always well received and did much to further the objectives of the Marine Corps at the time—to demonstrate the Marines' attentiveness to and expertise in amphibious warfare.

Lieutenant Colonel Heinl had written segments of the Norway problem and was greatly exercised when it was brought to his attention that some of his script had been altered. He seized the telephone, tracked down the lieutenant-colonel staff assistant who had committed the crime, and demanded an explanation. Heinl's definitive works (*Soldiers of the Sea* and *Victory at High Tide*) were as yet unpublished, nonetheless Bob was known throughout the Marine Corps for his extensive writings. His quarry was hard pressed for a satisfactory answer. Finally, Bob intoned that if that was the best that he could offer, he insisted that the matter be referred to the "staff grammarian" and the "staff rhetorician." The original text was promptly restored.

The Navy did itself proud that first summer of the Naval Gunfire Officers' School by making a superb, new cruiser with rapid-fire 8-inch guns, the USS *Des Moines,* available for our field-firing exercises. We had the exercises at the Culebra Shore Bombardment Range, about 20 miles east of Puerto Rico. Enroute, the ship went through the customary emergency drills of a fighting ship at sea. On one occasion, while we were at dinner in the senior officers' wardroom, the general-quarters alarm sounded. Heinl instantly leaped to his feet, his chair clattering to the deck behind him. He dramatically reached down to buckle on an imaginary sword or sidearm and took several steps toward the ladder topside. Even those of us who were familiar with his sometimes quaint behavior were startled. While the Navy officers attempted to bring their raised eyebrows down, Bob resumed his seat and explained that ever since the late '30s, when he had been a junior officer of the Marine Detachment aboard the USS *Tuscaloosa,* the sound of general quarters had galvanized him to action.

The skipper of the *Des Moines* was Captain Henry Crommelin of the famous Navy officer brothers. (The youngest, Quentin, had been a classmate of mine at the Academy.) Henry commanded a taut ship. Since I had taught conduct of fire at the Gunfire Support School in Little Creek, Virginia, Bob asked me to run the firing exercises from the observation post on a hill across from the range. He observed in the background in his old slouch hat, one of his old-timer mannerisms. (In those days only Marine drill instructors wore the field hat.) Firing was proceeding slowly due to the necessity of critiquing each fire mission for the benefit of the student officers before initiating the next one. Evidently, this deliberate pace irked Captain Crommelin, who was impatiently pacing his bridge. His mighty ship, which could deliver twenty-seven 8-inch rounds on target in less than a minute, cruised back and forth several miles offshore. Soon a message from the ship suggested that fire could be speeded up if we identified the subsequent target while the ship fired for effect on the current target. Annoyed by this attempted interference from seaward and assuming that it had come from the cocky young liaison officer we had left aboard, I responded that we were quite capable of conducting fire without advice from the ship. A stony silence ensued. Later, aboard ship for the night, we learned that it was the skipper himself who had made the unwelcome suggestion. Fortunately for me, neither of us had identified ourselves, the usual procedure when sending a message.

In the years between World War II and Korea, the military was under heavy budgetary pressure. Army Chief of Staff General Dwight Eisenhower had suggested that the Marines be restricted to regiment-sized units, and his boss, President Harry Truman, was well known for his anti-Marine Corps sentiments. The Marine Corps and its congressional allies were cognizant of the frequent instances throughout history in which Army and Navy leaders had been willing to sacrifice the Marine Corps on the altar of efficiency, organizational homogeneity, or some other appealing illusion that improved their own chances of survival. The pro-Marine Corps faction decided that statutory protection might prove useful.

At that time Senator Paul Douglas, who had been a field-grade officer in 1st Marine Division on Okinawa, was a power in the upper house. He was willing to lead an effort to enact a bill which would prescribe that the Marine Corps have no less than three divisions and three air wings. With politicking by the military services frowned upon, spadework for the bill had to be conducted with discretion. In the strategy sessions and related legwork, Bob Heinl was a key agent. Frequently, he would not show up for work at Quantico at all. Other times, during the morning, he would hit Colonel Wallace M. Greene's key on the intercom and advise him that he was off to the big city. Of course, Colonel Wally Greene was aware of Bob's clandestine activities and of his need to attend strategy sessions on short notice. Inasmuch as I had spent my ten-year Marine Corps career at the company or battalion level, these doings were a real eye-opener for me. They were even a little heady for Bob, I suspect, although lack of confidence or consideration for the finer points of conformity rarely deterred him.

Colonel Greene, the chief of the Combined Arms Section, had been Colonel Don Weller's roommate at the Naval Academy, in the Class of 1930, and Weller had been Bob Heinl's commanding officer on the USS *Tuscaloosa*. This link to his boss through Colonel Weller as well as his special status throughout the drafting of the Marine Corps Bill at times seemed to color Bob's judgment, which was never free from a touch of intellectual arrogance. One morning Bob called Colonel Greene on the intercom to ask if it was true that Wally, Jr. was uncertain whether to attend Yale or the Naval Academy. The colonel verified this. Bob forthwith launched into a passionate appeal for Yale coupled with a diatribe against the Academy. Although the reaction from the other end of the intercom was hardly warm, Bob did not let up, opining that this potential tragedy must be averted at all costs. Would the colonel object to Bob speaking to Wally on Yale's behalf? The colonel told him icily to be his guest. I was appalled by this performance and left our shared office to regain my composure.

About that time Bob showed me my annual Fitness Report. It was flattering enough, with only two marks less than the best. Why he had decided to mark me down in economy and cooperation, however, eluded me, so out of curiosity I asked him. His response floored me. He had marked me down in economy, he said, because he had witnessed me throwing some old papers away without saving the paper clips. As to cooperation, he could not imagine the son of Judge Parry being overly cooperative. (He had never met Father.)

Some months later Bob got orders to Korea. Although he had not overtly tried to forestall these orders, I had been privy to quite a few telephone conversations in which he had suggested that his talents might be better utilized elsewhere, such as in Europe. Now, with orders in hand, he called Colonel Don Weller at HQMC to advise of his impending departure.

From where I sat a few feet away, it appeared that Don asked him matter-of-factly, "Where to?"

"Where else but to the sound of the guns," Bob declared dramatically.

Advance Base Problem

In the early 1950s assignment to the Advance Base Problem team was coveted despite the fact that it was an additional duty beyond normal instructional responsibilities and involved considerable travel. Membership on the team brought one to the attention of the local generals and highly regarded colonels and, on occasion, to senior officers at HQMC as well. When the Denmark problem was in the final stages in 1954, a contingent of HQMC, including the commandant, General Lem Shepherd, journeyed to Quantico to give the final blessing. We were psyched up for a sparkling performance. When my turn came to deliver the ten-minute talk on naval-gunfire support, I stepped out from the podium to make a more dramatic impact. I was stunned to see that the commandant, in the front row, was sound asleep. The next ten minutes were the toughest of my three years on the team.

A few veterans of the Chosin Reservoir campaign were team members. Lieutenant Colonel Douglas B. Drysdale, who had commanded the 41 Royal Marine Commando, tried with limited success to civilize his colonial compatriots by insisting that we join him for gin and bitters before lunch on the road. His stage performance would invariably receive enthusiastic applause when he dead-panned that he was the only team member who spoke English.

Another was Major Hank Woessner, who had returned from Korea a few months after me and moved into government quarters across the street. He was one of the few officers in the Marine Corps with more children than I. Displaying the same unshakable poise he had demonstrated as Colonel Litzenberg's operations officer, Hank ruled his little-people kingdom without ever raising his voice, a feat at which I never ceased to marvel and, certainly, never remotely emulated.

Hank Woessner and I were long-time members of the Advance Base Problem team, whereas the full colonels who headed it usually spent little more than a year in the assignment. Colonel Herman Nickerson was our leader in 1952–53, after his return from command of the 7th Marines in Korea, where he had replaced Colonel Litzenberg. Hank had been his operations officer briefly before returning home. In one of the lighter moments of the presentation, Colonel Nickerson quaffed a full glass of tea that looked like whiskey in front of the audience. Who first got the idea to spike his drink I do not remember, although Nick always suspected Hank and me (and he was undoubtedly partially right). On cue, Hank, dressed in a steward's white jacket, handed him a glass, but this time it was a tumbler of bourbon. Nick quaffed it and never blinked. He continued with his monologue and, good sport that he was, he never even tried to find out who the culprits were. He let it be known, however, that such shenanigans would not be welcome in the future.

My three-and-a-half-year tour of duty at the Marine Corps Schools, including my work on the Advance Base Problem team and my close association with Bob Heinl and his sense of history, first opened my eyes to the perils of being a member of a small, elite force sandwiched into the Department of Defense. That the Marine Corps had survived the numerous assaults from the two larger, more powerful services throughout its 180-year history was, in itself, remarkable. It is attributable for the most part, I think, to our unique form of government, where congressional leaders with long memories and staying power can withstand administration raids.

It also taught me that survival of the Marine Corps depends upon its performance in action and readiness to undertake whatever task it is assigned. Further, I learned that amphibious-warfare expertise was a valuable part of readiness—an important national doctrinal responsiblity in keeping with the Marines' important role in the U.S. Fleet.

15

The Reserves

Units of the the Marine Corps Reserve had widely varying experiences during the Korean War based largely on the geographical area from which they were drawn and their individual talents. If certain specialties were needed, they were taken from anywhere, but many Reserve units mobilized on the East Coast never got closer to the war zone than Camp Lejeune. Contrast such mild commitment with that of West Coast units (such as the light artillery battery from Eugene, Oregon, which had been absorbed whole by 3/11). Within days, sometimes even hours, after activation these units were aboard ships bound for Inchon, many without even their pay records.

Awareness of the differing levels of war experience helps one to visualize the problems confronting the Marine Corps in its effort to resuscitate the Reserves in the mid '50s. In some cities and particularly in small towns where Reserve units had sustained heavy casualties, prudence counseled delay in reactivating units. In extreme cases the best course seemed to be to reposition units to remote locales.

I took over as inspector-instructor (I-I) of the 1st 105mm Howitzer Battalion, U.S. Marine Corps Reserve (USMCR), of Richmond, Virginia, in September 1954. I found a unit whose members had languished at Camp Lejeune throughout their "war" stint, an uninspired group that did little more than go through the motions. At the first two-hour evening drill, twenty-six Reservists showed up despite our paper strength of over two hundred. Following the next week's drill, at which the attendees numbered twenty-five, I drove up to Reserve District Headquarters in Arlington, Virginia, to confer with Colonel John R. "Pat" Lanigan, the district director. After apprising Pat of the sorry status of the battalion, I told him that I thought that a thorough housecleaning was necessary. Listening attentively, Pat agreed, with the proviso that battalion strength must not decrease. In other words, we could fire one Reservist with an indifferent attendance record for every new man we recruited. It would take a long time to invigorate the unit in this deliberate manner, but it was a sensible—if conservative—way to proceed since it forced us to try to motivate those on the rolls.

My assistant, 1st Lieutenant Bill Dietrick, a Reserve officer serving on active duty, was a slender, conscientious, imaginative graduate of Villanova. He and I racked our brains for ways to convince marginal participants to make a stronger commitment by rendering Reserve duty more attractive and meaningful. We recognized that there was no easy solution; the fact that we were both Damnyankees from the Philadelphia area made it a real challenge.

The battalion commander, Lieutenant Colonel Dick Peyton, a member of a respected Virginia family (his father had been headmaster of Staunton Military Academy) was a lawyer in his late forties. Easygoing, friendly, and cooperative, Dick was far from the dynamic, inspirational leader needed to lift the battalion from its moribund state. Nonetheless, his heart was in the right place, and he readily accepted advice as I steadily increased the pressure on him to make the officers measure up.

As we demanded attendance at drill on a regular basis, we ran into subtle resistance from an informal officer protective association that we came to call the VMI clique. A good percentage of the field-grade officers and captains were graduates of the Virginia Military Institute (VMI) who tended to view the battalion as their exclusive preserve. It constituted a source of not insubstantial income that required only minimal effort and represented little risk (especially for the more senior officers, whose pay was higher but whose chance of activation in an emergency was slim). Much of our effort in the early months was directed at trying to cajole or force these officers to produce.

Simultaneously, we sought to stimulate interest and esprit de corps by starting up a battalion club in our gymnasium for after-drill socializing at which we allowed 3.2 percent beer. We also instituted an intramural basketball league, with teams from each battery and the I-I staff, and built an obstacle course patterned after the one at Quantico to promote physical fitness. Each led to a modest, incremental advance in battalion interest and, as word of the shaking off of lethargy spread, our attendance and recruiting success slowly moved forward.

Richmond, however, was not an ideal recruiting ground for Marines. With a powerful Confederate tradition reinforcing deep-rooted Virginian loyalties, the National Guard held a strong grip on the high-school youth. The well-entrenched Richmond Light Infantry Regiment—locally known as the Richmond Blues—had, in an earlier incarnation as a battalion of the 1st Virginia Infantry, included such luminaries as Nathaniel Bacon, Patrick Henry, George Washington, and John Marshall. The Richmond Blues actively sought to ban us from the high schools, which were their prime sources of recruits. Despite these handicaps we made continuous progress in landing recruits and removing nonparticipants from the rolls. We also uncovered some deplorable administrative lapses. In one flagrant case we discovered that a Marine who had been on the rolls for four years had served a three-year hitch in the Army without our knowledge.

The leadership of the officers constituted a major obstacle to battalion rejuvenation. The senior officers either showed little interest in shaping up the battalion or were just incompetent. I convinced Peyton that some would have to go. He cooperated, albeit with some reluctance. As the year progressed, two of the three battery commanders were forced out, as were two of the three majors. One major, the battalion executive officer, had been a Navy Cross winner in World War II. The battalion operations officer, an outspoken major who had become increasingly troublesome, finally overstepped the bounds of propriety at our two-week field training at Camp Lejeune by repeatedly contradicting the battalion commander in front of several officers. I urged Dick Peyton to fire him on the spot, which he did.

The VMI clique was eventually rendered inoperative, although the ousted officers apparently attempted to retaliate through a Reserve brigadier general who made an unannounced inspection of the training center during our absence at Camp Lejeune. This proved fruitless, however, as he was unable to find anything out of order. All the officers and men now knew that we meant business and that it was time to build the battalion to respectable strength and competence.

Of course, you cannot replace somebody with nobody, so we had been canvassing the area all winter trying to unearth officer talent to bring aboard as vacancies were created. As cooperative as Dick Peyton was, it had been clear for months that he would have to go. His relatively advanced age gave us the excuse to ease him out once he had finished the unpalatable task of stripping the battalion of dead wood.

In our talent search I discovered a prime candidate for commanding officer in Lieutenant Colonel Jim Slay, USMCR. He had been an assistant G-3 to Lieutenant Colonel Victor H. "Brute" Krulak in 6th Marine Division on Okinawa. Jim was a handsome six-footer with the sort of leadership qualities we sorely needed. He was about my age (thirty-six) and a rising star on the Richmond horizon who would add prestige to the battalion and attract recruits. His only drawback was his busy schedule. As a vice-president and director of personnel of the Federal Reserve Bank, he had little time to take on new responsibilities. He had to travel out of town frequently and carried a significant speaking schedule. I worked for some time on Jim before he agreed to take on the task of leading the battalion to better days. We accepted the fact that he would only be able to attend about 75 percent of the drills, but I considered this a small price to pay for the dynamism he would bring to the unit. Dick Peyton retired soon after summer camp, thus completing the removal of all four field-grade officers as well as two of the three battery commanders. The battalion soon began to thrive under new leadership. Attendance rose steadily until it reached about 90 percent, a far cry from the 10 percent attendance we had inherited a year before.

16

The Pentagon

Action Officer

For a year after leaving Richmond, we had been living in Wellington, a small community on the Potomac between Quantico and Washington. For once I had predicted my next duty assignment accurately. After my student year at the Command and General Staff College was over in the summer of 1957, we did not have to move when I received orders for the Pentagon. I had only been working in the Pentagon for a few weeks when I heard that my sometime mentor, Brigadier General Bob Luckey, was in town. I asked him out to dinner.

During the cocktail hour the general asked me how I liked duty in G-3 Plans. Surprised, I responded that I was in Personnel Policy, Office of the Secretary of Defense (OSD). The general's reaction was unsettling; he flushed with anger. Apparently, he had arranged for me to be assigned to HQMC in one of the most prestigious positions—G-3 Plans—and had been unaware that someone had countermanded his wishes after his departure for Camp Lejeune. Naive to the internal politics of the Marine Corps, I thought little of his outburst at the time. But he knew, even if I did not, that my chances for promotion to general were severely crippled by denial of this duty—about half of all Marine generals are stationed at HQMC.

To me, joint-staff duty was fascinating. Brushing elbows daily with officers of the other services and high-ranking civilians was instructive and certainly broadened my outlook. It was clear that the Army consciously took more pains than the other services to assign high-grade officers. Of course, the Army had traditionally sought dominance in the joint arena and its large, well-educated officers' corps permitted it to pursue this ambition. About half of the officers in Personnel Policy were Army and all were colonels or lieutenant colonels or their Navy equivalents. I was a lieutenant colonel when assigned and was promoted to colonel in November 1958 during my second year of duty.

It had never occurred to me until that time that personnel policy was so important a field, particularly in peacetime. Obviously, this had not escaped the attention of the Army. In fact, a case could be made that personnel policy in peacetime is as important as plans and operations, which until then had been my main interest. Personnel policy involved a wide range of subjects from pay, to discriminatory practices, to joint-staff duty. I quickly realized that personnel policy could have long-term, significant effects on all the services.

In the Office of Personnel Policy, we were designated as action officers and were assigned actions according to our backgrounds and capability. As an officer demonstrated proficiency in the handling of minor personnel actions, he was given more significant ones.

The term *action officer* meant just that; you took action. You investigated the subject thoroughly, usually checking with all three military departments for their positions. Sometimes, if the stated positions appeared inconsistent with the facts, you probed further for contrasting views. You might seek expert advice on a specific subject from the chief of protocol. On rare occasions, you might even seek an audience with the military secretary to the President—at the time Brigadier General Andrew Goodpaster—to learn the President's opinion.

Having determined in your own mind the most desirable course, you wrote a one-page brief outlining the recommended action and the reasons therefor. (When General George C. Marshall was secretary of defense, he had instituted a policy of single-page briefs despite the complexity of the action, and ever after this practice had been followed as if it were holy writ. If the action required a directive to the military departments, this was included in final form for signature by the appropriate official. In all, it was excellent training for a field-grade officer.

The Director, Office of Personnel Policy, was at that time a disagreeable, eccentric rear admiral of pedestrian talent and obscure
motive. The Navy, it seemed, was slow in recognizing the advantage
of placing top-grade officers in OSD. The admiral's idea of his responsibility in overseeing the three million military and civilian
personnel of the Department of Defense was to side with the majority, without regard to merit. If two of the three military departments were for a proposal, that was good enough for him. Many of
us were unhappy with this simple-minded philosophy. We often penetrated into the military-department staffs to determine what was
really for the overall best rather than to accept a military secretary's recommendation per se, a recommendation that was often
tainted by politics. On one satisfying occasion I learned that the
three military-department staffs were for a proposition even though
the three official positions from the service secretaries were opposed; somehow I persuaded the reluctant admiral to sign off even
though the vote was 0 to 3 against him.

Evidently uncomfortable with his talented, multiservice staff,
the admiral imported two previous associates of questionable credentials. One was a Reserve lieutenant commander who had been
involved as a civilian contractor in some construction projects for
the admiral at the Naval Amphibious Base in Little Creek, Virginia. He was authorized to develop a study on the feasibility of
converting the Post Exchange Service to a cooperative. During an
information-gathering visit to the Army–Air Force Exchange Service in New York City, the lieutenant commander, who weighed in
at about 250 pounds, barged around like a bull in a china shop. He
so antagonized the local commanding officer that the CO appealed
to his superior in Washington to have the lieutenant commander
removed. A telephone call from an Air Force lieutenant general to
the admiral promptly halted further meddling in the exchange
service.

His second import was an Air Force Reserve lieutenant colonel
whose prior duty assignment, insofar as we could determine, had
been to attend to the emotional needs of itinerant flag-grade officers
who found themselves in Paris. He had done such a splendid job
pairing off the visiting brass with feminine companionship in the
middle and upper strata of Parisian society that the generals and
admirals felt constrained to provide him with some employment in
Washington when his tour of duty abroad was over.

To my knowledge this social butterfly, who briefly shared an office with me, spent his year of duty in the Pentagon arranging the Bal de Paris, a flashy, short-lived intrusion on the Washington social scene. He even managed to import for window-dressing a bona fide duchess whom the French Embassy certified as a genuine, albeit obscure, member of the old nobility.

Besides his bizarre choice of staff assistants, the admiral sometimes behaved childishly in the conduct of routine business. One brief that I had written was returned with the comment "Good God!" as the only clue to its inacceptability. Air Force Brigadier General Bob Hall, his deputy, who was barely able to hide his distaste for the admiral's behavior, took the paper back to get an interpretation of the comment. The admiral did not like the word *donee*—it sounded, he said, too much like *chinee*. The brief was retyped with the word *recipient* and he signed off.

The odd goings-on in Personnel Policy did not escape the notice of inspectors. The Office of Naval Intelligence began snooping into the admiral's after-hours activity; almost simultaneously, the administrative high command started investigating the manner in which the admiral conducted his office, including his oddball recruits. Finally, the Navy quietly removed the admiral from the scene, transferring him to a naval base in South Carolina.

The Operations Coordinating Board

The Operations Coordinating Board (OCB) was an outgrowth of World War II—an attempt to coordinate the numerous, varied activities of U.S. agencies overseas. At the time it was chaired by Undersecretary of State Christian Herter, ex governor of Massachusetts. Board members included such potent operatives as Allen Dulles, the boss of the Central Intelligence Agency. But the driving force of the OCB seemed to be Bobby Cutler, a workaholic, bachelor lawyer from Boston who was national security advisor. The national security advisor's role had not yet become as influential as it would in later years (no doubt because President Eisenhower did not feel the need for much advice), but Mr. Cutler was active nonetheless.

In 1958 the OCB was assigned the task of developing a comprehensive report on U.S. administrative practices abroad, to include recommendations on how these might be bettered to improve the reception of U.S. military and civilian personnel stationed in foreign countries. Entitled "United States Employees Overseas," the two-volume report drafted by a working group chaired by the State Department was accorded the unusual distinction of being presented directly to the President. As the Defense Department representative, I spent most of my time for about six months attending meetings and helping to draft the report, conclusions, and recommendations. This interesting experience introduced me to the inner workings of the federal government and prepared me for the remainder of my tour in OSD, for duty in Saigon in 1966, and for my later career in government in the Departments of the Interior and Energy.

The working group was composed of representatives from the Departments of State and Treasury, from the U.S. Information Agency (USIA), the Agency for International Development (AID), and the OCB—all allies of the State Department. Also represented were the Bureau of the Budget (BOB), the White House staff, and the Department of Defense. The White House staff and BOB members, however, were absent more often than not, so I frequently found myself alone on an issue with the State Department and its satellites arrayed against me. Even though defense personnel accounted for about 95 percent of U.S. employees abroad, the 5:1 pressure in working-group arguments was difficult to contend with. On several occasions, I called the White House and BOB members before meeting to ensure their presence in an effort to redress the balance. I found that neither felt much empathy for the State Department clique; they invariably voted with the Defense Department on controversial issues.

One controversial issue regarded the discriminatory practice of allowing embassy employees a far more liberal policy with respect to the possession of foreign currency and purchase of foreign goods than military personnel. I refused to sign off a chapter unless it stated that an effort would be made to eliminate such discrimination or justify its practice openly where deemed necessary. I won the round as far as the report was concerned. Whether this ever translated into action in the field I have no idea.

For all its bureaucratic weaknesses, the OCB was a useful forum. It soon became victim to one of the periodic purges of such groups, this time by President Kennedy. Some thought that its abolition was a mistake. In my opinion it could well have helped to avoid some of the cross-purpose activities of U.S. agencies in Vietnam in 1965 and 1966.

Waffling It

For much of my first year in the Pentagon, I shared an office with Lieutenant Colonel Betty Smith, who might have been head of the Womens Army Corps (WACs) were it not for her portliness. Previous assignments as top WAC in Europe and head of the WAC Training Center had rendered her overqualified for available WAC jobs, so her assignment at OSD was periodically extended. An ex English teacher from Ohio, Betty was known as the Master of the Waffle. When it was believed appropriate to issue a directive on some subject but authorities did not want to be bound too tightly by the written word, it was turned over to Betty to "waffle it." She would water it down with subtle ambiguities so that one was free to interpret it pretty much as one chose. So much did I prize her counsel that in my first year in OSD I regularly showed my briefs to Betty.

Betty could not protect me from all mistakes, however. I had been forced to withdraw a simple personnel directive because I had neglected one agency in the sign-off procedure. Due to this experience, I was determined to clear the new directive on joint-staff duty, which had been mandated by the President, with everyone with a conceivable legitimate interest.

President Eisenhower had become increasingly aggravated by the periodic outbreaks of interservice rivalry. (The controversy over which was the more vulnerable strategic weapons system, the Navy carrier task force or the Air Force's B-36 bomber, had particularly irritated him.) He believed that a better understanding of one another's responsibilities, capabilities, and problems was essential for senior officers. The President believed that duty on the joint staffs fostered such awareness. So the word came down from the White House that the President wanted a directive issued that would require field-grade officers to serve on a joint staff before they would become qualified for promotion to general or flag rank. I drafted such a directive. It was crystal clear and fully captured the President's intent.

It then started up the chain of command. The Assistant General Counsel (Manpower) added a comma; the Deputy Assistant Secretary for Manpower and Personnel, an adjective; the Assistant Secretary, a phrase; the Controller, an adverb; the Military Secretary to the Secretary of Defense, a modifier here and there. And so it went. By the time my crystal-clear directive had been fully approved for publication, it was so obscure that I had to issue a two-page memorandum to clarify it.

Once again the obfuscators had triumphed; the bureaucracy obliquely thwarted the President's wish. Had I waffled it in the first place, I would have saved everyone a lot of trouble.

Representing the Marine Corps

Although the Marines had been offered opportunities to move their headquarters into the Pentagon, they had declined to do so, believing that they were better off a mile up the hill on Arlington Heights. Considering the lack of communication between HQMC and the Pentagon from 1957 to 1960, this short distance could well have been a mile-wide moat teeming with alligators. In fact, the mile could not be negotiated as the crow flies because of a road network that defied pedestrian traffic. The journey consumed nearly an hour for those who had to travel by their own vehicle. The apparent closeness of HQMC was a delusion that effectively forbade OSD interaction with the Marine staff as contrasted to the Army, Navy, and Air Force staffs.

In one instance a Marine memorandum on a proposed personnel action was so ambiguous that I could not determine whether the Corps favored the proposal or not. Believing that I had a responsibility to represent the Corps whenever I could without tarnishing my service-neutral joint-staff status, I visited Major General Don Weller, the Marine Corps G-1, for enlightenment. He explained that those officers who could express themselves clearly and to the point in writing were few and far between at HQMC. General Weller then invited me to attend his weekly staff conferences to learn Marine positions on personnel matters for myself. This proved impractical, but the liaison with the general and his staff that I had established served well enough for the remaining two years of my Pentagon tour.

An unexpected opportunity to do something for the Marine Corps presented itself during the preparation for the ceremony of the burial of the Korean War Unknown. Although the Military District of Washington handled all the details of the burial procession, there were some controversies that were referred to OSD for arbitration. One was the precedence of limousines bearing the government's most powerful personages. The issue was whether the Chief Justice of the Supreme Court and his fellow justices should precede the Speaker of the House of Representatives. The Speaker of the House was not demanding precedence over the Chief Justice, but he would not defer to the associate justices. On the other hand, the Chief Justice contended that the Court always moved as a body. This monumental struggle was finally resolved by having the Speaker and Chief Justice travel side by side in adjacent limousines. Some members of the Court rode with the Chief Justice, the overflow in a trailing limousine.

While seeking this compromise in the best Washington tradition, I delved into protocol. I learned, to my horror, that the commandant of the Marine Corps ranked below assistant secretaries of the Navy. I telephoned the chief of protocol to ask how he dealt with precedence of Defense Department and military-department luminaries at official functions. As far as he was concerned, the chiefs of service ranked right after the military secretaries. I rewrote the directive on precedence, got the chief of protocol to endorse it, and in one fell swoop had the commandant officially elevated over not only the assistant secretaries of service but the assistant secretaries of the Defense Department as well.

A less successful action involved John R. "Russ" Blandford, chief counsel of the House Armed Services Committee. I had known Russ slightly as a lieutenant on Guadalcanal with 2/11. He had stayed with the Marine Corps Reserve through the years and was now a colonel. Seeking to ensure that there were no pitfalls lurking in the path of an action I was handling, I called Russ for help. He assured me that the proposal would have clear sailing. In all honesty it was difficult to see how so meritorious a proposal could have otherwise.

A big-shot Washington financier who had served on General Eisenhower's staff in Europe wanted to do something to promote international understanding, so he had formed the Olmstead Foundation. He proposed to donate more than a million dollars to finance it. The foundation would select two meritorious graduates with language facility from each of the three service academies and foot the expenses for two years at a foreign university. He believed that living with a foreign family while attending school; speaking the language; and participating in the social life, sports, and other activities would forge lifelong friendships among future leaders that could only promote harmonious relations.

A rear admiral from the Navy Department was designated as the witness for the legislation, which would authorize the services to accept money from the foundation. I tried several times to brief the admiral before the scheduled hearing, but he could not spare the time. Nonetheless, I was not overly concerned because it seemed hardly possible that the Congress would object to Mr. Olmstead's magnanimity, a worthy cause that did not require one dime of the taxpayers' money. Besides, Russ had assured me that there would be no difficulty.

The hearings had just gotten under way when an aide whispered to the chairman that he was needed elsewhere. He turned over the chair to his senior colleague, summoned Russ to accompany him, and away they went. The acting chairman seemed favorably inclined to the proposal until the admiral responded to a question by referring to its legal aspects. The chair immediately perked up. "Oh," said the chairman, "perhaps it would be well to defer action now and refer this legislation to the Judiciary Committee." Within seconds the bill was sidetracked.

Salvaging the Olmstead Foundation, I learned later, took two years. Because candidates for the first year had already been selected and sent to language-refresher courses, the services had to find the funds to proceed or shut down a program that had been enthusiastically embraced by the service academies. The Army, Navy, and Air Force decided to eat the costs.

What the admiral did not know when he inadvertently mentioned the legal aspects of the bill was that the chairman had only recently sidetracked a pet project of his senior colleague by referring it to the Judiciary Committee. The opportunity to get even, a time-honored Washington strategy, was too tempting for the acting chairman to pass up.

In 1959 I was made available by OSD to serve as a member of the captain-to-major promotion board at HQMC. A valuable experience, it alerted me to the fragility of the promotion system. The Fitness Report, the principal instrument for measuring an officer's potential for performing in a higher grade, was only marginally adequate. Many of the categories upon which an officer was marked, such as "loyalty," were meaningless. Loyalty to whom? To the marker? To his regiment? To the Marine Corps? To the country? To his own ethical standards?

Periodically, the Marine Corps goes through the evolution of "improving" the Fitness Report, with most of these manifestations striving for greater objectivity. Whereas this is laudable, it is also a snare and a delusion. The Fitness Report is one officer's opinion of another officer's competence and future potential. It is personal; mechanical efforts to make it objective are doomed to failure, tending only to render it more meaningless.

In 1957 General Randolph Pate, the Commandant of the Marine Corps, spoke to the Senior School in Quantico. He reminisced about the time he was commander of the Marine detachment aboard a warship. One of his additional duties was as legal officer, and his responsibilities included processing Fitness Reports. He said that the best report he had ever seen was by a crusty old skipper who ignored the traditional markings, writing in firm hand across the paper, "This is the best damned officer in the Navy." The officer in question: Arleigh Burke.

Another unfortunate effort to make the job of promotion boards easier is the ranking of officers of the same grade within the unit. This is absurd. Is a brilliant staff officer or a dynamic troop commander more valuable to the Marine Corps? All the captains in one battalion may be superior to any of those in another, but only one can be ranked as number one. In a division staff with numerous colonels, what chance do those colonels not ranked "number one" have of becoming generals, even though several may be outstanding officers? Among other things, this ranking requirement penalizes officers whose commanders are collectors of talent. How would I have adequately ranked my talented captains in 3/11?

Yet another inadequacy was the option the RCT commander had with respect to making out reports on attached unit commanders. For example, in Korea in 1950–51 field-artillery battalions were attached to infantry regiments for long intervals—they frequently never even saw the artillery regimental commander for weeks on end. Our Fitness Reports were, nevertheless, submitted by the CO of the artillery regiment. There should have been no option; the infantry-regiment commander should have been required to submit a supplemental report.

Too much reliance on such impersonal, dubious measurements of officer potential, as the GCT, is also dangerous. Whereas GCT scores serve a useful purpose in aiding the selection of candidates for technical schools, they are an uncertain indicator of an officer's value. Some officers with GCTs of 145 or higher, for example, tend to get into trouble in relatively unstructured assignments such as the Reserves or in recruiting. On the other hand, one of the best troop officers I ever knew had a GCT of only 118, supposedly below the level required for officers.

Another point of interest was the relative ease with which one could distinguish the bottom 8 to 10 percent of those in the promotion zone. If attrition beyond that percentage was called for, however, selection at this early stage in an officer's career degenerated quickly into an inexact science. Late bloomers who might eventually become the most competent staff officers or dynamic troop leaders could be weeded out before having had sufficient opportunity to prove themselves. Our promotion board was held up as an example to later boards, I was told, because we picked one officer from above the zone and one from below. These selections, while far from indiscreet, did illustrate two concepts that the Marine Corps wanted to stress. The first was that selection boards are not infallible, and officers should not give up hope when passed over the first time around. The second was that outstanding officers who have demonstrated both ability and maturity beyond their contemporaries have a chance of being promoted early.

Despite inadequacies, the Fitness Report survives in spite of itself largely because promotion boards rely primarily on the written comments and on board officers' personal knowledge of the candidates. Hence, officers who are largely unknown to the board members, such as those who have served on tours with the Army, Navy, Air Force, or joint commands are liable to be handicapped. Of course, there is no way to eliminate completely personal prejudice and favoritism from the selection process, especially in the selection of general officers, where so many are well qualified for so few billets. All in all, the three weeks spent at Headquarters grappling with the promotion system were instructive, if disturbing.

The Issue of Special Pay

One of my assignments toward the end of my Pentagon tour was as watchdog over those seeking special pay. It was my view that special pay was already out of hand and that line officers such as battalion commanders or ship captains were the ones who suffered. And yet various proposals for command pay, which might have reduced the problem, had consistently been turned down by the services (primarily the Army and Marines) because of what they believed to be insuperable problems inherent in the administration of such a system. The submariners, who received extra pay only when actually assigned to sea duty on a submarine tended to resent the aviators, who received it whether assigned to an air squadron or not. That medical officers received extra pay along with special treatment in entry-level rank (they started as first lieutenants instead of second lieutenants) as well as promotion (medical officers were rarely passed over) rankled many and further distorted the pay scales. The situation made a mockery of the concept that one was paid according to level of responsibility.

Using the muscle of the American Medical Association, the doctors had bullied the Defense Department into having their own assistant secretariat, which in my view was unjustified and performed no useful service. It did, however, upset the lawyers, and they would periodically machinate for equal treatment. But they were fighting a losing battle, it seemed—there always appeared to be a shortage of doctors and an abundance of lawyers.

One afternoon the assistant general counsel for manpower, Frank Bartimo, called to ask me to attend a meeting in the general counsel's office in which he expected personnel matters would be discussed; he thought someone other than lawyers should be present. When Frank and I arrived, the three Judge Advocate Generals (JAGs) were already there. Also present was a member of the Philadelphia Bar, the chairman of the American Bar Association's committee on lawyer's pay. He was enroute to the ABA annual meeting in Florida and was seeking DOD endorsement of a resolution on special pay for military lawyers, for which he intended to seek ABA sponsorship. The three JAGs gave hearty approval. Robert Dechert, a Philadelphia lawyer serving as the Defense Department's general counsel, nodded his agreement, and it looked as if the meeting was about to adjourn. Receiving Mr. Dechert's permission to speak, I stated that the JAG endorsement did not represent the official DOD position, that the service chiefs had repeatedly opposed special pay for lawyers, and did so now. If the glares of the two generals and the admiral could kill, I was long dead. The meeting broke up on this sour note.

While I waited for Frank Bartimo to join me for the return up the hall, he whispered a few words to Bobby Dechert. Apparently he advised Mr. Dechert that I was a son of Judge Parry of Philadelphia. Dechert, the son of the National Guard colonel who had appointed Father a second lieutenant in 1900, beckoned me to join him saying, "Colonel Parry, you come by your outspokenness naturally." Then he proceeded to tell me of the purple prose that had been exchanged between his father and my father, his captain adjutant, in the early 1900s.

This brief exchange brought back poignant memories, for Father had died in dramatic fashion just a year before at age 86. He had been unable to restrain himself from participating as an attorney in a case in which he was emotionally involved as cotrustee of a close friend's estate. After vigorously cross-examining a witness, he turned to resume his seat and dropped dead on the floor of the courtroom. Of the numerous acclamations that poured in from members of the Bar, I quote President Judge Klein of the Court of Common Pleas (Father's court before his retirement at age 80):

> Newspapers called him a controversial figure of the Bar and that he was. As a judge he neither sought or cared for public acclaim. He never used his judicial office for self-exploitation. He was not gregarious. His wants were few and he was almost Spartan in his way of life, but he had a capacity for deep and loyal friendships. He had the sterling virtues of loyalty and integrity—loyalty to colleagues, friends and family and an integrity that was firm and unbending. He always had the courage to do what he thought was right and he never trimmed his sails to the shifting winds of popular opinion.

That was Father's legacy to his sons. Needless to say, the military lawyers did not get extra pay in 1960.

The Government at Work

What did I learn from over three years of service in the military headquarters of the most powerful nation on earth? Not much that was inspirational. It was instructive to see how the bureaucracy worked or did not work, according to your viewpoint, to observe the federal departments and agencies pursuing their own agendas, and to realize how little effect a President really has on the functioning of government. It was both disturbing and reassuring—disturbing to contemplate how easy it was for the headless bureaucracy to subvert the wishes of those in authority and reassuring to understand that the government operates almost oblivious to the machinations and posturing of the leadership. I learned that integrity and perseverance are as valuable traits in dealing with agencies of government as they are in private life, that government bullies—administration and congressional alike—often back off when confronted by a strongly held position based on integrity.

It was also interesting to observe how few of the individuals in positions of authority do anything constructive. Oh, they keep the vast and senseless paper mill running, they attend endless conferences, and hold staff meetings to deliver themselves of bright remarks that suggest that they are in the know. Most of them could go on a leave of absence for a year and would not be missed. The necessary business of government would continue. And these are the good guys.

There were some offices right within the Manpower and Personnel secretariat that performed no useful function at all. But no one had the initiative, persistence, and guts to phase them out. When I suggested that we recommend closing them down, there was little enthusiasm: Why create a controversy or why risk retaliation from their friends and allies? So these hangers-on drank coffee, occupied space, drew salaries, even signed off on an occasional document— but they performed no useful service. How could a bona fide housecleaning fail to smoke these people out?

Once there was a so-called 10-percent reduction in Department of Defense personnel, the meat-axe approach. But the bureaucracy had dealt with such administration tantrums before. So the trash piled up in the corridors and the lavatories went uncleaned, but not a single GS-13, or -14 or -15 was told to seek employment elsewhere. And soon the crisis was over, it was business as usual as the lowest, most vulnerable end of the work force, the janitorial service, was resuscitated and the world's largest office building tidied up again.

All of my impressions of the federal government were not negative. I was associated with a highly respected civil servant, the director of the Office of Civilian Personnel Policy, who refused promotion from GS-16 to GS-18 because he believed that he could accomplish more of a useful, enduring nature by staying where he was. I was impressed by the intelligence and dedication of a number of congressmen and by the desire of many field-grade and general officers to do what was in their view best for the country rather than cling to some parochial, single-service bias.

By the time I left OSD in the autumn of 1960, I believed that I could operate successfully within the framework of government. You could always find someone—if you looked hard enough—who would be willing to help you get some worthwhile action accomplished. In spite of the many excesses and inconsistencies of our federal system, you could make the system work if you had a worthy, needed program, had developed a sensible strategy, and if you persevered. Although this knowledge would benefit me little during the remainder of my military service, it would be of real value to me later, in civil service, my second career.

17

Troop Duty

Regimental Commander

In consideration of our mentally retarded fifth son, HQMC—in a typical demonstration of taking care of its own—changed my orders upon request from 2nd Marine Division in North Carolina to 1st Marine Division in California. California was reputed to have a far more enlightened program for dealing with mentally handicapped children. We left the Washington area in September 1960.

Arrival at Camp Pendleton in late September meant that all the coveted regimental command and general-staff jobs had long since been filled. For about eight months I was assigned as director of the Exercise Control and Inspection Group (ECIG). Although the position lacked the stature of the prized colonel billets, ECIG did have its compensations. I had the opportunity to make myself as valuable to the commanding general and chief of staff as I was inclined.

With a staff of about twenty, my principal role was to plan and conduct major field exercises. The exercises usually involved amphibious assault over the three main Pendleton beaches, helicopter redeployments, and follow-on inland phases at the vast Twentynine Palms desert training area.

ECIG was also responsible for division command-post exercises, and it was as a result of this responsibility that I was asked to critique the Marine division's dual-headquarters organization. The concept of Alpha and Bravo headquarters derived from the desire to provide more command-control flexibility and staying power in the face of tactical atomic weapons. In my opinion it was an operational monstrosity. Not only did it split communication and staff resources, it also introduced needless command-control uncertainties. Major General Henry Paige agreed with this view, and our recommendation to HQMC detailing the liabilities of the dual arrangement was accepted. The table of organization was revised accordingly.

I took command of the 11th Marines on August 1, 1962. About a week later I asked Major General Jimmy Masters, the new division commander, for permission to reorganize the regiment to improve readiness. When the general expressed surprise at so drastic a suggestion just after assuming command, I explained that Major General Paige had promised me the 11th months earlier and that I had closely observed the regiment for about six months. I had come to firmly believe that the current organization would be impractical in combat. Primarily, none of the infantry regiments would accept the 4.2-inch mortar battalion for direct artillery support. Indeed, the regimental commanders were violently outspoken on this point, and with good reason. Among other things the mortars had only half the range of the howitzers, a serious deficiency for a direct-support "artillery" weapon.

I explained to the division commader that if I used the three 105mm howitzer battalions in direct support, I would have no general-support artillery at all since the 4.2-inch mortar was a weapon for special situations only. I told the general that I would like to form an advisory committee of the four battalion commanders with the mission of proposing a practical temporary reorganization that I would then present to him for approval. General Masters gave me his somewhat reluctant consent.

Two weeks later I proposed an organization of three direct-support battalions of two 105mm howitzer batteries and one 4.2-inch mortar battery each. The general-support battalion would consist of the three remaining 105mm howitzer batteries. The weapons, prime movers, and other equipment would be transferred between battalions on a temporary basis. The battalion commanders and I recognized that this would amount to an equipment accountability nightmare, but we were willing to live with it to render the regiment operationally viable. The justification for having the mortar battalion as part of the artillery regiment—if indeed there had ever been one—was the fact that it was transportable by helicopter. Now that modern helicopters could carry 105mm howitzers without difficulty, this "justification" had evaporated. The general gave his approval, and throughout the year we operated on this organizational basis. (About eighteen months later HQMC revised the Marine Division Tables of Organization back to their Korean War status: three 105mm howitzer battalions and one 155mm howitzer battalion.)

"You of All People"

Soon after I became the 1st Marine Division G-3 in June 1962, Major General Herman Nickerson assumed command of the division. Herman the German was a rugged six-footer from Massachusetts who had been a first-rate ice-hockey goalie at Boston University. Somewhat stubborn and with a low boiling point, the general would, nonetheless, listen to reason and was not difficult to work with so long as you did not cross him in public and allowed his blood pressure to return to normal after bringing up controversial subjects. Our relationship dated from duty together on the Advance Base Problem team in 1952 and 1953. We were not close, but our relationship was friendly and relaxed.

One of the division's important responsibilities in the early '60s was to supply a well-trained and well-equipped infantry battalion about every six weeks to 3rd Marine Division, which was based on Okinawa. The objective of the "transplacement" system was to maintain 3rd Marine Division in top readiness for deployment to trouble spots in the western Pacific, from Korea to Southeast Asia. Because of this training responsibility, 1st Marine Division was always short a battalion and frequently short of two since the returning battalion lost many of its men upon arrival to other duty stations or discharge from the service. Such units had to be remanned, re-equipped, and retrained before they could be considered operational. Other than the debilitating effect on 1st Marine Division, it was considered a successful system, the pride of its architects in the Fleet Marine Force, Pacific, Headquarters. After intimate involvement with it for a year, however, I believed that it had two flaws in addition to 1st Marine Division's lack of readiness: The battalion commander was assigned by HQMC, and the system ignored the importance of regimental integrity.

In a regimental amphibious assault training exercise in which we were using the soon-to-be-deployed transplacement battalion as the aggressor force, the battalion commander disregarded written

and verbal instructions to withdraw from a key hill that was blocking the entire assault force. I helicoptered in and ordered him to
follow the script. The eight-hour delay had thrown the entire exercise into disarray inasmuch as the schedule had been designed to
utilize all suitable terrain by the operation's conclusion. It was not
the only instance of the battalion commander's questionable behavior over the four-day exercise. I recommended his replacement, but
nothing came of it because HQMC had assigned him. So the unimpressive officer was soon one of the battalion commanders in the
brigade deployment to Laos where, fortunately for the Marine
Corps, he was not tested.

When a regimental commander has little to say about who his
battalion commanders are to be or, indeed, what battalions are to
constitute his regiment from month to month, how is he to foster
regimental esprit de corps?

In 1963, HQMC decided that more troops were needed at Twentynine Palms, so 4/11 was ordered to permanent duty there. The
11th Marines commander had nothing to say about one of his four
battalions being taken from under his wing, moved into the desert a
hundred miles away, for all intents and purposes just another independent Force Troops battalion. How was the 11th Marine Regiment supposed to learn how to integrate the fires of its 155mm
general-support battalion with those of its three 105mm direct-
support battalions? How could the regimental commander ensure
that his four battalions were uniformly well trained? Marines need
to identify with a regiment. Somehow the system should take into
account this need, this important source of cohesiveness.

At a briefing prior to a 1st Marines two-week training exercise
in the desert at Twentynine Palms, General Nickerson questioned
the task organization. What was the 3rd Battalion, 11th Marines,
doing as direct-support artillery to the 1st Marines? Didn't 3/11
traditionally support the 7th Marines? Lieutenant Colonel Tom
Randall, who had replaced me as CO of 11th Marines, looked to me
for support. Both Tom and I knew that Colonel Charlie Hodges, the
CO of 1st Marines, had refused to accept 1/11 as direct support since
at Tom's direction 1/11 had reverted to its authorized status as a
4.2-inch mortar battalion. Hence, Tom had to assign either 2/11
(traditional direct support of the 5th Marines) or 3/11. I rose to
defend the troop list.

By then, however, the general's indignation had been aroused.
Before I could explain the reason for abandoning tradition, Nick—

who had commanded the 7th RCT in Korea in 1951—invoked the glory days of the inseparability of 3/11 and the 7th Marines. He spoke of Inchon, the Reservoir, and beyond, when 3/11 had been such an integral part of the 7th Regiment that it was routinely known as 4/7. He declaimed, "Fox! You of all people!" I knew then that it was time to back off. When Tom appealed to me privately after the briefing, I told him that I would not go to the mat with Herman the German on that issue—it was bigger than all of us.

18

Cuba

The Reality

From the viewpoint of 1st Marine Division in Southern California, the Cuban missile crisis contained almost all the elements of an overseas military expedition. The bulk of the division was positioned by air and sea in the target area, and the final elements were readied for commitment by air. The only element lacking was the command *execute* from the Joint Chiefs of Staff. That the order never came is history.

When tension began to mount in the Caribbean in the late summer of 1962, the division was directed to reinforce the naval base at Guantanamo Bay, Cuba, with an infantry battalion. The battalion was augmented by all the usual support troops as well as additional field artillery and antitank increments. The mount-out was staged from El Toro Marine Corps Air Station about 50 road miles north of Camp Pendleton. At El Toro the Air Force Air Transport Command assembled cargo and troop carriers from around the world. It was an impressive and sobering experience to observe the Air Force go into action—impressive in regard to the efficiency with which the lift-out was conducted by the Air Force control team and sobering from the standpoint of the great effort necessary to mount out just one reinforced infantry battalion by air (about 2,000 men in all).

Guantanamo Bay had been defended for many months by a reinforced battalion from 2nd Marine Division, which was based at

Camp Lejeune, North Carolina. As the crisis deepened, another battalion of 2nd Marine Division had been deployed, and a Navy provisional battalion was organized from sailors who could be spared
from their regular duties. This defense group was now swelled by
the battalion of 1st Marine Division to a healthy regiment-sized
force with beyond-normal augmentation of field artillery, antitank,
and air units. The sprawling base was interlaced by numerous bays
extending from the main anchorages. How well the ad hoc regiment
could have defended it from a determined attack is conjectural. It
certainly could have given a good account of itself and, of course,
reinforcement by sea if not by air was certain.

While this force dug in, a brigade of some 15,000 Marines was
readied for deployment by sea from the San Diego–Long Beach
area. Under command of Brigadier General Willie Fairbourn, the
1st Marine Division assistant commander, this brigade constituted
most of the operational division troops. To the brigade was added a
strong composite air group of fighters, attack planes, and helicopters. Four infantry battalions and a replacement battalion of infantry "fillers" formed the maneuver complement. These battalions
were backed up by light and medium field artillery, tank, antitank,
engineer, motor-transport, and shore-party units and all the other
combat and combat-support elements required for an amphibious
assault and protracted offensive operations ashore. This formidable,
near-division-sized task force "quietly" sortied from San Diego,
transited the Panama Canal, and took up station in the Caribbean
just over the horizon from eastern Cuba. When ordered, it would
land in the vicinity of Guantanamo Bay and join forces with the
three battalions ashore to conduct operations inland.

Remaining at Camp Pendleton were two battalions of the 5th
Marines, the 5th Marines headquarters, the 11th Marines headquarters, the division headquarters, and separate battalions
largely denuded of troops. At the height of the missile crisis in late
October, 1st Marine Division (minus) received a dispatch from the
Joint Chiefs of Staff directing, on order, the air deployment to Guantanamo Bay of the 5th Marines (minus one battalion) and Division
headquarters. The commanding general, 1st Marine Division, upon
his arrival was to assume command of all forces in the area, including the brigade (when landed). He was to prepare for further offensive operations to the north and west.

I joined General Nickerson in his quarters around midnight at
the height of the tension. I asked his judgment as to when we would

receive the order to execute. He replied, "If we don't get it within the next few hours, I think the operation will be called off."

Eventually the seaborne brigade and the airlifted battalion were returned to Camp Pendleton, and the division went back to business as usual, with one exception. Because of 2nd Marine Division's commitments in the Mediterranean and Europe, responsibility for defense of Guantanamo Bay was assigned to 1st Marine Division. After discussions with officers of the battalion that had recently returned from there, the G-3 section developed a base-defense plan. Although it might have been desirable to have flown to Guantanamo to view the terrain first hand, the keepers of the newly depleted division coffers thought this an unnecessary expense, what with the availability of current defense plans, detailed maps, and recent returnees. I had been in Guantanamo Bay twice before. Once, in the summer of 1940, as a midshipman aboard the battleship USS *New York,* we had languished in the anchorage for about a week. I went ashore on several occasions and took an overnight run on a Navy destroyer to the picturesque inland harbor of Santiago de Cuba about 50 miles to the west. I was there again in 1947, while enroute to inspecting the shore-bombardment range facilities at Culebra. Although these visits hardly qualified me as an expert on the shore-defense characteristics of the base, I was at least generally familiar with the terrain and harbor. In any event, the defense plan was just a contingency plan, one of thousands developed by the U.S. armed forces through the years.

What Might Have Been

We will never know whether the decision to abort the invasion after deployment of over 300,000 troops, hundreds of ships, and thousands of planes to the target area was the right one. To assemble so vast an armed force at the cost of billions of dollars and then to parlay its presence to only temporary gain certainly raised questions around the world as to U.S. judgment and determination. If the world's mightiest nation hesitates to use its power in a cause so close to home and so readily justifiable, where and when—if ever—will it use it?

Perhaps it was the failure to follow up the advantage clearly won by this awesome display of armed might rather than the standing down of the invasion itself that should bear the principal blame. For, as everyone knows today, U.S. muscle flexing did not succeed in deterring the Soviet Union from turning Cuba into an aggressive satellite. Thus, the aborted invasion or bungled follow-up—to whichever one ascribes the blame—has resulted in who-knows-what long-term damaging effects to the United States, not only in the Caribbean but throughout Latin America and the world. Further, the psychological reaction to this pull-back decision may well have played a determining role in our leaders' future actions, which drew us into the ultimate debacle in Vietnam.

For me, the opportunity of a lifetime—to be operations officer of 1st Marine Division, reinforced, as it slashed north and westward out of the Guantanamo Bay beachhead to link up with the main-assault forces in the vicinity of Havana—was lost forever.

Before we would have been ready for such a breakout, however, there would have been some interesting problems to resolve. The first would have been the reorganization of the division after arriving on the scene. Two battalions and the abbreviated regimental headquarters of 2nd Marine Division composed the bulk of the Guantanamo Bay defense force. These battalions, with our heavily reinforced battalion (which had been airlifted there) constituted a regiment. The 5th Marines, which would accompany us there in the airlift from the West Coast, was minus a battalion and would have had to pick one up from the brigade, which had four. Assuming that we retained indefinitely the two battalions of 2nd Marine Division, our infantry would have been at full strength.

The artillery would not have been so easy to piece together. The remaining 105mm batteries at Camp Pendleton would have had to be flown to Guantanamo Bay on a priority basis, as would the 11th Marines headquarters. The lack of any general-support artillery— 155mm howitzers—would have constituted a serious deficiency. The issue would have been whether to bring 1/11 armed with 4.2-inch mortars or only the FO and liaison teams needed to convert 4/11 into a direct-support battalion. The 155mm howitzers available from Force Troops would have been a higher priority than the mortars.

The headquarters and service elements of the division's separate battalions as well as any remaining companies—such as tanks, engineers, or motor transport—would all have been needed. In contrast to an amphibious assault, these units were not sitting offshore prepared to land on call; they were at Camp Pendleton, some 5,000 sea miles away. And much of their equipment would have had to come by sea.

As soon as the brigade had landed, we would have had to make plans for the rapid absorption of its headquarters back into the division headquarters and the air group. We would have had to piece together temporary headquarters for the artillery and combat and service battalions for operational control and planning. My experience at Guadalcanal and Inchon suggested that we might have been committed to action almost immediately, ready or not. For if we were to be of real assistance to the main assault in the Havana area, we would have had to move out of the beachhead and strike north and west promptly. There was little question that the general staff would have had its work cut out for it, planning and operating with temporary headquarters and jury-rigged units.

These handicaps would have added spice to the operation. That the division would have landed in or adjacent to a secure beachhead was, on the other hand, a huge plus. Amphibious-assault divisions usually have no plans beyond the landing and seizure of initial objectives ashore, and we had no plans for the subsequent breakout from the Guantanamo Bay area. The development of plans concerned me a lot less than the orderly organization and positioning of the combat and service forces within the beachhead for the initial breakout—the piecemeal commitment of the division in the objective area by air and sea represented a unique experience for a Marine division.

I did not discuss any of these thoughts with General Nickerson, whom I was sure had been committed to the strictest secrecy by HQMC. I know, however, that for an hour or so, while we held our breath in the general's quarters awaiting the President's invasion decision and the order *execute* from the Joint Chiefs of Staff, we were eager to accept the challenge.

PART V

Vietnam

19

Military Assistance Command, Vietnam

From Newport to Saigon

The landing of a Marine brigade in the Danang area of central
Vietnam in the spring of 1965 signified the beginning of full-scale
U.S. involvement. Our involvement would swell to over a half million troops within Vietnam and almost that number in supporting
naval, air-strike, and logistics elements stationed from Thailand to
the West Coast. The modest toe wetting on the southeastern littoral
of the Asian continent in 1965 scarcely caused a raised eyebrow in
the United States. At the time I was comfortably situated at the
Naval War College in Newport, Rhode Island.

It was an ideal assignment. As director of the Strategic Plans
Division, I was responsible for one third of the senior course, which
comprised Navy captains and commanders; Marine, Army, and Air
Force colonels and lieutenant colonels; plus a handful of senior
foreign-service military officers and Department of Defense
civilians—about 160 in all. In the summer I was charged with running a two-week course for senior Navy Reserve officers, including
many big-shot businessmen and professionals who had retained
their status as Reserve admirals or captains. Being senior Marine
on the staff and chairman of the Athletic Committee rounded out
my interesting, pleasant, and not unprestigious duties.

The city of Newport was a charming fishing village and yacht-
ing center with an overlay of money and class, fabulous mansions,
and lingering social status from the days when it was society's play-
ground. To a tennis buff, the Newport Casino is a sparkling green
gem. With sailing and seafood, invigorating summer weather, and
proximity to New England's treasures, no duty in our quarter century in the service was more pleasurable. Even our living accommodations were superb. We lived in Fort Adams on a narrow peninsula
guarding the channel entrance to Narragansett Bay. The original
plans for our Quarters 9 had been approved in 1848 by 2nd Lieutenant Robert E. Lee, U.S. Army Corps of Engineers.

Vietnam was a war that, for me, was easily avoidable. I had
been passed over once by the committee that selected generals.
With at least another year to go on my War College tour, I could
have served until the following year's selection board, at which time
I would automatically have been retired if I failed to earn a promotion. But I had spent almost thirty years preparing for and following a military career, and I felt compelled to strive for the top as
long as there was a chance. And what better place to make a name
for myself than this new war? So, for the third time in my career, I
ventured to Washington and volunteered for war service.

Although my dispatch orders to Vietnam came a few weeks
later, we were allowed enough time to check out of government
quarters for the last time and move Vera and John, our only son left
at home, across the country to our house in Oceanside, California.

It was with a heavy heart that I said goodbye to Vera and John
in the Los Angeles airport and started westward across the Pacific
for the fifth time. After an overnight layover in Honolulu, I flew via
Okinawa and Clark Field in the Philippines to Saigon. I spent the
better part of two days on Okinawa, where I had to get a full complement of immunization shots for tropical Asia. We proceeded to
Tan Son Nhut Airbase, arriving in midafternoon, Sunday, October
30, 1965.

Saigon and Points Afield

My first day in Saigon was not an auspicious one. The war had not
yet heated up, and Sunday was still a day of leisure. Okinawa must
have failed to notify the Military Assistance Command, Vietnam
(MACV) of my arrival or the notification was sitting on someone's
vacant desk. In any case, no one met me. After repeated inquiries of

the stoical Vietnamese in English and halting French, I found a MACV directory and telephoned the G-1 duty officer. In about forty-five minutes an apologetic Army lieutenant colonel arrived, and we set off for downtown. The inroads of a lowland tropical climate (Saigon was built over a swamp) were evident in many places. Stucco facing on brick walls was everywhere peeling off in picturesque decay. He took me to the Rex Hotel in the center of Saigon and showed me to drab but adequate accommodations on the fifth floor. As I sat in the gathering dusk, my loneliness was promptly compounded by the first of many electrical blackouts—the electrical system in Saigon was becoming increasingly overburdened. The realization that I had no candles or flashlight and did not know where to get potable water intensified my sense of disquietude. At that moment, however, Major Jim King, senior Marine in J-3 (the staff responsible for short-range plans and operations), called on the telephone to welcome me aboard. Within twenty minutes Jim was in my room with candles, flashlight, and two bottles of drinking water.

The Rex Hotel, though unprepossessing, was reasonably comfortable by Asian standards. It housed senior officers—generals without villas, colonels, visiting firemen, and some senior lieutenant colonels. I stayed there for about three months. Other hotels downtown housed lower-ranking field-grade officers. Most of the company-grade officers and enlisted men were billeted farther out, toward Tan Son Nhut. The dining room on the roof of the Rex, with a large outdoor patio, commanded a panoramic view of Saigon from about twelve stories up. The elevation provided some relief from the noise and gasoline fumes of the heavy vehicular traffic below, including thousands upon thousands of unmuffled, motorized two- and three-wheelers.

Despite the racket and choking fumes on the main arteries, Saigon in late 1965 still retained much of the charm that had earned it the title "Paris of the Orient." You could still stroll the broad boulevards, appreciate the stately mansions, and visualize what French colonialism had wrought in its heyday. An unceasing joy was the slender Vietnamese woman in her graceful *ao dai*, a long, tight-fitting dress with the skirt split to above the knee.

The social center of Saigon was the Circle Sportif. Here the French overlords, the foreign big shots, and—more recently—the elite Vietnamese, refreshed themselves in an olympic-sized pool or relaxed on the surrounding terraces with drink in hand. There were about twelve tennis courts for the athletically minded. It was a charming place to have a light lunch or dinner and contemplate the French and Vietnamese females disporting themselves in mini bikinis.

One of my first discoveries in Saigon was that General William Westmoreland had changed his mind about the advisability of a joint Vietnamese-Allied command. (The Allied forces were primarily American, but they also included Korean and Australian troops.) Inasmuch as I had been ordered to Saigon to head up the Plans Division of the joint command, I was now without a job. Fortunately for me, the executive assistant to the J-3, to whom I reported for duty, was a sharp young Army lieutenant colonel who had been a student of mine at the Naval War College. He gave me a strong boost to Brigadier General William DePuy, the J-3. So I was taken into the J-3 family without portfolio. I set about learning the ropes.

Bill DePuy was slight, of small stature, and—as is often the case—of Napoleanic cast. He had graduated from South Dakota State College in 1940 and put in for the only available Marine commission. He lost out and threw his lot in with the Army. He had prospered and within a few months of my arrival in Saigon was promoted to major general. Eventually he was an Army vice-chief of staff with four stars. A brilliant staff officer, Westmoreland leaned on him heavily. It often seemed that they took little counsel of anyone else.

The deputy commander, Lieutenant General John Heintges, spent much of his time visiting Special Forces outposts and had little input to strategic plans and operations. The chief of staff, Major General Bill Rosson, concerned himself primarily with administrative and logistic matters. So there was much truth in the assertion that the chain of command was Westmoreland to DePuy to the field. It soon became apparent to me that part of the Westmoreland–DePuy mystique derived from their detailed knowledge of Southeast Asian geography and Vietnamese topography and place names. To be able to understand DePuy, much less prove useful to him, it was essential to gain comparable grasp.

Fortunately, I love geography. It was no chore for me to spend hours poring over maps. To reinforce this study, field trips to each of the four corps areas were scheduled for the better part of three weeks. At IV Corps in the Mekong Delta, there was a little excitement when the Viet Cong (VC) half-heartedly harassed the Vietnamese division advisor's compound at My Tho. Two days later, after visiting the corps advisor in Can Tho, I flew by helicopter to observe a B-52 raid on a reported VC staging area in the jungle by the coast. We landed after the B-52s had devastated the target, only to find not a single trace of VC. Unfortunately, many B-52 raids, despite their accuracy, had similar results. The B-52s, hours away at their base on Guam, were hardly an appropriate weapon to use against a transitory target, and the VC always seemed to anticipate us by a few hours.

The II Corps area, including the Vietnamese highlands, was by far the largest operational area. Initially, General Westmoreland committed most of his elite Army troops to this region. In fact, it seemed that Westmoreland had some sort of a high-plateau fixation, a conviction that this spacious tableland would play a dominant role in South Vietnam's future. Perhaps this was wishful thinking inasmuch as it was an ideal test site for the Army's new vertical-envelopment equipment and tactics.

Brigadier General Dick Knowles, assistant commander of 1st Air Cavalry Division—which was stationed at An Khe, on the eastern edge of the highlands, about 30 miles east of Pleiku—had been a classmate of mine at Fort Sill in 1950–51. I spent the night in his tent and helicoptered around the highlands with him. First Air Cav was an impressive outfit. It proved itself at the battle of the Ia Drang Valley a few weeks later, when it surprised a good part of a division-sized unit and mauled it. A few months earlier, the Marines had trapped and wiped out a VC regiment on a peninsula in southern I Corps—the northernmost military region in South Vietnam. This encounter and Ia Drang Valley were the only times that the VC and North Vietnamese Army (NVA) ever tried to engage large U.S. combat units during my tour. The enemy was far more effective in small-unit action, where vastly superior U.S. firepower and air mobility could not be brought to bear.

I seized every opportunity to accompany General DePuy on his frequent one- and two-day jaunts, mostly to II Corps. We visited Field Force I Headquarters at Nha Trang, the major logistical port of Qui Nhon, airstrips at Tuy Hoa, Phan Rang, and Kontum, and the huge harbor at Cam Ranh Bay, where a crack Korean Marine brigade provided security. We also toured the front lines of a Korean Army division. The Koreans looked sharp and proved themselves to be good defensive fighters a few months later, when the VC tested their lines. (From then on the VC gave them wide berth.) I also made many trips to I Corps, which was the responsibility of the Marines. Since I knew many of the key players, from Lieutenant

General Lew Walt on down, I was always well received and hospitably ferried around by helicopter or jeep. Since Saigon resided within the III Corps area, I had many opportunities to see the key sites there. Within a month I gained a fair working knowledge of the terrain and troop situation and easily outdistanced the Army and Air Force colonels in J-3. Doing so, I impressed DePuy.

The Combat Operations Center

From my first days in J-3, it became clear that the overgrown advisory staff, which had been adequate before the days of major U.S. troop deployment, was now totally inadequate. As troop units began to arrive, corps-sized U.S. headquarters started forming—III MAF (Marine Amphibious Force) in Danang, FFI (Field Force I) in Nha Trang, and FFII (Field Force II) in Bien Hoa. The need for an operations and short-range planning staff became urgent. Westmoreland and DePuy had anticipated this requirement and conceived the idea of a major staff organization called the Combat Operations Center (COC). It would be the nerve center of headquarters and located in the small compound with the commanding general. During 1966 the COC grew to 112 officers and ninety enlisted men, or about half of the J-3 division. The COC also included elements of J-2 (intelligence), J-4 (logistics) and J-6 (communications). It quickly crowded most of the J-2 section out of the command compound. J-1 (personnel), J-4, J-5 (long-range planning), and J-6 had long since been scattered to other compounds, mostly on the way to or at Tan Son Nhut Airbase.

Approval of the formation of the COC by the Joint Chiefs of Staff was considered pro forma. However, it soon became the center of interservice rivalry. The Air Force demanded that the director be from that service rather than from the Marine Corps. This infuriated Westmoreland. He needed an effective operations center right away. He also wanted a closer tie to his major forces in the north, the U.S. Marines. No Marine general was in Saigon, yet it was obvious that the rapidly arriving Marine forces would soon constitute about half of his combat strength. Westmoreland remained adamant while the Joint Chiefs of Staff, not an instrument of quick decision, deliberated.

DePuy reasoned that turning the COC over to a Marine general would be facilitated if a Marine colonel started it up, and in the unhappy event that an Air Force general was issued to them, they would want a Marine deputy. DePuy also saw the need to focus short-range plans and operations immediately and Westmoreland agreed that not another day should be wasted. The COC was activated in late November 1965 with me as its first director—the only director who was a colonel. Brigadier General William Jones, USMC, would not arrive until January 1, 1966 and would not take over active direction until late February. So, for me, the next three months were pressure packed and hectic.

The COC was composed of four elements: short-range plans, operations, air, and the Command Center. It was the Command Center that became the focus of day-to-day activity, the showplace of headquarters, and the sine qua non for all visiting firemen of consequence. Tim Brown, an Army colonel who had commanded a brigade (regiment) of 1st Air Cavalry Division during the battle of the Ia Drang Valley, was selected to head this division. He was a West Point graduate, Class of 1943, and quietly competent. (I remember him primarily for his reaction to the Letter of Commendation offered in recognition of his six-month stint with the COC. He considered it an insult. Verifying the inflation that had taken place in Army medal giving, we later offered him a meritorious Bronze Star.)

The Command Center was manned twenty-four hours a day with nine officers on duty much of the time. These were the J-2, J-4, and J-6 watch officers, one watch officer for each of the four corps areas (these were cut to two at night), and one each for air and naval matters (these were combined at night).

As the war heated up during the winter of 1965–66, the National Command Center in Washington demanded more and more information, regardless of the twelve-hour difference in time zones. Modern communications soon became a real curse. It had been a time-honored ploy of overseas commanders to disregard stupid or inconvenient orders by saying they had not been received or understood. The convention was not readily available to Westmoreland; LBJ could get him anywhere within Vietnam within minutes. This led to micromanagement of the war by politicians, which—as much as anything—guaranteed ultimate disaster.

An early fratricidal battle within J-3 developed over responsibility for short-range plans. Should the J-3 plans group or the COC plans division call the shots? Inasmuch as J-5 had responsibility for long-range plans, there was presumably not much turf to divide up. This was resolved without undue bloodshed by giving COC responsibility for plans up to one year since short-range plans could not be readily separated from operations—at least that was my argument. J-3 Plans then concerned itself with medium-range plans of one to three years. J-5 was not too happy with this arrangement but was unwilling to bring the issue to Westmoreland, where DePuy invariably emerged as the winner. So, in effect, DePuy absconded with Plans as well as Operations, and J-5 subsided into a dream world.

Our air division was the scene of some unforgettable sessions. Here, a favored few would assemble to select targets for B-52 raids, or—to be more accurate—to watch Westy select the targets. These sessions illustrated the difficulty confronting a modern industrial power trying to apply sophisticated intelligence-gathering and analytic techniques to a guerilla situation in the enemy's agrarian homeland. There was just no way that we could find a suitable target for B-52s except by sheer chance. The reason was simple: There were no targets because the Viet Cong saw to it that there were none. Even in their forest hideaways, which were hundreds of square miles in area and almost unpenetrable by any means, they rarely presented targets of rewarding size for any length of time. But Westmoreland had a weapon at hand, the B-52, which he wanted to use, so he elected to use it pretty much the way an artillerist employs harassing-and-interdicting fire. Based upon the best intelligence he had available, he guessed where likely targets might be a half day later, by the time the B-52s were briefed at Guam and flew across thousands of miles of Pacific Ocean and South China Sea to make their strike. To me, the deployment of the B-52s (at least during my time in Vietnam) was the first indication of the futility of conventional U.S. tactics against an enemy who was everywhere, yet nowhere, and almost indistinguishable from friends. Strategic bombing was used in South Vietnam because it was available—not because there were any appropriate targets for it.

In early December, as the COC was experiencing severe growing pains, a personnel situation developed that had a resounding effect on the organization for many months. One afternoon after I had come in from a field trip, the sergeant major closed the door to my office and reported that a serious argument had taken place within full view of several enlisted men. A crusty old Army tank colonel and a precocious Army lieutenant colonel had engaged in a violent confrontation, which ended in a shoving match. After hearing both sides of the story separately, including the colonel's demand that his subordinate be fired, I decided to seek advice from DePuy. Not only were these both Army officers, but the colonel was only slightly junior to me.

DePuy evidently saw this as an opportunity to demonstrate support for me as director, as well as to assure our integrated command (Army, Navy, Air Force, and Marines) that no unofficerlike conduct would be tolerated, regardless of service affiliation. He fired them both, sending one to FFII and the other to J-2. He then asked me if I had any other officers who were not performing up to snuff. Seeing this as a golden opportunity to unload two Army majors who were not producing, I mentioned them. They were promptly dispatched to other staffs. When the dust settled there was little disposition in any service to question my authority in the COC—for a few months at least.

Alsop and Walt

This was a heady period for me. The COC, through its air division, had access to both helicopters and small twin-engine, propeller-driven planes (U-8s). This ensured me a high degree of mobility, permitting flights throughout Vietnam on short notice. I took advantage of this mobility often to familiarize myself with the various parts of the country, although these excursions were invariably tied to necessary liaison trips to field headquarters. My profound impression from these safaris was of the vast, almost impenetrable jungle areas, and the enormous mountainous sections of the country. These areas were almost uncharted, much less inhabited.

One evening in mid winter, DePuy called me in to ask me to take Joe Alsop, the so-called Dean of American War Correspondents, on a trip I was making to Danang the next morning. I picked up Alsop early in the morning at the Hotel Majestic in downtown Saigon and drove him to my U-8 at Tan Son Nhut. Soon after we were airborne on the four-hour flight to Danang, we entered into a discussion of the war. This quickly turned heated when I charged that the buildup in Vietnam was denuding the U.S. Army in Germany of many crucial technicians who were then in short supply. Alsop denied it. I said that I had talked to many who substantiated the fact. Alsop would not listen. We rode the remaining three hours to Danang in silence. Upon arrival, we proceeded in separate sedans to Lieutenant General Lew Walt's III MAF headquarters. We both talked to the chief of staff, explaining our desire to see Walt. In a few minutes the chief invited me into the general's office. After a brief discussion concerning Westy's instructions, Lew took me by the arm and we proceeded out the rear door to a waiting helicopter. I saluted and he was off to visit his troops. He had not bothered to see the Dean of American War Correspondents.

I am not sure why he decided to give Alsop the brush-off. Perhaps he was aware, as was I, that Alsop's stout defense of administration policy was not what you should expect from a respected journalist. Perhaps Walt had developed a hearty contempt for the press. In any case, the incident was a matter of some amusement to me and of extreme annoyance to Alsop.

The Loft

A few weeks after the COC was activated, DePuy invited me to attend the super secret meetings in The Loft (the top floor of the MACV building). These were almost exclusively restricted to generals, with others in attendance only on request. I told DePuy that I did not have the "celestial" clearance required for attendance. He said that as COC director, I should attend; he would get me temporary clearance. (My official clearance arrived in two weeks, the fastest I have seen such action. I never did get permanent "super" clearance for the communications facility during my fourteen-month tour as G-3 of 1st Marine Division because Major General Herman Nickerson had thrown the apple-cheeked FBI investigator out of his office for asking "stupid questions" about me.) For the next month—until General Jones settled in—I was taken into the inner circle and attended the weekly "seances."

The seances were eye-openers, dealing largely with out-of-country activity in Laos, Cambodia, Thailand, and North Vietnam. There was a dreamlike quality to these sessions, with Westmoreland often leaning back in his chair with his eyes apparently closed and delivering lengthy monologues. I carried away an uneasy impression that was similar to my reaction to the bombing-target meetings. I suspected we were groping in a milieu that we understood only partially and that we were doing so amateurishly.

Generals Jones and DePuy

In late December word arrived that Brigadier General William K. Jones had been assigned as director of the COC and would arrive in

Saigon by the end of the month. I had never served with him or even met him. I did learn, however, that he had an outstanding combat record as an infantry commander in World War II at Tarawa, where he was the youngest battalion commander (1st Battalion, 6th Marines) in the Marine Corps. He also served with distinction at Saipan, Tinian, and Okinawa, and was highly regarded as a staff officer.

I was soon to discover that Bill Jones had recently lost his eldest son in an automobile accident. The general was still visibly affected by this trauma and for a few weeks suffered melancholia. For the next month he was withdrawn. I later came to understand that his behavior was uncharacteristic.

Jones, a slender, good-looking six-footer, had been carefully selected for assignment as the senior Marine in General Westmoreland's headquarters. Knowledgeable in the ways of high-level staffs, he was also a confidant of Lieutenant General Victor "Brute" Krulak, commander of all Marines in the Pacific. The Brute had strong views on how guerilla wars should be fought (as did most Marines weaned on the trails of Haiti and Nicaragua during the '20s and '30s). These views differed dramatically from the Westmoreland strategy.

Although there was no outward friction between Jones and DePuy, they were never close. Perhaps this was the only possible accommodation considering DePuy's rapport with Westmoreland and Jones's with Krulak. Beyond that loomed the far broader subject of the commitment of each service to an exhausting war in mainland Asia. We had seen a fading French Empire hastened to its demise in this ancient cockpit. Yet despite the danger of crippling losses, no service could allow itself to be viewed as less than a full partner in the enterprise. The dilemma was real. To hang back was to endanger the roles and missions (and budget support) so long fought for in the Joint Chiefs of Staff. To become overcommitted or badly mauled in this arena could weaken one's capabilities to perform elsewhere. So the services watched each other closely and searched for hidden motives where there often were none.

This put me in a delicate, if not awkward position. DePuy had drawn me into J-3 and had assigned me to organize and direct the COC—the Marine Corps had not. Throughout my first half year in Vietnam I felt that the Army (excepting DePuy) watched me closely; the Marines, who should have known better, seemed to have reservations about anyone close to Westlmoreland's man, DePuy.

Even General Jones sometimes gave the impression that he was more an observer than a full-fledged participant. This impression was probably a reflection of the nature of Westmoreland's modus operandi, where all real decision making was at the Westmoreland–DePuy level. The staff served as implementers, not advisors.

In my opinion DePuy was also in a slightly ambiguous position. Although a faithful and ardent supporter of Westmoreland's combat philosophy—if not the architect—he was also a deep-down Marine admirer. His admiration went well beyond the obvious fact that the strength and quality of Marine forces would be a necessary ingredient to MACV success. DePuy leaned over backward to demonstrate support for Marines in Vietnam. There were many instances of this support throughout the fall and winter of 1965–66.

Consider, for example, what happened when DePuy accompanied Westmoreland to a conference with the President in Hawaii in February 1966. DePuy called me to his office and announced that he would be going to Hawaii for three or four days. During his absence I would be acting J-3. I mentioned the fact that several Army and Air Force colonels within J-3 were senior to me. He said he knew that, but it represented no problem (as it would have in the Navy or Marines) since I would be officially designated. DePuy did not return for about a week. In the meantime Colonel John Chaisson, operations officer of III MAF, called to ask for armed helicopter support for a brigade-sized operation in I Corps. I promised him eight armed UH-1s (Hueys). (Although Marines had pioneered the use of helicopter-borne troops, their devotion to fixed-wing aircraft for ground support had blinded them to the potential of armed helicopters; hence the Army had stolen the march on them, and the Marines had to borrow armed Hueys or go without.) I directed Colonel Eduardo Soler, head of our COC air division, to provide the eight Hueys on station in I Corps at dawn the next morning. At about 4:00 A.M., John called to report that the Hueys had not yet checked in by radio; where were they? I phoned Soler, who had been a classmate at Fort Sill in 1949–50, to inquire as to their whereabouts. He informed me that the Hueys had not been sent because the brigadier general commanding the helicopter brigade and he had decided against it. I was taken aback for a moment. Then, in language as cold and forthright as I could make it, I said, "Colonel Soler, I don't give a damn what you and the brigadier decided; get those Hueys on their way to I Corps immediately or I'll report you both to the chief of staff!" The helicopters arrived on station in I

Corps at about noon. Upon DePuy's return, I reported this disobedience. I doubt if the brigadier general and Soler ever recovered from
General DePuy's fierce tongue-lashing.

Marine House

A few weeks after General Jones's arrival, we began to actively
pursue the idea of acquiring a villa. As senior Marine in Saigon
there would be many occasions when a villa would be a real asset to
Jones, if not a necessity. He would frequently have to entertain
visiting firemen or high-ranking Vietnamese. The problem was
that, with the influx of senior officers into Saigon, the appropriate
housing had already been occupied. There were, of course, several
villas still occupied by groups of colonels and lieutenant colonels,
holdovers from the advisory-staff days. After a little snooping we
discovered an excellent house in a perfect location two blocks from
the U.S. Embassy and six blocks from MACV headquarters. It was
occupied by a coterie of dentists. The senior dentist was a lieutenant colonel. Furthermore, the house obviously saw the frequent
comings and goings of Vietnamese ladies of questionable virtue, as
we discerned one afternoon on an impromptu inspection. Upon return to MACV headquarters, we decided we had found our mark.
The general said that he would ask the chief of staff for permission
to take possession of the house first thing next morning. Knowing
the speed with which information spread in such matters and the
subtle pressure that resourceful field-grade officers could bring to
bear to sabotage our wishes, I suggested that we strike immediately. After all, they had possession, they were Army, and we did
not know what allies they might have in high places. The general
moved swiftly. He talked to the chief minutes later, well before the
dentists could mount a counterattack.

The success did much to cheer the general up. He coined the
name Marine House, and the large living room was soon decorated
with Marine division and wing plaques and other memorabilia.
One notable touch of class was provided by the Army COC sergeant
major. His year in the country was nearing an end, and he was
eager to return to Baltimore, where he was an enthusiastic follower
of the horses at Pimlico. On weekends in Saigon he had had an
opportunity to test his luck at the local track and in so doing had
become friendly with the sort of folk who frequent such ventures.
Being well aware of his interest since I had excused him from duty

on several Sunday afternoons, I told him that there was one condition to his release from COC duty to return home. I had his undivided attention. He was to provide Marine House with a brass nameplate for the front door, suitably inscribed, before he could be considered eligible for release. No funds were available. True to his resourcefulness and artistry, he not only produced a brass nameplate engraved "Marine House," but he balanced the Marine Corps emblem on one corner with the head of a horse in the other. It was, he deadpanned, the Vietnamese Year of the Horse.

The general invited four other colonels to join us in residence, with representation from the other J staffs and the senior advisor to the Vietnamese Marines. In this way we had a sort of Marine headquarters for the exchange of information and general camaraderie in Saigon. By any reckoning, however, the most indispensible resident of Marine House was Gunnery Sergeant Metoyer, who had come with the general from Twentynine Palms.

Gunny Metoyer was a gem. Not only was he a master chef and a polished major domo, he was a compassionate father figure to our young Marine steward, who had a spotty past. Metoyer's talents did not end there. He was also an expert mechanic. When the Saigon electrical system faltered, our stand-by generators were quickly brought into service. When the air conditioning system in the general's sedan went on the blink, only the gunny could make it work. As the months went by and Marine House became the site of many eventful social occasions, Metoyer faultlessly presided over all. Naturally, his talents did not go unnoticed, and this talented Marine—who could have earned a comfortable living in any number of ways—ultimately ended up in the commandant's quarters in Washington, D.C., ministering to the nation's elite.

Premier Nguyen Cao Ky, Ambassador Henry Cabot Lodge, General Westmoreland, and many lesser luminaries were dinner guests at Marine House. In the early summer of 1966, General Jones conceived the idea that it would be appropriate to honor the commandant, General Greene, with an award for the Marine Corps' all-out support of the war effort. He suggested this to General Khang, the commandant of the Vietnamese Marine Corps, who in turn commended it to Premier Ky. Ky liked the idea and offered to liven up the ceremony with a military band. The courtyard of Marine House was narrow and fenced in by a high masonry wall. When the band struck up the usual martial music, including "The Marines' Hymn," the whole neighborhood reverberated with the sound amplified between Marine House and the wall. The Embassy, which was only two blocks away, wanted to know if a coup was underway. Westmoreland, who had not been informed of the ceremony, was not pleased and General Jones was forcefully advised that such high-jinks at Marine House were over.

The Links of Cooperation

By the spring of 1966, General Westmoreland had begun to harbor grievances about the support being rendered by the 7th Fleet. I told General Jones that I thought that Westy was needlessly concerned. I had known of Vice Admiral Johnny Hiland, the 7th Fleet commander, in the Pentagon, and he had a reputation for being smart and easy to get along with. I suggested that I could straighten out the emerging difficulties in a hurry if I could deal directly at the staff level. Westy agreed to our proposing a MACV–Pacific Fleet meeting in Okinawa and to my heading the MACV contingent. An Army colonel from FFI was included to keep an eye on me.

The first night in Okinawa I was met by Colonel Hank Woessner, now G-3 of Fleet Marine Force, Pacific. I had seen Hank only once since our days together on the Advance Base Problem team. After Quantico, he had been a battalion officer at the Naval Academy, CO of 1st Reconnaissance Battalion, a member of the Naval Advisory Group in Korea, at the Marine Corps Recruit Depot in San Diego, and a student at the National War College. He now had the unenviable job of being General Krulak's operations officer. But anyone who had prospered as Homer Litzenberg's operations officer in Korea was not going to be cowed by The Brute.

Hank had hunted me down to warn me that General Krulak wanted a dispatch from me that outlined my instructions. During the evening Hank reminded me twice more in his friendly, insistent way that The Brute was expecting to hear from me. I told Hank as often that I had no instructions from Westy. To reinforce Hank's point, Brigadier General Mike Ryan, the senior Marine on Okinawa, flew in by helicopter early the next morning and ferried me back to his headquarters, where I drafted a dispatch. I outlined what MACV hoped to accomplish at the conference but emphasized that I had no instructions from Westy. This episode, however, alerted me to the serious view that Pacific Fleet was taking. My awareness was soon amplified when I returned to camp where the conference was waiting for me to get under way. I stopped to pick up my briefcase in the anteroom set aside for the MACV and Pacific Fleet contingents. There I noted a tall stack of documents on the Pacific Fleet side. Naturally, I glanced at them. They were strongly worded position papers on every issue that was even remotely expected to surface at the conference. Realizing that the Navy–Marine Pacific Fleet team was loaded for bear, I kept my own counsel but decided to promptly defuse the situation.

After an hour of briefing by MACV on the incountry troop situation, I suggested that the best way to get at the issues was to set up committees to address air support, amphibious operations, naval gunfire support, and naval support of the Vietnamese. Captain Johnny Thrum (Pacific Fleet operations officer and a year ahead of me at the Naval Academy), Captain Bob Pond (7th Fleet operations officer and a student of mine at the Naval War College the previous year), Hank Woessner, and I then repaired to the Kadena golf course. While establishing excellent rapport, we allowed the lieutenant colonels and majors to work things out.

There is little question that our hours on the golf course over the next two days did as much as anything to ensure the success of the conference. In any case, all matters were resolved smoothly, harmony perhaps unexpectedly reigned, and the get-together turned out to be a material as well as an artistic success. When we briefed General Westmoreland upon return to Saigon, I believe that he was not a little surprised at the degree of cooperation achieved. Years of hard-won Navy–Marine teamwork paid off!

20

The War

From the Theater Level

War as viewed from the theater level is so far removed from the experiences of the combat units as to be almost unrelated. My insight into the war had no relationship whatsoever to that of a patrol leader or battalion commander and not much more to that of a regimental commander or division staffer. Even on those occasions where I had an opportunity to see troops engaged with the enemy firsthand, I knew that in a few hours I would be miles away, eating a hot meal and with a comfortable, safe lodging. Security vastly influences one's perspective.

As often as I could find a valid excuse, I visited ongoing combat operations. On one occasion in the spring of 1966, Brigadier General Jones and I flew into Binh Dinh Province in northern II Corps and watched a brigade of 1st Air Cavalry Division sweep through a village. Most of the villagers, VC, and NVA had departed. No matter what enormous mobility edge the helicopter gave to American combat units, it was still nearly impossible to surprise and pin down sizable enemy forces. And the search-and-destroy missions did not do much toward winning the hearts and minds of the villagers, who absorbed much of the punishment.

During the winter I accompanied General DePuy to a Marine brigade-sized operation west of Tam Ky, in southern I Corps. Again, no significant number of enemy troops was killed or captured. The visit, however, was unlike most in that we arrived by helicopter only a few hours after the brigade commander had been replaced. Although General DePuy and I had no firsthand information about the cause of the abrupt relief (which had occurred only a day into the operation), there appeared to be extenuating circumstances. The brigade staff had been patched together from various sources. As a result, some of the officers and NCOs scarcely knew one another. With capable, experienced leaders, this is an acceptable practice, but the brigadier general was not an experienced field commander. The support of a steady, knowledgeable regimental staff might have been more appropriate. It was another case of the casual way in which task forces are too frequently thrown together without regard for regimental integrity. Had General DePuy not been a strong Marine supporter, this lapse could have been embarrassing.

In June I flew out to the small aircraft carrier USS *Okinawa* off northern II Corps and observed the landing and initial operations ashore of the Special Landing Force (at that time the 3rd Battalion, 5th Marines and a helicopter squadron). Again, it turned out to be little more than a training exercise—the force encountered only a handful of the enemy.

In July I helicoptered into a search-and-destroy operation by 1st Infantry Division east of Saigon. Major General Bill DePuy, who by then was trying to put his combat philosophy into practice in the field, commanded the operation. Despite its sound and fury, it produced few tangible results.

The actions that I witnessed were brief and inconclusive. It was no accident that I saw little. The VC and NVA chose the time and place that they would commit important forces to action.

During 1965–66 a controversy over strategy developed between the Marines and the Army. The Marines held that pacification—the deliberate winning over and stabilization of villages in slowly expanding safe, productive enclaves—was essential to any ultimate winning of the war. The Marines' view was that search-and-destroy missions, without hard intelligence to give them a good chance of being productive, diverted limited resources from the pacification effort. MACV contended that until the major VC–NVA units were tracked down and destroyed, pacification efforts could not be expected to bear much fruit. During late 1966 two factors dissolved the disagreement: the accelerated introduction into South Vietnam of NVA divisions and the adoption of an overall MACV pacification strategy to go along with the search-and-destroy strategy. As the war in South Vietnam expanded ominously, there was need for an energetic effort to bring units of NVA to combat on terms as favorable to us as possible—even while we pushed pacification. Of course, even significantly reinforced U.S. and Allied units could not have implemented this dual strategy effectively, but recognition of this fact had not surfaced by the summer of 1966.

Despite the lack of any notable field successes since 1965, the rapid buildup and deployment of forces generated a euphoric state at MACV headquarters. One of the outgrowths of this increased U.S. commitment was the need to show progress to solidify support back home. In true bureaucratic fashion a monthly report called The Indicia of Progress Report was required by Washington. In this, various indicators, such as the number of miles of highway or railroad brought into service, were to be reported. Unfortunately, such a report is almost guaranteed to misinform because of the inherent pressure on the preparers to show progress. It also tends to misguide those who do not understand the nature of guerilla strategy. Nonetheless, many hours were committed to rendering these reports, from which undoubtedly false conclusions of real progress were derived in Washington.

This reminded me of a previous McNamara-directed effort at determining the combat readiness of troop units. While I was CO of the 11th Marines in California during 1962, a Rand Corporation investigator visited 1st Marine Division in an attempt to estimate the combat readiness of individual battalions. He looked at two of mine and employed such criteria as presence of necessary skills, manning level, and materiel availability and condition. I told him that he was wasting his time trying to mechanically determine what was a largely emotional issue. In my opinion, I advised him, the single most important factor in combat readiness is the quality of leadership, particularly the quality of the commander. The most up-to-date equipment and best trained men avail little in a combat situation if the action is directed by an incompetent or spineless leader. On the other hand, superb leadership can overcome almost any deficiencies. This Defense Department passion for reducing military matters to quantitative measurement was a characteristic of the McNamara regime and could well have been a factor in obfuscating the true combat situation.

Another problem in Saigon was the discrepancy in the apparent degree of commitment of the MACV and Vietnamese General Staffs. The Americans were trying to wage an around-the-clock war, seven days a week. On the other hand, the Vietnamese held the weekends inviolate. If General DePuy wanted to rouse his opposite number on the Vietnamese staff on Saturday afternoon, it took special effort and was not always possible. It was difficult to escape the conclusion that we were fighting different wars.

From the Field

For more than fleeting glimpses of the war in the field—that is, outside Saigon—we have to look to my colleagues of the war generation.

Jimmy Callender had served as an ordnance instructor at the Naval Academy, attended the Senior School, and then reported to 2nd Marine Division at Camp Lejeune. There he became CO of 2/10 (my old battalion) after a few weeks as the division naval gunfire officer. He had subsequent duty at the Marine Barracks, Pearl Harbor; the Marine Corps Schools in Quantico; and research and development in the Navy Department. Then Jimmy attended the National War College. He arrived in Vietnam in late July 1965 and had been assigned as CO of the 12th Marines, 3rd Marine Division's artillery regiment.

Jimmy found the 12th Marines, which had come from Okinawa, in terrible shape—poorly trained and unmotivated. Battery and battalion commanders were woefully inexperienced. He had a monumental task on his hands to improve their gunnery to the point that their firing was consistently safe. After struggling with the inadequately trained officers for some weeks, Jimmy persuaded the commandant, who was incountry on an inspection trip, to send field artillery lieutenants through Fort Sill after The Basic School and prior to assignment to Vietnam. (After the first year of World War II, all field artillery lieutenants went to Field Artillery School in Quantico before being sent to the Fleet Marine Force. In Korea, we survived because of our experience in World War II, which overcame the initial lack of trained lieutenants. In Vietnam there was no such reservoir of experience.) This shut down the pipeline of artillery lieutenants for three months, but Jimmy accepted this inconvenience and filled the gap with an intensive training program for NCO FOs. There was probably no one in the Marine Corps better equipped to straighten out the shooting problems of the 12th Marines, which he did with alacrity and strong positive action, but it took Colonel Callender his best efforts for most of his eleven-month tour as regimental commander to bring the Okinawa-based artillerymen to a uniformly excellent level of performance. The only time I saw Jimmy in Vietnam was just before his return to the States in June 1966. We could do little more than reminisce about the glory days at the Chosin Reservoir over a few drinks in the crowded, noisy III MAF officers' club.

Jimmy's predicament with respect to officer competence revived my concern about military policies, which insisted that all officers serve as battalion commanders to have a chance for promotion. Other popular terms for this policy are *ticket punching* and *careerism*. It is a dangerous practice. Not all officers are troop leaders, just as all officers are not cut out for high-level staff duty. Some are good troop leaders; some are good staffers. Few are both. Who in his right mind would have insisted that Chesty Puller pull his share of staff duty? We must be more selective about the officers who lead our troops. Who suffered when we ran officers in and out as battalion commanders every six months to get their career tickets punched? I believe that this shortsighted policy was partly responsible for troop disenchantment later in the war.

Westy

General Westmoreland labored under great handicaps. He was viewed as a theater commander without really being one. He was considered by many to be responsible for the prosecution of the war when, technically, he was only assisting the South Vietnamese with the war in South Vietnam. Others were running the air war against North Vietnam and the out-of-country operations in the rest of Southeast Asia.

Consider also that Westmoreland was only in command of U.S. military forces. The State Department still clung to the illusion of a coordinated Country Team. This team operation was headed by Ambassador Henry Cabot Lodge, who was ostensibly in charge of all other U.S. activities. Country teams may work well in less violent, less confused environments, but in Saigon in 1966 there was little coordination and much confusion. For example, the fertilizers and other materials that Agency for International Development (AID) people were distributing to the Vietnamese were a primary source of VC explosives.

It would be unreasonable to lay much blame on the ambassador, however, because the independent agencies such as AID, the U.S. Information Agency (USIA), and the Central Intelligence Agency (CIA) took their orders from Washington, not Saigon. Each in time-honored fashion, was trying to get a larger piece of the action, to justify its existence, and expand its budget. So it is difficult to escape the conclusion that Washington itself was responsible for the ultimate debacle in Vietnam. The White House, the State Department, and the Defense Department were a hydra-headed monster.

In fact, Westmoreland's job was close to impossible. He was responsible for developing a strategy for winning the war in South Vietnam, but he had no control over the influx of NVA forces that continually altered the enemy order of battle upward. Neither the disrupting influence on the war effort of dissident political activity nor the competing political ambitions of the generals of the Army of the Republic of Vietnam (ARVN) could be ascribed to General Westmoreland. Nor could the questionable fighting qualities of some ARVN units.

Although Westmoreland's search-and-destroy strategy enjoyed some modest early success, it was never viable because we never had reliable enough intelligence to locate and track significant enemy forces. The pacification strategy required enormous resources and years of effort, neither of which we were willing to expend. Given the silly ground rules about the inviolability of national boundaries—rules that were contemptuously ignored by the North Vietnamese—and the national ambivalence about prosecuting the war to the fullest, it is hard to conceive of a strategy that General Westmoreland could have devised that would have made much difference.

Should he have made a more serious effort to help clean up the contradictions in U.S. activities in Saigon? Perhaps, but it really was not his responsibility. His inclination was to be a field-army commander, as his almost continuous field inspections and strategy sessions around the country attested. Even the COC seemed to be a monument to his yearning to be a field commander. But though the COC looked impressive, it did little. After all, the ground action in South Vietnam was managed by the three U.S. corps headquarters—III MAF, FFI, and FFII.

If Westy is to be faulted at all, it is perhaps because he postured as the man in charge. How much did one hear of Admiral U.S. Grant Sharp, Commander-in-Chief, Pacific, who was technically

Westmoreland's Defense Department superior? How often did one hear of Ambassador Lodge, his superior in Saigon, or the CIA, which sponsored the supporting operations in Southeast Asia, particularly in Laos? They were all willing to let Westy bask in the limelight, and he was eager enough to be credited with successes. By the same token, when problems developed, he was out there in front to draw fire.

Two occurrences during the spring of 1966 threw a little light on General Westmoreland's character. The first was Westy's almost continuous pique at the press, a pique that reflected his intolerance of criticism. For all its deficiencies, the press was reporting frustrations at the squad and platoon level that bore scrutiny. Even if the overall performance of the press was below par or unfair in reporting the war situation, as Westy often charged, there were surely clues to later difficulties in these low-level reports.

The other incident centered around a staff conference I attended in General Jones's stead in the spring of 1966. Because of the nature of theater staffs, there were few present who were not general officers, and they were well in the background. I was the only colonel at the long conference table. The subject under discussion was interdiction of the NVA above the Demilitarized Zone (DMZ). The NVA had been steadily infiltrating to the south over the Ho Chi Minh Trail for many months. Now there was evidence that they would move directly through the DMZ as well. Westy was talking about a greatly intensified air-interdiction effort from the DMZ north for about 40 miles to Dong Hoi. There was no mention of naval-gunfire bombardment, although this narrow strip of Vietnam to the Laotion border was only about 30 to 35 miles deep, and the main roads were within range of medium- and long-range naval guns. Brashly, it soon appeared, I suggested a combined interdiction effort by air and naval gunfire. You could have heard a pin drop. Who was this neophyte who presumed to suggest strategy to the commander in chief? The subject was quickly changed. Several weeks later a plan for interdiction by air and naval gunfire was agreed upon. It was manifestly clear that there was only one strategical-tactical genius in residence at MACV headquarters.

General Westmoreland was certainly an outstanding product of the Army system. He kept himself in excellent physical condition (a la Patton), and at age 52 he made an impressive appearance as a young, articulate commander. He visited the troops in the field at an aggressive pace. His success in the Army had been so meteoric, that the only positions in the Army hierarchy superior to his own (chief of staff and chairman of the Joint Chiefs of Staff) might, at that time, have held little appeal. Successful prosecution of a war obviously could have far greater political rewards, as it had for generals throughout history. This ambition and the string of prior successes that had fed his ego had not prepared Westy, in my opinion, for any sort of failure. Perhaps this is an indictment of the Army system, which speeds select favorites to the top and does not give them opportunity along the way to develop those emotional resources that only adversity strengthens.

Dak To and the Rung Sat

Two brief field trips, one in late March and another in the early summer, illustrate two of the many difficulties presented by the enormous Southeast Asian area in which we were trying to conduct a pacification effort.

Heated action involving an Army airborne battalion in the mountainous terrain north of Kontum in II Corps signaled a serious increase in NVA strength in the area. DePuy, some FFI officers, and I flew into Kontum to find out more about it. After meeting the ARVN II Corps commander, we flew on up to Dak To, a Special Forces outpost near a known NVA infiltration route. We thought Dak To might be an early NVA target. General DePuy flew with the Vietnamese general while an Army FFI colonel and I took his U-8.

Our landing on the short strip at Dak To was an interesting one. Although the pilot protested to the contrary, the Army colonel and I were convinced that he failed to put the wheels down for landing. Whatever the cause, we landed amidst a shower of sparks with the belly directly on the pierced steel planking, without benefit of wheels. We came to rest on the far edge of the strip overlooking a deep ravine. Although the plane was a total wreck, it did not catch fire, and we walked away without a scratch. Withour further ado, ARVN Rangers pushed the carcass off the runway and into the ravine. After a brief inspection tour of the outpost, we rode back to Pleiku with the two generals and were picked up by another U-8 from Saigon.

This experience brought the whole matter of outposts into focus. The maintenance of isolated outposts is an expensive business. And to what purpose? If heavily manned so that worthwhile, extensive patrolling can be done, then they seriously deplete mobile combat or pacification forces. They also require extensive logistic support. If lightly held, as was Dak To, the NVA bypass them with hardly a second thought, and the outposts serve little purpose beyond displaying a friendly flag on the situation map.

My experience in the Rung Sat, a vast mangrove swamp between Saigon and the South China Sea, underlined my suspicions concerning our strategy. Cargo vessels in the shipping channel were being fired at from the jungle recesses. The Army Chemical Warfare Service had been authorized to try its hand at extensive defoliation to deny the VC hiding places along the riverbanks within 50 feet or so on either side of the shipping lanes. The areas that we observed were well denuded of vegetation. When we helicoptered down for a look-see, we were shown fighting holes and other evidences of VC passage through the area, but no VC. Here again, I saw the unequal contest between a sophisticated, industrial giant and native ingenuity. No matter what material and treasure the giant expended, one would be foolhardy to bet against native resourcefulness.

The COC: Reorganization and Realization

Prior to relinquishing the mantle of J-3 in mid March 1966, General DePuy became insistent that the COC, his creation that represented over half the J-3 empire, not be an exclusive Marine enclave. He wanted an Army as well as a Marine deputy to back up the COC director. So in April I recommended to General Jones and Major General John C. F. Tillson, DePuy's successor as J-3, that the two COC deputies divide up their duties. The Marine deputy was to be responsible for I Corps, II Corps, and air and naval matters while the Army deputy was to be responsibile for III Corps, IV Corps, and Special Forces operations both in and out of country. This scheme retained a Marine hand in those areas of most interest to Marines, and it was not an unsatisfactory arrangement to the Army. Implementation of this division of responsibility actually took place in June 1966.

At about this time I began to realize that the beefy COC was destined to be largely window dressing. It had been a challenge to organize and activate so large a multiservice staff team and be its first director. But once this 200-odd man organization was in place and operating, we subsided into a relatively inconsequential routine. We issued orders as directed by the J-3. We developed plans of a broad general nature that often proved to be wishful thinking, such as the incremental opening up of key highways and railroad segments. The Command Center hummed along, kept us well informed of activity in the corps areas, and fulfilled a useful public-relations purpose. But General Westmoreland did all the real decision making. He was his own planner, and he decided by himself where to deploy incoming troops or redeploy units already incountry. His top staff officers—Rosson, DePuy, and the rest—undoubtedly had some input. But we at the lower level, who were contemporaries with almost comparable levels of experience, were not asked for recommendations and only rarely had an opportunity to make any significant contribution to the war effort.

I had commanded troops in combat and during peacetime, had been operations officer of a Marine division, had attended and taught at a plethora of military schools up to the highest level. I had served at the highest level of the military establishment and learned how to operate successfully on the staff level at the center of government. Now, at the height of my capability to prove useful in this complex, many-faceted war, I was little more than an observer. I was unable to make a meaningful impact. It was galling. It was also a deplorable waste. And what of the other hundred-odd officers in the COC and many others distributed elsewhere throughout the bloated MACV headquarters? Were any of us making worthwhile contributions to the war effort?

Had a joint Vietnamese-Allied war plans office been formed when I was ordered to Saigon in September 1965 as its first director, I might have been able to perform a useful service. Perhaps this early decision not to try to integrate the forces into a single command, complicated though it undoubtedly would have been, guaranteed that the U.S. and the Vietnamese would fight separate wars. On the other hand, it might not have been as easy for General Westmoreland to ignore a joint staff as it was for him to ignore his own U.S. staff—including his own creation, the COC. But this is all the stuff of dreams.

The glaring fact that faced me in the spring of 1966 was that after almost thirty years of grooming as a professional military man, I would spend the last days of my career in Saigon's no-man's land, buried in a largely unnecessary staff organization, going through the motions of planning and controlling U.S. combat operations. It might well have been that the war was predestined to come a cropper, but misuse of valuable personnel resources did little to alter that outcome.

Vietnam, Farewell

In July, for the second time, I was passed over for selection to brigadier general. This signaled an end to my Marine Corps career and seriously deflated me.

An incident at dinner at Marine House poisoned my last few days. We had just started the main course when the subject of the Marine Corps promotion system reared its ugly head. Colonel Hank Reichner, a talented, outspoken, sometimes abrasive fellow Philadelphian whom I had known since childhood, offered the opinion that John Chaisson, one of the finest Marine officers ever produced, was promoted to brigadier general the second time around only as the result of a special rehabilitation effort to place him in a key billet—as III MAF G-3.

General Jones flushed with anger and called upon me to agree with him in denying this damning criticism of the system that had just promoted Jones to two stars. The four colonels at the table looked at me as silence pervaded the room. The general had asked the wrong man to defend a system that had just terminated his military career. Only months earlier General DePuy, in signing off my Fitness Report for the months served under him, had written in bold hand that if Parry "were an Army officer I would have him promoted to general-officer rank without reservation." Other flashbacks crossed my mind. I thought of retired Colonel John Saxten, my first classman at Annapolis, who was a four striper and number two Marine in his class. His principal disqualification in the general-officer sweepstakes had been his indispensability as an amphibious-force logistics officer in World War II, which prevented him from getting a battalion in combat. Even General Wally Greene, our current commandant, had been passed over the first time for major general.

Instead of declining comment, as I have often wished I had, I admitted into the hushed atmosphere that I thought that there was some truth in what Hank had said. Jones threw down his napkin, glared at me as if to say that I had failed to stand by him as a trusted deputy should, and stalked out of the room. Fortunately, only a few days remained before my departure.

There was one more trip I had to make—to Danang—to bid fare-well to friends, but primarily to congratulate John Chaisson on his selection for brigadier general. I also wanted to see Colonel Ben Read, who had taken over command of the 12th Marines from Jimmy Callender.

John and I sat in his quarters and talked of old times over a beer. It was bittersweet. His career would go forward brilliantly; I had no idea what I would do after retirement. We bid each other a fond farewell. (John stayed in Vietnam for almost two more years. He took over the COC from Bill Jones upon his promotion to briga-dier general.)

I had run into Ben Read from time to time through the years since he had been flown out of Koto-ri on a stretcher in December 1950. Ben still had a slight limp, a relic of his magnificent stand with How Battery on the road from Hagaru-ri to Koto-ri. I found him as hard-charging as ever. Again, it was painful to bid farewell to an old comrade.

In Retrospect: Vietnam

What went wrong in Vietnam? Although it was not clear in 1966 that the war would turn sour or that we would not be able to bull our way through to some sort of acceptable accommodation, there were surely more than a few indications of trouble ahead.

North Vietnam had largely negated our vast superiority in fire-power and mobility by her guerilla strategy. She had demonstrated her willingness to deploy south whatever troops were necessary to offset our buildup, despite a potential U.S. threat to mount an am-phibious invasion of the north. Weren't these indications of a ques-tionable war strategy? Wasn't it apparent even at this early hour that the North Vietnamese were not behaving according to our stra-tegic script?

The so-called national strategy in 1966 was known as Flexible Response. It overlaid the old strategy of containment, which called for stopping Communism in its tracks whenever it threatened im-portant free-world interests. The Flexible Response strategy visual-ized punishing the enemy just hard enough to bring him to heel. It was a sophisticated strategy, appropriate to the world's greatest power, and it reflected the brilliance of its author, General Maxwell Taylor. Perhaps it would have worked in Europe. But against an agrarian peasant economy and fiercely nationalistic Asian culture, it did not fare well. It was already clear in 1966, as we incrementally stepped up our bombing attacks on North Vietnam, that this strategy was hardening, not softening, enemy resolve. Despite this selective assault on their communications, command, and industrial centers, they steadily pushed reinforcements south to match our own.

In a far more easily managed war in Korea more than a decade earlier, we had seen that the American people would not long support a war of attrition on the Asian continent, and we had accepted a stalemate. But in 1966, with even less commitment at home, we were rushing down the same path. Wasn't our strategy with respect to North Vietnam based on an inflated view of our own armed might, politically constrained as it was?

The bright young men in the Pentagon and the White House seemed to be bemused by our superpower status and contrasted it to North Vietnam's status as a third-rate power. This was sheer delusion. If you subtract capabilities, which were largely ineffective, and factor down the value of mechanical mobility and firepower in the guerilla environment, you are not talking about a first-rate power versus a third-rate power. Add to this equation the high quality of enemy troops, the fact that they were on home soil, the enemy's widely held conviction that they were defending their homeland from exploiting western imperialists, and the lack of any similar motivation on the part of U.S. troops, and you can see that the contest was not one-sided at all.

As a corollary to superpower arrogance was the idea that the war would be fought by the professional Regular forces unaugmented by significant Reserves—in contrast to the Korean War. It ignored the fact that this country's armed forces have always been (and are still to a great extent, despite their volunteer label) a reasonable cross-section of the nation and reflect the strengths and weaknesses of the nation. One of these strengths is not supporting lengthy wars on distant fronts where the national interest is not manifestly at stake.

Given a free hand with only the prohibition of nuclear, biological, and chemical warfare, could we have subdued North Vietnam in the two or three years that the U.S. home front might have sat still? Perhaps we could have achieved some sort of Korea-type stalemate. But surely China would have reacted to any major incursion into North Vietnam. China may have viewed with indifference, perhaps even satisfaction, the working over of her ancient enemy by

U.S. air bombardment. But the establishment by force of a U.S.-dominated state on China's southern border is a totally different matter. The weapons rattling that MacArthur had done in the Korean War did not deter China. Why should she have been deterred by similar threats with respect to North Vietnam? Of course, we heard of plans to take out China's nuclear facility at Lop Nor if she intervened, but these never seemed convincing to me. There is always residue from such surgical strikes. When the strike is nuclear, the residue could be incalculable. What fallout would have accrued to the leader of the Western world, already tarnished by equivocation over Cuba?

The Korean stalemate, with many features relatively favorable to the U.S. (an industrializing society, proximity to a major U.S. ally, and both flanks dominated by the U.S. Navy) requires to this day a substantial U.S. troop commitment. Would we have been able to maintain a similar or even larger force in Southeast Asia to ensure the peace?

So, even as early as 1966, the handwriting was on the wall, if we had only looked, and it had nothing to do with the popular phrase "war morality." With China unwilling to allow North Vietnam to be reduced to impotence and the Soviet Union eager to provide whatever material resources were necessary to prolong a struggle so debilitating to her chief adversary, North Vietnam primarily needed leadership, fortitude, and resourcefulness to endure. She had already demonstrated these in abundance.

Add to this major U.S. blunders, such as ignoring the time-honored principles of war: unity of command, surprise, mass, and the rest. Consider also the fact that the United States artificially limited the war to the enemy's great advantage, and you can see that all the ingredients of failure were present.

This disaster was so injurious to the United States in so many ways that the sorry aftereffects are still with us and promise to be for many years to come. What lessons can we learn? They should be self-evident, but let me enunciate them.

Consider carefully the likely results of a successful war strategy. Do you really want to win? What commitments will be needed to guarantee victory? What national benefits and ongoing costs will success confer?

Know the enemy and the willingness and capacity of his allies to support him. Never underestimate him.

When you decide on war, go for the win. Motivate your armed forces. Rally the nation behind them. Give the commander in chief all the resources he needs to win decisively. Do not interfere with his prosecution of the war and, in particular, do not tie his hands by artificially restricting his courses of action or limiting his weapons.

Hit hard, hit fast, hit with all the power necessary to ensure success. Be ready with all the resources you need to consolidate the victory promptly.

Epilogue

Despite growing disillusionment with America's role and strategy and the way in which the military system rewarded its practitioners, my war generation had been faithful to the last. We had moved to the sound of the guns in the 1960s as we had in the 1940s and 1950s. We had given our best, and many would now seek other fields to conquer.

My final months of active duty were marked primarily by the effort to readjust my thinking after thirty martial years to the pursuit of a civilian career. This was not an inconsiderable task for one with no obviously employable skills, such as engineering or communications. How many artillerists are needed in the private sector?

On May 1, 1967, two months short of thirty years, I retired from military service. After a pleasant, instructive three-year stint with Ordnance and Specialty Manufacturing Company, Aerojet General Corporation, I returned to government as a civil servant with the Interior Department. Here I was fortunate to get in on the ground floor of the major federal push in energy research.

During the '70s the electric energy systems research program that I initiated grew from less than a million dollars annually to over sixty million. The research encompassed such problems as the development of high-capacity underground power cables and 1,200-kilovolt power equipment, the development and control of large interconnected power networks, the integration of new technologies (such as solar and wind generators) into the power system, development of distributed source generators (fuel cells) and electric-storage power plants, and assessing the environmental effects of high-voltage electric and magnetic fields from power lines. In 1981 I retired as director of the Office of Electric Energy Systems, Department of Energy.

As to my close associates of the war generation, John Chaisson returned from Vietnam in June 1968 and rapidly rose to lieutenant general and Marine Corps chief of staff. John was a prime candidate for commandant, but President Nixon selected a past military aide, Lieutenant General Bob Cushman. John retired July 31, 1972 and took a civil-service job with the Atomic Energy Commission as director of licensing—an important and demanding assignment. Before he could make his presence felt, however, he died of a heart attack on September 20, 1972, while playing badminton at the Pentagon Athletic Club.

Ben Read came home from Vietnam in the summer of 1967 and was assigned to the staff of the Joint Chiefs of Staff in the Pentagon. Retiring in January 1969, he also took a civil-service job with the Small Business Administration as the deputy director of procurement. It soon evolved that he had cancer, which was probably incurred during his exposure to radiation during the atomic weapons tests in Nevada in the summer of 1957. Never without pain the last years of his life, Ben retired from the SBA and died a year later, on March 29, 1975.

Following his return from Vietnam in July 1966, Jimmy Callender served for two years on the staff of the Armed Forces Staff College in Norfolk, Virginia. In his final year of active duty he served as chief of staff of the Marine Corps Base, Camp Lejeune. In spite of discrimination in the academic community due to his military background and age, Jimmy earned his Ph.D. at the University of Florida. He served for about five years in a high administrative capacity at a Florida junior college before he soured on academia. He found it fraught with intellectual dishonesty, and he resigned.

Following his tour with Fleet Marine Force, Pacific, Hank Woessner served in Vietnam as chief of staff of 1st Marine Division, then retired in 1968. He also decided to try the academic world. He taught algebra and social studies at Fallbrook Union High School near Camp Pendleton while he took graduate courses at San Diego State University. Hank earned his teaching and administrative credentials. When the assistant principal's job became vacant at Fallbrook in 1973, he was selected. Hank was promoted to principal in 1977, and earned his Ph.D. in 1979. In 1983–84, Fallbrook was selected for national secondary-school recognition.

The war generation—my generation—has all departed from military service and, in most cases, from public service of any sort. For those of us who stayed until the end, I can say that we remained true to our calling, true to our ideals, and true to our nation. It was a good life on balance, a life in every way worth living, for it was filled with associations with men larger than life and encompassed a sweep of our national history in no way overshadowed by other periods.

Acknowledgments

I regret that this memoir was not started earlier, when some of my closest comrades could have helped. My two Guadalcanal tent-mates, John Chaisson and Bob Sack, left us many years before I embarked on this project. So did Reds Miller. Hence, it is to Jimmy Callender that I owe a great debt for enriching my reminiscences with his own recollections. In numerous letters and conversations, Jimmy gave continuing encouragement as well as substantive suggestions on ways to render this book more significant.

I would also like to thank Marvin Pugh and Dave Berger for taped accounts of their last days at the Chosin Reservoir and Ray Miller and Dr. Bob Shoemaker for contributing their photo collections of our time together in Korea.

For his early encouragement, I would like to mention the late Bob Heinl. The continuing professional assistance of Brigadier General Ed Simmons and his staff at the Marine Corps History and Museums Division is greatly appreciated. Dr. Richard Sommers of the U.S. Army Military History Institute is to be thanked for his prompt response to inquiries, as is my brother, Ted, for his knowledgeable contributions regarding our family's history and for his critique of the manuscript.

Finally, the importance of Eric Hammel's advice and guidance in helping to consolidate my various writings and ideas into an integrated, flowing book is immeasurable. He has my heartfelt thanks, as does our highly competent editor, Toni Murray, for her painstaking efforts to make this book more readable.

B PARR PARR
Parry, Francis Fox.
Three-war Marine :